Thinking A Modern Landscape Architecture, West & East

Marc Treib

Thinking
A Modern
Landscape
Architecture,
West & East

Christopher
Tunnard,
Sutemi
Horiguchi

ORO Editions
Novato, California

Published by ORO Editions
Publishers of Architecture, Art,
and Design
Gordon Goff: Publisher
www.oroeditions.com
info@oroeditions.com

Research for this book was
supported in part by a grant
from the Graham Foundation
for Advanced Studies in the
Fine Arts.
Production was supported
by a grant from the
Hubbard Educational Trust.

Book Design: Marc Treib
ORO Project Coordinator:
Jake Anderson

10 9 8 7 6 5 4 3 2 1 First Edition
Library of Congress data available
upon request.
World Rights: Available

ISBN: 978-1-943532-78-0

Color Separations and Printing:
ORO Group Ltd.
Printed in China

International Distribution:
www.oroeditions.com/distribution

Dedication

For their support and friendship
over the years...

In England:

Alan Powers,
architectural historian

In Japan:

Makoto Suzuki,
Professor of Landscape Architecture,
Tokyo University of Agriculture

David B. Stewart,
Professor of Architectural History,
Tokyo Institute of Technology

Contents

1. >

Thinking a Modern Landscape Architecture

This book examines the initial conceptualization and realization of modern landscape architecture in England, Japan, and to a lesser degree the United States. Although these nations stand nearly at geographic antipodes, with vast distances separating them, they shared certain ideas that instigated the formulation and making of landscapes appropriate for the twentieth century. In both England and Japan, landscape designers confronted the burden of tradition to free themselves from it, in its place creating a landscape expression to suit contemporary times and lives. In terms of thinking and practice, the two subjects of our story—the Canadian-born Christopher Tunnard (1910–1979) and the Japanese Sutemi Horiguchi (1895–1984)—serve as ideal representatives. Each, however, was conditioned by the cultural, economic, and political contexts in which he worked. Although Horiguchi was over a decade older than Tunnard, who by 1950 had left landscape architecture for city planning and conservation, both stand as seminal figures in the quest for a modern landscape architecture to fit their respective cultural situations. Rather than a monograph then, this book is structured as a "duograph" that presents the parallels and divergences in the formation, philosophies, and design approaches of its two protagonists. Although a true step-by-step comparison is neither required nor possible, sufficient parallels reveal the convergences and divergences in their respective contributions.

Those formulating a landscape architecture for the twentieth century pursued differing, if related, paths. In the West, the path rejected the geometry and naturalism of historical traditions, looking instead to designs free of meandering paths punctuated by irregular clumps of trees or geometric landscapes populated by axes and clipped shrubs. Rather than retrieving historical precedents, landscape architects looked to modern art for their inspiration and formal sources, while simultaneously turning their attention to the greater landscape beyond the garden or the boundaries of the immediate commission. Within this story Christopher Tunnard stands as a central and influential figure, especially in the first half of the century when the rise of a modern consciousness also infiltrated the design of landscapes. This consciousness and intellectual attention came late. By the 1930s, when the subject of the modern landscape entered theoretical discussions, modernism in painting and sculpture already possessed a history of almost half a century; in architecture, key publications such as Le Corbusier's *Towards a New Architecture* and Henry-Russell Hitchcock and Philip Johnson's *The International Style* had been published, and buildings representing the new thinking had already been constructed.[1] Tunnard's epochal *Gardens in the Modern Landscape*, first published in 1938, provided the clarion call for innovative landscape design, landscape design that solved the needs of the current era but also looked to the future. Despite his insights into the modern garden, however, Tunnard remained very much linked to the past, in particular the eighteenth-century picturesque that had shaped so much of the English countryside. Yet even in the very title of his book, Tunnard directed his readers to look beyond the garden, to the cultural landscape shaped by habitation and use, of which the garden was only a small constituent. Curiously perhaps, Tunnard also looked to both the historical and contemporary landscapes of Japan as a model for a new, modern, "empathic" landscape architecture for the West. Among the illustrations used in Tunnard's manifesto was the 1932 Kikkawa house and garden by Sutemi Horiguchi.

Unlike Tunnard, who had studied horticulture and had only rudimentary training in landscape design, Horiguchi was an architect who had graduated from the prestigious Tokyo Imperial University, today the University of Tokyo. Like other architecture students around the world at that time, Horiguchi bristled against the strictures of Western neoclassicism which suppressed Japanese architectural traditions as well as the very idea of architectural modernism. With a small cadre of classmates he first organized a group known as the Bunriha—usually translated as the Japanese Architectural Secession—its model being the Viennese Secession that preceded its Japanese progeny by some two decades. In place of the use of the classical orders, in their architecture Bunriha members sought personal expression supported by advances in such construction materials as reinforced concrete. Following graduation, after a year's journey in Europe, Horiguchi was forced to return to Japan in the wake of the 1923 Great Kanto Earthquake. In a small group of houses constructed by decade's end, he moved from expressionism to modernism—the Kikkawa house by Tunnard cited above being one example.

Despite this youthful fascination with the West and its architecture, over time Horiguchi's sensibility shifted toward a greater appreciation of Japan's past, and like novelists Yasunari Kawabata and Jun'ichiro Tanizaki, in Japan's cultural history he found the source for an architecture—and landscape design—addressing contemporary times. Tunnard looked to contemporary art for inspiration and a possible vocabulary; quite to the contrary Horiguchi looked to the past, in particular to the eighteenth-century Rimpa School of painting. In their aesthetic, most evident in screen paintings, the Rimpa artists realistically rendered flowers, grasses, and trees, but set these depictions against a simple ground, usually covered in gold or silver leaf. To some degree in parallel with Tunnard's and Garrett Eckbo's call for a "structural" use of plants in landscape design, Horiguchi set plants and grasses in at least partial isolation against the neutral surface of a white boundary wall. His 1934 Okada garden in Tokyo best represents the most precise and beautiful application of this thinking.

Tunnard realized few projects, probably fewer than a dozen, and even those landscapes that survive only in documents probably total fewer than two dozen. After teaching at Harvard University's Graduate School of Design for about five years, in 1945 he moved to Yale University to develop its program in city planning. By 1949 his last landscape design—the Warren garden in Newport, Rhode Island—had been completed, although his writings on planning continued to reflect a landscape consciousness that persisted in his thinking and description of case studies.

Horiguchi, it must be admitted, never became a landscape architect; he remained an architect, and in time a professor of architecture as well. By war's end, like the novelists cited above, he turned from modernism, and in its place sought an architecture and landscape architecture that drew more consequentially on Japan's history rather than on foreign imports like neoclassicism or the so-called International Style. In the postwar years Horiguchi became well known as a literary figure and an authority on the teahouse and other structures of the *cha-no-yu* (tea ceremony). Several of his later architectural commissions, however, involved the design of their accompanying landscapes, and so his involvement with landscape design continued until late in his life.

Thus, these two figures—Christopher Tunnard and Sutemi Horiguchi—fittingly represent those searching for a modern landscape architecture, West and East. They are linked by mutual interests such as Tunnard's belief in historical Japanese gardens as potential design sources for the modern Western garden, and Horiguchi's initial fascination with modern Western archi-tecture that may have instigated his reinvestigation of Japan's own historical architecture and gardens. Together, these two designer/professors mark two distinct and important attitudes toward the creation of landscape architecture for the twentieth century in their respective countries, and their work is instructive.

Over the last three decades the body of scholar-ship addressing the definition and history of modern landscape architecture has grown considerably, enriched by both generalized and monographic studies (although, it must be said, compared to studies of modern art or even modern architectural history, publications on the modern landscape remain meager). Modern landscape architecture in the United States and abroad has been my own principal area of investigation, centering on American subjects but accompanied by studies on modern landscapes in Italy, Sweden, and Japan. My interest in the ideas and design work of Christopher Tunnard and Sutemi Horiguchi, the subjects of this book, began decades ago as a part of a wider international study; however, it is only in the last few years that I have intermittently returned to continue work on these subjects. Now it is time to shape and present my findings and interpretation.

Remaining problematic, however, is the thorny question of how to define "modern landscape architecture." In 1993 I offered six "axioms" by which modern landscape architecture could be qualified. After some years, however, I found that my initial definition of the term was too rooted in American landscape architecture, and somewhat inapplicable internationally.[2] More recently, I updated these initial categories by breaking down the broad notion of "modern" into four subcategories.[3] The first, *transitional*, describes the work of such important figures as G. N. Brandt in Denmark, Erik Glemme in Sweden, and Christopher Tunnard in England. Then there were landscapes such as the so-called Cubist gardens in France, about which Dorothée Imbert has written so insightfully.[4] At first glance, these landscapes look "modern" in their use of zigzag motifs, mirrors, and minerals. Yet in their spatial structure, frequent reliance on symmetry, and use of clipped shrubbery, they belie their continuance of the classical French tradition.[5] Because the designs of these gardens do not truly deliver what at first look they promise, I termed these "modernistic" rather than modern—although I suspect a better term can be found.

Then we come to the class "modern." Among those projects that stymie attempts at a comprehensive history of modern landscapes are those that embody or respond to a modern program—the improvement of health and life expectancy or the use of new materials, for example—but in their vocabulary, often naturalistic, they appear to be traditional, perhaps following in the wake of the eighteenth-century English landscape park. How, for example, to categorize the extensive Stockholm park system with its origins in the 1930s under the directorship of Holger Blom? Certainly, as landscapes intended to provide leisure grounds and extend the life expectancy of the Swedish populace, these were modern works. Yet in form they seem virtually undesigned, appearing as some atavistic woods kindly left standing among the recent construction that surrounds it. Certainly these were *modern* landscapes in their programs although they did not *look* modern in their form. Also in this group of "modern" landscapes would be those that incorporated novel materials such as asphalt, fiberglass, and glass, or introduced new plant species or cultivars. Their plans, sections, and spatial configurations may harken back to earlier times but they could never have been realized in just this way without these modern materials. Thus, the category of "modern" remains broad and in some ways a catchall.

Lastly, are the landscapes I would term truly *modernist*. In *All That Is Solid Melts into Air*, Marshall Berman established the three categories of modernization, modernity, and modernist. Modernization is the process by which traditional societies and their cities were converted to industrial metropoles, accompanied by drastic increases of population resulting from an influx drawn from the countryside and immigration. Modernity is the resulting state of these cities and those living within them. Berman then advances as modernist that art that uses, or at least incorporates, the state of modernity as a crucial aspect of its aesthetic expression. James Joyce's investigation of language, Georges Braque's and Pablo Picasso's expression of time through cubism, perhaps Frank Lloyd Wright's "destruction of the box," and Le Corbusier's conflation of space and time in the *promenade architecturale*—all incorporate to a greater or lesser degree aspects of modernity in their work.[6]

How, then, could one formulate a modernist landscape architecture? Plants and trees are hardly novel in and of themselves. They can be left to grow naturally or cut to shape, and can be planted in geometric arrangements or in irregular stands. So how then can vegetation in any form be used to express modernity when these vegetal forms and their configurations in gardens and landscapes have been used for millennia? In all, how can one express modernity in the design of a landscape?

While new materials, hybrids, and species contribute to the making of the modern landscape, in my estimation its key defining aspects are space, movement, and vocabulary. Garrett Eckbo once famously claimed that the axis had run out of steam in the seventeenth century, and like formal arrangements in general, especially those symmetrical, he asserted it had no place in a truly modern landscape.[7] Likewise, naturalism is too mimetic, with insufficient distance separating it from its source in nature. The denial of both these traditions was part and parcel of the modernist argument. Arguments are not landscapes, however, and a linguistic pronouncement differs markedly from one uttered in vegetation, minerals, and synthetic materials. It could also be argued that it is impossible to deny completely the institutions of naturalism and formalism, which will remain in some form, even as a remnant or thought. These were the formal parameters that contributed to the making of the modernist landscape.

Landscape architects pursuing modern tenets also attempted to enact social and economic reforms while blazing new trails in terms of space and form. The truly modern landscape, they argued, should envision new, multidirectional spatial constructs bolstered by appropriate ideas and forms inspired by contemporary art—together these would forge its structure and vocabulary. If we accept these as constituting a working, if not conclusive, definition of modern landscape architecture, there is little question of the significant roles played by Christopher Tunnard in England and the United States, and Sutemi Horiguchi in Japan, whether we ultimately judge them as transitional, modern, or fully formed modernist.

NOTE: *It has become customary among scholars of Japanese studies to adopt the ordering of names following Japanese usage, that is, with family name first and given name thereafter. However, to avoid issues of confusion and problems with cataloging, I have opted to follow Western ordering, that is, with given name first and family name thereafter.*

Unless otherwise noted, all place names in the Christopher Tunnard chapter are in England; those in the Sutemi Horiguchi chapter are located in Japan.

There have been several ways to Romanize the long o sound in Japanese: oo, ou *(following the Japanese convention using the syllabary),* oh, ô, *and the macron (a bar over the letter o). While I would have preferred to use the macron, it is not available on this font. Therefore* ô *has been used throughout the text and captions.*

Gordon Cullen.

2. >

Christopher Tunnard:
Gardens for the Modern Landscape

Always ill-defined in scope, with apparently limitless boundaries yet surrounded by economic and social restrictions, the landscape architect's work has been fragmentary and unclear, riddled with dilettantism, often venal in its commercialism and lack of concern for the needs of the public's use and enjoyment. The landscape of the 20th century is littered with frustrated masterpieces and much that is at best plain hack-work. The profession has not kept pace with social development.

Christopher Tunnard
"Landscape Architecture in the U.S.A."[1]

2-0
Christopher Tunnard.
"Shrubs for the Roof Garden."
[*Gardens in the Modern Landscape*, 1948]

The 1938 publication of *Gardens in the Modern Landscape* was a watershed event in the history of landscape architecture—primarily in the English-speaking world, of course, but with repercussions in several foreign countries as well.[2] The book's Canadian author, Christopher Tunnard, was young, knowledgeable, and ambitious, trained in horticulture but possessing keen interests in art and architecture; his original focus on the garden had expanded into the greater realm of landscape planning [figure 2-1]. While in the book Tunnard cast a broad vision for the present and the future, it was a vision that maintained an appreciation for both the European and Asian pasts. Its scope ranged from the historical evolution of the English landscape to plant selection, and called for both an art *of* the garden and art *in* the garden. In all, Tunnard's manifesto staked out for landscape architecture what modernism had already brought to architecture and art. Inherently a conservative practice due to the nature of its living materials, landscape design was chronically hampered by inertia. Tunnard sought to breach that stasis by investigating parallels in other design disciplines and, somewhat curiously, by advancing the landscape art of Japan as a model for the new Western garden.

Like Tunnard, the Japanese architect Sutemi Horiguchi, the subject of the second half of this book, sought a modern garden for his country as he expanded his vision to include the design of the landscape as well as the building. *Gardens in the Modern Landscape* included photographs of one Horiguchi garden, reusing plates from architect Raymond

McGrath's *Twentieth-century Houses*, illustrations also used in Tunnard's first article several years earlier.[3] Just where and how Tunnard first acquired an interest in, and knowledge of, things Japanese remains speculative, although in *Gardens in the Modern Landscape* he acknowledges the potter Bernard Leach as a major source of his information and understanding. Whatever its ultimate origins, it is obvious that by 1935, when Tunnard published "The Influence of Japan on the English Garden" in *Landscape and Garden*, the young Canadian horticulturalist was already taken by Japanese landscape design—a subject to which we shall later return. The article was also the first of Tunnard's to cite the work of Sutemi Horiguchi, his Kikkawa house in particular—hence the tenuous link between the two landscape designers.

> Early Years & Formation

At the time of Arthur Christopher Tunnard's birth in Victoria, British Columbia, the city had a population of only 30,000 and was, in fact, hardly seventy years old. Despite its remove from major urban centers in the United States, Canada, and Europe, Victoria was nonetheless the territorial capital, a status that fostered a certain richness in cultural activities and in the architecture that accompanied the calmer years after the late-nineteenth-century Gold Rush, as logging became British Columbia's primary industry. Although the English crown colony became a province when it joined the Canadian Confederation in 1871, its citizens still turned to Britain for their cultural identity. In *The Book of Small*, a memoir of her childhood in Victoria, the artist Emily Carr recalled how her father "wanted his place to look exactly like England. He planted cowslips and primroses and hawthorn hedges and all the Englishy flowers. He had stiles and meadows and took away all the wild Canadian-ness and made it as meek and English as he could."[4] Despite the change in governance that accompanied entry into the Confederation, however, even decades later—as the young Tunnard came of age—the citizens of Victoria continued to look directly across the Atlantic to England for manners and manufactures, and took little note of the thousands of miles of Canadian wilderness and water that lay between. Like many of the citizens of Victoria, Carr's father "stood still, torn by his loyalty to the Old Land and his delight in the New." Around the turn of the century "nearly all the people in Victoria were English and smiled at how they tried to be more English than the English themselves, just to prove to themselves and the world how loyal they were being to the Old Land."[5] That so many young Canadians gave their lives fighting for England in the First World War illustrates how these ties endured into the early decades of the twentieth century.[6] Given these cultural conditions, that Christopher Tunnard turned to England for further education in horticulture seems almost preordained.

Despite its latitude, the climate of Victoria is remarkably mild, while the rain-shadow effect of the Cascade Mountains makes the city the driest on the British Columbian coast—rainfall averages only about 24 inches per year. Vegetation can be lush, particularly in the understories of the great conifer forests that blanket the region. At the turn of the century the city's leading architects were Francis Mawson Rattenbury, who designed the Parliament Buildings and the venerable Empress Hotel, and Samuel Maclure, known for his commercial and residential work [figure 2-2]. Their architecture was formally eclectic, although as might be expected, oriented toward Victorian Britain as the source of their architectural styles. Like architectural tastes, the local garden tradition had also been imported from Britain, as indeed were most of the city's arts and social values. Having exhausted the limestone for Portland cement on his property, Robert Pim Butchart, at the prompting of his wife, began to convert the exhausted quarry into a series of gardens, beginning around 1906.[7] In time, the Butcharts added a panoply of gardens that reflected the traditions of Italy, Japan, but most of all, the English love of plants. The gardens are today more remarkable for their horticultural richness than for their structure, however, illustrating the effects of benign climatic conditions on the abundant plant growth characteristic of Vancouver Island. The Butchart Gardens remain British Columbia's best-known garden and its most visited.

2-2
Francis Mawson Rattenbury. Houses of Parliament. Victoria, British Columbia, Canada, 1893–1897; 1912–1916. [Marc Treib]

As part of their turn-of-the-century quest for a regional and national identity, Canadian artists adopted but adapted international movements such as symbolism and expressionism when painting their native landscape. Tom Thomson (1877–1917) was the first of these artists to devote his later life to capturing the power of the wilderness in paint, executing his visual impressions in an enormous number of small, quickly executed oil sketches, a selection of which he later worked up into finished paintings. *Spruce and Tamarack* (1916) features the ragged profiles of two of the country's most characteristic tree species set against dense woodlands, hills, and a pale blue sky [figure 2-3]. The Group of Seven, for whom Thomson remained the inspiration long after his early death in 1917, was based in Toronto but made frequent excursions to the northern forests and lakes, seeking a national essence in its landscape. Over time their styles evolved from one more influenced by turn-of-the-century Scandinavian painting to one—at least for members like Lawren Harris—more highly stylized and abstract.[8] Closer to Tunnard's home, Emily Carr (1871–1945), today the province's most highly regarded turn-of-the-century artist, worked in a post-impressionist style as she interpreted the landscape of British Columbia and the material culture of the First Nations. It was a time particularly rich in intellect and achievement and remains to some degree the Golden Age of Canadian art. This was the artistic milieu into which Christopher Tunnard, the

boy who would become the landscape architect, was born in Victoria on 7 July 1910 and in which he was educated thereafter.

Christopher Tunnard's father, Christopher Coney Tunnard (1879–1939), had emigrated from Lincolnshire in England, his family homestead being a place called Hampton House.[9] Tunnard's mother, Madeline Kingscote (1881–1977), had lived in Gloucestershire although she had been born in New South Wales, Australia.[10] Marriage, moving, and emigration scattered the Tunnard family members across England and over two foreign continents, even to distant places like the Canadian Pacific coast.

The Tunnard family, whether in England or abroad, displayed few artistic leanings, the sole exception being the landscape architect's cousin, the painter John Tunnard (1900–1971), who was born in Bedfordshire. His father, Jack, had painted as well as hunted; his son John hunted as well as painted, thanks to the financial support of his wife's inheritance.[11] Maturing after studies at the Royal Academy of Art in London, John painted in a style that mixed abstraction, surrealism, and landscape in what has been described by one writer as "plein-air abstraction"; textile design augmented his income. In the 1930s and 1940s, John Tunnard enjoyed modest success in both Britain and the United States but he is today almost completely forgotten.[12] Presumably as a favor, Christopher Tunnard brought several of his cousin's paintings to the United States in August 1939 as he was about to begin his teaching appointment at Harvard. As a result, *Fugue* (1938) was later purchased by the Museum of Modern Art, one of the few

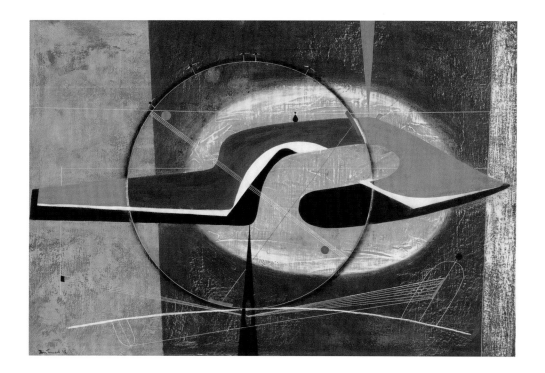

of his paintings in North American collections [figure 2-4].[13] Thus, although a small artistic strain appeared in the Tunnard lineage, only John and Christopher truly achieved any notice and celebrity in that arena.[14]

After completing his secondary education in Victoria, Christopher Tunnard enrolled in the fledgling Victoria College, founded in 1903 as a branch of McGill University based in Montreal. Graduating with a bachelor's degree in liberal arts in 1928, he seems to have headed to England almost immediately for intensive studies at the Royal Horticultural Society's Wisley School of Horticulture in Surrey, a program that had been founded in 1907.[15] In a letter published in the *Journal of the Royal Horticultural Society* the following year, F. G. Ogilvie reported that the school's two-year training program included "instruction in the sciences bearing on horticulture," and noted that "this instruction has, at present, to be made very fundamental and in some respects very elementary, as few of those admitted to the course of instruction have received a satisfactory training previously in the rudiments of science."[16] Being the program's inaugural year, the entering students' ignorance of horticulture was understandable. Ogilvie hoped that during its second year the program would offer more advanced coursework in various subjects than it did at that moment. He also cautioned that the diploma would be awarded only to those students who had completed the full two-year program, passed written and oral examinations based on the syllabus of study, "present[ed] an essay upon some approved Horticultural or Scientific subject"—and submitted

2-5
Percy S. Cane.
Tilt Yard,
Dartington Hall.
Devon,
late 1940s.
[Marc Treib]

2-6
Percy S. Cane.
"Terrace Garden for
a Modern House."
[*Garden Design
of Today*]

an album of "at least 200 properly dried, named, and localized plant specimens" collected *outside* the school's gardens. Lastly, the candidates for the certificate would need to "submit a collection of insects either injurious or helpful in Horticulture."[17] Each student was given laboratory space and allotted "a small plot of land."[18]

Required subjects featured, as one might expect, extensive training in botany—but also incorporated studies in physics, chemistry, and soil sciences. Advanced coursework included plant life and genetics, insect life, a more detailed investigation of soils, fertilization, and in the "Fruit and Vegetable Department," plant cultivation in the open air and under glass. Rounding out the program was practice in flori- and arboriculture, and even the study of meteorology. Compressed into two years, this was a rigorous curriculum. The demanding requirements for graduation suggest the thoroughness of the program as well as the use of student effort to bolster the Royal Horticultural Society's research activities and collections. Graduates from this rather elite program would be suited for practical on-site landscape management as well as potential scientific investigations. In the 1929 *Royal Horticultural Society Gardens Club Journal*, Christopher Tunnard is listed as one of only a handful of students accepted that year. He was not the top student: in his second-year examination he received a second-class pass, the grade he also received in his senior year.[19] He graduated with the Wisley Diploma in 1930.[20] No printed evidence suggests that garden or landscape design was included in the program of study, however, and the origin of Tunnard's interests in these areas is open to speculation.

After graduation Tunnard's initial employment involved testing seeds for Sharp & Company Agricultural Suppliers. After two years wrestling with this highly technical employment, he left to join the office of the landscape architect Percy S. Cane, where he remained from 1932 until about 1935. Cane was one of the better-known landscape architects practicing in London, proficient in the modeling of terrain and the composition of herbaceous borders [figure 2-5]. His practice was wide, and included sizable estates in northern England and Scotland. Seen today, Cane's designs are squarely in the arena of post-Edwardian practice, and suggest little of the modernity Tunnard would call for in his later writings; but there is little doubt that considerable thought lay behind Cane's design practice. His several books, published both pre- and postwar, include *The Earth Is My Canvas* and *The Creative Art of Garden Design*, and as one would expect, featured portfolios of his landscapes. Less typically, they also contained more generalized comments about such subjects as the approach to the site, the appropriateness of certain plants, and the care and use of selected flowers such as roses.[21] In *Garden Design of To-day*, Cane includes suggestions for planting a "modern house" and notes, "Trees such as silver birch seen against white walls make a delightful composition, as also do the vertical lines of Lombardy poplars or the dark columnar growth of many of the junipers, and either would tend to emphasize the rather severe lines of the house" [figure 2-6].[22] Interestingly, he also devoted an entire chapter to Japanese gardens, suggesting that the subject was known, and possibly appreciated, among British garden makers at that time.

While working for Cane, Tunnard acquired "experience in draughtsmanship, designing, surveying and all outdoor and indoor routines connected with the above." After two years, however, he seems to have felt that he had learned what he could learn and chomped at the bit to open his own office, which he did in Cobham, Surrey, in 1934. Although now independent, Tunnard felt that his graphic and construction skills were not up to snuff as he undertook a six-month course in "perspective drawing and pencil sketching" with one Harold White, and "an elementary course in building construction at the L.C.C. School, Westminster."[23] Regardless of this coursework, Tunnard's graphic skills appear to have remained limited as only one drawing signed by, and presumably drawn by, him has come to light. Over time he relied instead on H. F. Clark for much if not all of his drafting, and Gordon Cullen for his presentation sketches while working in England.

Seen from our perspective today it seems clear that even within two years of graduation Tunnard's interests extended far beyond the seed, seedling, and flowering shrub upon which his study and practice had focused to that point. Although armed with a technical knowledge virtually unmatched by any twentieth-century landscape architect since, he clearly had much broader visions, both in terms of landscape architecture and social and cultural issues.[24] How he made these profitable professional connections is not clear, but by the time of establishing his independent practice Tunnard was already hobnobbing with some of Britain's leading architects—and some artists as well. Among these were the artists and designers represented in *Circle*, members of the Modern Architecture Research Group (MARS), and the staff and contributors to the *Architectural Review*.

> An Era of Associations

Seen today, 1930s Britain appears as an era of associations. In 1933 the artists Ben Nicholson, Barbara Hepworth, Henry Moore, Edward Wadsworth, Paul Nash, the critic Herbert Read, and half a dozen others formed Unit One: its purpose to promote modern art, in this case painting and sculpture that inched toward nonfiguration [figure 2-7]. Also affiliated were the architects Colin Lucas and Wells Coates. In 1934, to accompany the publication of Herbert Read's *Unit One: The Modern Movement in English Architecture, Painting, and Sculpture,* the group held its sole exhibition, at the Mayor Gallery in London. While short-lived, Unit One nonetheless set the stage for the other groups to follow, all of which were broadly defined, loosely structured, and fluid in membership. The primary accomplishment of the *Circle* group, in many ways a successor to Unit One, was the major publication with its eponymous title that appeared in 1937.

The cover of *Circle: International Survey of Constructive Art* announced that its contributors comprised "painters, sculptors, architects and writers."[25] The stable of contributors was huge—the book presents the work of over 80 creative individuals whose texts and projects were assembled from previously published writings, projects, and artworks; accompanying these older contributions were several essays seeing print for the first time. Although extensive in number, the writings remained secondary to the copiously illustrated

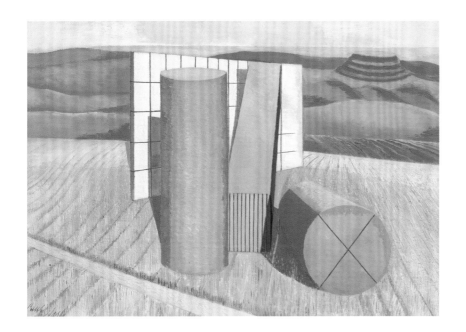

portfolio of works that represented "constructive" art and architecture. Gabo, Nicholson, Lázló Moholy-Nagy, Piet Mondrian, and Antoine Pevsner represented a more geometric approach while a more organic aesthetic was evident in sculptures by Barbara Hepworth, Henry Moore, Constantin Brancusi, Alexander Calder, and the young Alberto Giacometti. The architects published included Alvar Aalto, Serge Chermayeff, Walter Gropius, Richard Neutra, Erich Mendelsohn, Maxwell Fry, and even Le Corbusier.[26] The roster was impressive.

By the date of publication, the editors—the architect Leslie Martin, the painter Ben Nicholson, and the sculptor Naum Gabo—were established figures in their respective fields. Their individual talents and networks of associations guaranteed a breadth of interpretations of what constituted the "constructive" tendency. Two things it was not, however. The authors were careful to distinguish "constructive" from "constructivist," although the works of certain artists—the Russian-born brothers Naum Gabo and Antoine Pevsner among them—shared aspects characteristic of Soviet revolutionary art. *Circle* also distanced itself from surrealism. Surrealism investigated the internal workings of the mind, perhaps through automatism, perhaps through the remembrance of dreams. Constructive art, in stark contrast, dealt with the actual. Yet despite this stress on what exists rather than what is dreamt, the ultimate purpose was to touch the inner mind through the senses. Several writers suggested that the Continental linguistic term "concrete" rather than "constructive" better explained the group's intentions.[27]

While there is no evidence that Christopher Tunnard read *Circle*, either before or after he began publishing his own essays in the *Architectural Review* in 1937, there are certainly parallels between his regard for the physical elements of landscape and the "empathic" approach he advanced as the path to the future of landscape design. In terms of design idiom, however, Tunnard seems to have been remarkably untouched by the shapes and spaces of the new art. His ideas at that time resonate more closely with writings found on the Pacific Coast, at the San Francisco Museum of Art, where the first international exhibition of "contemporary landscape architecture" was displayed from 12 February to 22 March 1937.

In his introductory essay to the exhibition's catalog, *Contemporary Landscape Architecture and Its Sources*, the emergent architectural historian and critic Henry-Russell Hitchcock mirrored Tunnard's vision for the modern garden, although there is no evidence that they had ever been in contact. Hitchcock had been a co-curator of the Museum of Modern Art's epochal "Modern Architecture: An International Exhibition" in 1932, which proselytized for the International Style. But his vision for landscape hardly equaled in force and innovation his vision for architecture. In the catalog essay "Gardens in Relation to Modern Architecture," Hitchcock shared Le Corbusier's vision of greenery unformed: "The most successful contemporary technique is neither embellishment nor 'improvement'; it is the frank addition of those necessary features for the owner's use which no natural site can offer." Like the architect Reginald Blomfield writing in the 1890s, the American architectural historian suggested plans more geometric near, on, or under buildings, which would thereafter dissolve into unshaped greenery as the garden moved outward from the structure.[28] Clearly, landscape design—except adjacent to modern architecture—was to keep to itself, and its historical order, as a foil for the new shapes of modernism.

With the possible exception of his last garden, in Newport, Rhode Island—discussed later in this essay—no Tunnard garden radically departed from the English landscape tradition nor from Hitchcock's limited vision. To place these ideas in perspective: By 1939 Thomas Church was already enfolding the biomorphic curve into several of his residential gardens as well as experimental gardens at the Golden Gate International Exposition in San Francisco [figure 2-8]. Garrett Eckbo and James Rose, recent graduates of Harvard's Graduate School of Design, were propelled in their search for a new landscape design from reading Tunnard's book, but both of them had already far excelled the master in the freshness and dynamism of their designs. Looking back to the years 1938–1939, it appears obvious that Tunnard was, and would remain, far more influential as an author and theorist than as a practitioner. He would shout the call to arms and establish many of the parameters for modern landscape design, but it would be the task of other designers to render those ideas in concrete form. In some ways Tunnard was just not equipped, having little or no training in landscape design per se. Although we may look critically at his work from the 1930s, this is not to say he didn't try to design and to construct, as well as to formulate, a modern garden. One way to develop the ideas for the new landscape was gained by associating with architects already working in the modern idiom.

If the 1930s appears as an era of professional associations, it was equally an era of exhibitions. Keep in mind that radio and cinema were the primary entertainment media; television, still in its infancy and a rare household item, and even popular publications about architecture and design, were limited. Exhibitions, however, were common and drew crowds of considerable number. The *Daily Mail*'s annual Ideal Home Show attracted several hundred thousand visitors each year, a figure that rose rapidly during the 1930s.[29] For the design professional, the exhibition provided the opportunity to present three-dimensional spatial displays that resembled, at least to some degree, works they envisioned for places beyond the exhibition hall.

The Modern Architecture Research Group (MARS) was a loosely affiliated and somewhat motley crew formed primarily as the English branch of the Congrès International d'Architecture Moderne (CIAM, 1928–1959). The noted architectural historian John Summerson was a charter member, yet even he could not with accuracy assert just who had founded the MARS Group and when they had done so. In one iteration of the story, MARS was founded in 1933 to prepare a plan for London as a presentation at that year's CIAM meeting. As the initiating forces Summerson credits Wells Coates, the architect, critic, and writer; the bon vivant, aesthete, and critic P. Morton Shand; and Hugh de Cronin Hastings, publisher of the *Architectural Review*—although Coates' partner, David Pleydell-Bouverie, was also among the inaugural crew. Over time the membership expanded to include figures on both sides of the Atlantic: among them, Serge

2-9
Modern Architecture
Research Group
(MARS) Exhibition,
1938.
Catalog cover.
[Frances Loeb
Library / Harvard
University Graduate
School of Design,
hereafter Loeb
Library, HUGSD]

2-10
Modern Architecture
Research Group
(MARS).
Exhibition plan.
[Loeb Library /
HUGSD]

2-11
Modern Architecture
Research Group
(MARS) Exhibition.
"Architecture
Garden Landscape"
section.
[Loeb Library /
HUGSD]

Chermayeff, Hugh Casson, Marcel Breuer, Walter Gropius, Berthold Lubetkin, F. R. S. Yorke, Basil Ward, and "reluctantly" Frederick Etchells.[30] Its purpose was fourfold: "1. To formulate contemporary architectural problems; 2. To represent the modern architectural idea; 3. To cause this idea to penetrate technical economic and social circles; 4. To work towards the solution of contemporary problems in architecture."[31] An exhibition at the New Burlington Galleries planned for 1937, but ultimately held in January 1938, was the group's sole major contribution to English and international architecture; its purview proselytized for modernism in all aspects of living, from the chair and the table to the room and home—and even the garden, the city, and the region [figure 2-9].

Most of those mentioned above formulated the exhibition, but the committee also included J. M. Richards, E. Maxwell Fry, László Moholy-Nagy, and the Australian-born Raymond McGrath—with whom Tunnard would later collaborate on his best-known landscape project. "The Martians," as they were referred to in at least one review, solicited a catalog introduction from none other than George Bernard Shaw, who was 82 years old at the time. In his contribution, Shaw traveled backward in time to Baalbek in order to recover what he called "impressive architecture," noting that this was an architecture to be experienced primarily from the exterior. "The MARS group represents a violent reaction against impressive architecture," he claimed. "It has no religion to impose; and however it may operate incidentally as an advertisement of wealth and respectability, this is not its object." And just what was its object? The "health and convenience not only of individuals but also of their neighbors"—one must consider the whole town as well as its constituent buildings. In the twentieth century, new materials and new techniques have yielded a new architecture. It was of little consequence, Shaw believed, that their forms were uncomfortable in their novelty. "No matter: we shall have to get used to them, even if the only way to escape from their unusualness is to get inside them."[32] Unlike Baalbek, the significance of these new buildings lay in their interior spaces.

Each room of the exhibition presented architecture in relation to certain themes, with an overriding idea that good building has commodity, firmness, and delight [figure 2-10].[33] A brief introduction presented historical buildings: Heritage. From there the Martians presented their ideas on building for habitation, work, leisure, the community, transportation, and town planning.[34] The long corridor linking the two main rooms was co-opted for additional exhibition space and lined with panels that presented "the technician's contribution": mass production, standardized quality control, prefabrication, and scientific research among other issues. The second room contained the exhibits on "Form and Purpose" and included a section called "Architecture in the Landscape," perhaps at least in part the product of Tunnard's involvement [figure 2-11]. The charming line drawings illustrating the catalog were probably by Gordon Cullen, who drafted the pictures for Tunnard's *Gardens in the Modern Landscape* at about the same time. Nonstructural bents of an unspecified material joined wall and terrace floor; a tree grew—or at least stood—between two of them; perforated screens complemented the patio paving, suggesting that architecture

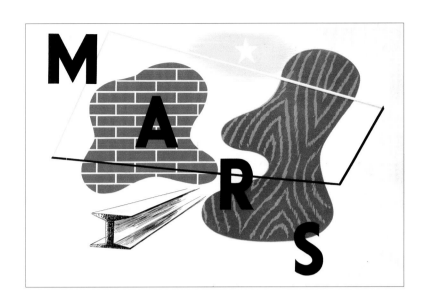

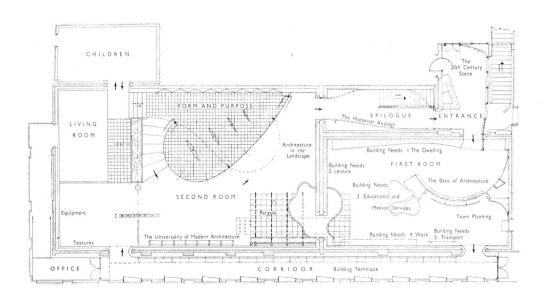

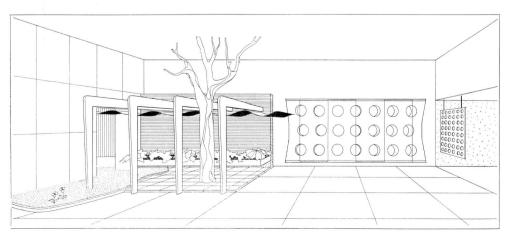

itself could be made more permeable. "There must be no antagonism between architecture and its natural setting," the catalog read. "The architecture of the house embraces the garden. House and garden coalesce, a single unit in the landscape."[35] Certainly, this pronouncement was fully in accord with Tunnard's ideas then being publicized in his essays for the *Architectural Review*. But just where did vegetation enter into the design? The spaces appear rather barren.

Tunnard's role in making the exhibition is ambiguous and was probably limited. In the catalog he is credited only with "flowers and plants" and nothing more consequential. He is not even listed as a MARS member, suggesting that like Misha Black, the actual designer of the installation, Tunnard hovered on the periphery of the organization. As intended, the show did make a mark and it received extensive newspaper coverage, much of it tepidly positive.

An anonymous review titled "Mars versus Jupiter" appeared in the Spring 1938 issue of *Landscape and Garden*, the journal of the Institute of Landscape Architects. Linking Shaw's "impressive" architecture to Jupiter, the unnamed reviewer contrasted monumental work against that of the MARS Group: "There is nothing rude or violent about the criticism of Jupiterian architecture but a confident assertion of their new principles."[36] Architecture must serve its social purpose. Town planning is a necessity. "The centre is repulsive, population and industry are migrating to what was once the open country, vast enough to form towns of fifty thousand people every four months," the review continued. "This fact, which cannot be disputed, makes the rescue of London from its doom an urgent problem, for unless the outward movement is intelligently thought out, the resulting chaos will make us all more uncomfortable." One solution proposed a "central nucleus" of "older cultural and commercial buildings, a broad band of higher buildings for residential purposes, well separated, should come next and thirdly the widest sphere of all, the cottage units: then the real green belt." If Tunnard had not already reached the same conclusion, he shared sympathies with at least the ideas concerning the countryside. The review concluded with the call to "Let us remember that the background and foreground of Nature are 'given'; we cannot dispute with them. What we add must be *adapted* or assimilated to what we have already."[37] This sentence could have been extracted in toto from *Gardens in the Modern Landscape*. In fact, an article signed by "A Member of the MARS Group" appeared in the following issue under the rubric "Modern Architectural Research and Landscape Planning."

While no evidence credits Tunnard with its authorship, there was no other landscape architect among the exhibition's participants. In any event, whether written by Tunnard or not, its content was fully in accord with other writings by the young landscape architect in those years, arguing for the discarding of prior styles and manners, the appropriateness of high-rise development if it preserves the landscape, and praise for the Amsterdamse Bos.

> The demand for contact with Nature under contemporary conditions is a foremost concern of MARS, and if it can help to make the countryside available to the masses instead of to the few by suggesting means of replanning, rebuilding, and relandscaping hopelessly crowded and badly developed areas, the Group is not going to let restrictive interpretations of laws governing densities and heights pass without challenge.[38]

Despite such claims, the impact of the MARS Group as a collective was meager, although their exhibition and the publicity it generated may have advanced the cause of modern architecture in the United Kingdom and the careers of some of its members.

If John Summerson wavered in his beliefs when joining the group, his reticence only grew over time. By 1940, in a letter to Ben Nicholson, Summerson wrote, "I think modern architecture will have to beat a retreat, simply because the public can't understand it, never will, and hates it like poison." The breach had been made, however: "On the other [hand] the modern movement has completely and irretrievably bust up all the old concepts of architecture. There's no going back." More emphatically he asserted that "Everybody who realizes that the flat-roofed, white-walled, over-glazed buildings which created such a stir on the continent in the twenties have not the slightest appeal to the ordinary Englishman, and that no architecture is likely to make much headway in this country which cannot make some sort of emotional contact with the ordinary educated man and woman—let alone the rather less educated masses."[39] On the subject of landscape design he was mute. But one can easily extrapolate his pronouncements on architecture to the landscape: the English landscape garden would endure, although perhaps be allowed a modernized touch here and there.

The clouds of war were gathering over Europe at the time of the MARS exhibition, and in less than a year Britain, too, would descend into the maelstrom. Paired with the diaspora of European architectural talent departing for the United States to escape the war and in search of greater professional opportunities, the MARS Group went into hibernation and ultimately disappeared. In Summerson's view, the efforts of this activist group of modernists had produced only Wells Coates' Lawn Road, or Isokon Flats—for which Tunnard designed a small garden [see figure 2-29], Tecton's Highpoint towers and Penguin Pool at the London Zoo, and one or two other projects of note. Little else. "The MARS Group continued in existence for some years after the war, but at midnight on 28 January 1957 it voluntarily extinguished itself."[40] For Christopher Tunnard the association with MARS seems to have been primarily social, cementing associations with the leading architects and designers working in Britain in the late 1930s. Walter Gropius and later Marcel Breuer departed for the United States to become faculty members at Harvard University's Graduate School of Design. In short order Tunnard would follow them, supported by Gropius in his bid to modernize the program at the Graduate School of Design under Dean Joseph Hudnut. It could be that the greatest benefit of Tunnard's association with the MARS Group was his invitation to join the Harvard faculty in 1939.

Before leaving England, however, Tunnard helped organize a major exhibition of work by the members of the Institute of Landscape Architecture shown at the Royal Institute of British Architects in London in June 1939, as well as the Broadway department store in Worcestershire. The London location of the exhibition *Garden and Landscape* at the RIBA in itself could be considered a coup, bringing the work of the younger society to the heart of the older professional association. In addition to contributing his own projects,

Tunnard was responsible for the overall planning of the exhibition and its layout, and he divided the material into three sections: Garden (private gardens and estates), Decoration ("emphasizing the character of the materials of landscape architecture"), and Landscape (work affecting the community as a whole).[41] In his introduction to the catalog, Tunnard explained that "Contrasts of form, subtle gradations of colour, and sensitive associations in group planting belong to the province of landscape architecture."[42] At the opposite extreme, landscape architecture also concerns the larger landscape: the arterial road, the parkway, and even the "aerodrome." He closes with a plea for the "maintenance of the manmade order in the landscape in the face of increasing destruction and irresponsible planning."[43] The review of the exhibition featured three photographs of models, but the last page reproduced three panels whose shapes and typography recalled those used on the cover of the MARS exhibition catalog.[44]

By 1937, just a handful of years since receiving his diploma, Tunnard had become a rising star on the horizon of British landscape architecture, primarily as an author but also as a practitioner.[45] His association with the MARS Group had been fruitful, one might even say pivotal, as it not only brought him into contact with those applying the most advanced ideas in architecture and planning but also introduced him to several future collaborators. Among them was Hubert de Cronin Hastings, the publisher of the *Architectural Review*, in whose pages Tunnard would first publish the essays that would form the core of *Gardens in the Modern Landscape*. Through MARS he probably also met Raymond McGrath, the Australian-born architect with whom he would collaborate on the gardens for at least two houses, including one in which he himself would live for a short time. And it is probable that it was through the MARS get-togethers that he first encountered the housing expert Elizabeth Denby, with whom he would also collaborate shortly thereafter.

From his association with the MARS Group and work with the Institute of Landscape Architects it is obvious that Tunnard actively sought to broaden his artistic and professional horizons from the moment he left Wisley, if not before. Participation in these groups brought him into contact with many of the leading voices in English architecture, design, and criticism, influential contacts that paid off in collaborations and publicity. Without doubt he profited by being the MARS Group's sole landscape designer, especially given his views, shared with several of its members, toward the countryside and regional planning. In March 1938, Tunnard appeared with the *Architectural Review* editor J. M. Richards on a BBC television program presenting his ideas for developing the landscape of a small suburban house [figure 2-12]. The program, billed as "Garden Planning," addressed differences of approach for two types of sites: one, a small suburban plot, the other, "a larger garden of about an acre." "Emphasis was laid on the need for a considered relationship between house and garden, and the advantages stressed of an increased cooperation between architects and landscape architects in all planning schemes."[46] Like the American landscape architect Fletcher Steele in his 1923 book *Design in the Little Garden*, Tunnard clustered the intensive planting near the house and left much of the land to rough grass, planted also with fruit trees to amplify the sense of space.[47] Mown paths through the grass would be planted with "spring bulbs in order to make the layout interesting yet easy to maintain."[48] Tunnard's co-presenter, J. M. Richards, claimed that they made the "BBC's first television broadcast on architecture."[49]

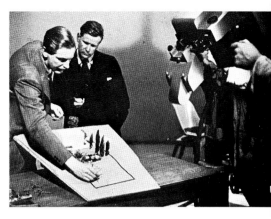

These ideas were given greater depth in "The Sectional Layout of a Small Garden Plot," published in the *Architectural Review* in March 1939, one installment in a series entitled "Garden and Landscape."[50] In the article, Tunnard further developed his discussion of ideas and issues addressed in the earlier "The Suburban Plot" and "The Country Acre," parts of the same series. In this article, however, he treats the issues and the garden's design with increased detail [figures 2-13, 2-14]. It will be a three-year project, he tells his readers, and provides specifications and instructions for the tasks to be undertaken each year. Tunnard cautions that the first year will be the most costly, as it involves investments for site work, basic planting, and paths; the provision of a sandbox shows that children have not been forgotten in the planning. Some basic flower beds will be planted near the house and configured to define an area that extends outward the rooms of the house. Year two sees the site more fully planted, with lines of fruit trees planted along the western lot line, further enriched by a kitchen garden, while still keeping much of the site as lawn. In year three a more naturalistically planted zone to the southeast completes the picture, "making possible a walk round the garden in which all sections can be visited without any retracing of steps." As in his almost coeval scheme for Bentley Wood, Tunnard suggests that bulbs and wildflowers be planted to enhance that quadrant of the garden.

The design vocabulary illustrated in the plans and perspective suggests the influence of Tunnard's Belgian colleague Jean Canneel-Claes, which is evident in the overall zoning of the site, the shaping of the flower and vegetable beds, the play of formal areas against those more natural, and especially in the use of square concrete pavers to construct the paths. One might even read behind-the-scheme suggestions from Canneel's Heeremans garden in Liedekirke, although given the proportions of the small garden site, the extenuation of the Belgian garden has been compressed into a squatter figure [see figure 2-48]. The benefits of the approach explained in the article are many, claims Tunnard, asserting that despite any consistent approach to configuring the many private gardens of a housing estate, the individual tastes of the owners would be sufficient to guarantee a varied and vibrant overall landscape.

> As Author: Japan as Model

From what sources Tunnard acquired his interest in Japan is not known but it was an interest that appeared very early in his career and remained lifelong. In what was probably his earliest essay, and written under the name Arthur C. Tunnard, he first explored the lessons to be learned from Japan in the summer 1935 issue of *Landscape and Garden*. In that article, he cited three areas in which the impact

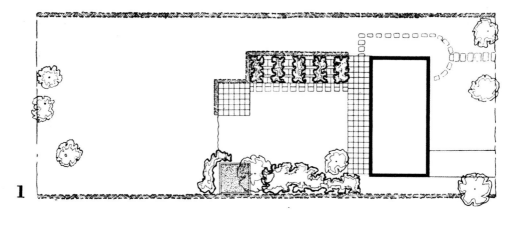

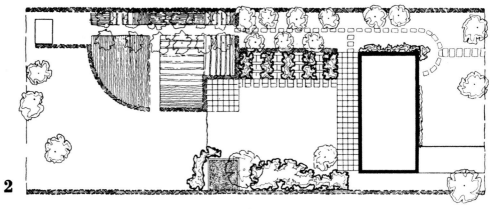

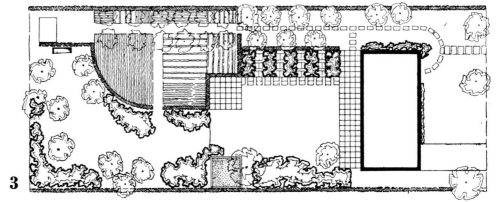

2-13
Christopher Tunnard.
"A Small Garden,"
1939. Plan.
[*Architectural
Review*]

2-14
"A Small Garden,"
1939.
Perspective.
[*Architectural
Review*]

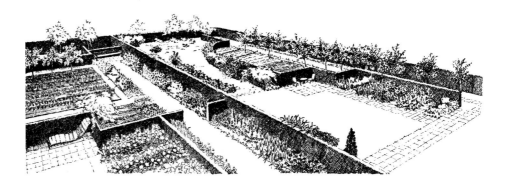

of Japan had been felt in the British Isles. First, the imported plant species themselves, in particular the *Azalea amoena* and the *Acer palmatum* (Japanese maple), whose popularity had grown rapidly, departing from their early use only as hothouse or specimen plants for broader applications in the English garden. Second, Tunnard described the nearly complete integration of house and garden found in Japan, noting the new possibilities offered by modern architecture, in particular how with its "girder construction we can now make sliding or folding walls of glass almost wherever we please on the outer walls."[51] In several ways, of course, the polemic was quite strained, especially if we consider the vast differences in lifestyles—including domestic spaces and furnishings—between Japan and Britain. Lastly, Tunnard examined the parallels between the two countries in their "recreating natural scenery." At this point in his career—consider that he was then only 25 years old and had completed his studies fewer than five years before—Tunnard can be faulted for presenting the Japanese garden tradition as monolithic, at the very least not completely understanding the considerable differences between the dry and stroll garden types and the historical evolution of the country's garden forms. "The trend in all art," he believed, "is slowly moving towards an acceptance of form, line and economy of material as being of first importance; some of our gardens are beginning to show signs of this change of opinion." While the rise of the English landscape garden has been assigned by most historians to a path in the Western arts, Tunnard believed that "There can be no doubt of the influence of Japan here."[52] Yet despite these shortcomings in his argument, the article does display a profound respect for Japanese aesthetics, and the subjects he presents will reappear in the empathic approach proposed in essays in the *Architectural Review* begun in 1937 that would coalesce as *Gardens in the Modern Landscape* the following year. Although Tunnard's early article focused exclusively on historical landscapes, its illustrations were restricted to those of Sutemi Horiguchi's Kikkawa house built in Tokyo in 1932. [The project, whose alternate reading is Kitakawa, will be discussed in greater detail in the Horiguchi section of this book].

Although the sources of Tunnard's interest in Japan have not been determined with certainty, he is known to have read a number of books on Japanese gardens and flower arrangement.[53] In the acknowledgments to *Gardens in the Modern Landscape*, Tunnard credits Bernard Leach for "information concerning Japanese art"—a connection probably more consequential than his reading, as Leach would have shown him artifacts such as ceramics in addition to discussing aesthetic ideas.[54] Leach, Britain's most celebrated potter, had been born in Hong Kong in 1887, but after his mother's death, he accompanied his grandparents in their move to Japan, where his grandfather would teach English at Dôshisha University in Kobe for about a decade.[55] He returned with them to England in 1908 and studied at the Slade School of Fine Art in London. There he met Kotaro Takamura, a sculptor, and with an introduction from the young Takamura to his father, Leach headed back to Japan. He soon met Sôetsu Yanagi, the founder of the *mingei* (folk art) movement that had been formed to preserve native craft traditions, including ceramics, from the onslaught of Western art forms.[56] In the ensuing decades, Leach would alternate periods of stay in Japan and St. Ives in Cornwall. He established a deep friendship with master potter

Shôji Hamada, with whom he shared aesthetic values, and became attached to the pottery community of Mashiko north of Tokyo, where Hamada lived and worked. Over time Leach became a peripatetic ambassador who traveled between England and Japan, his own work influenced by the surface quality and glazes of Mashiko pottery, although the exchanges were mutual. Leach is credited, for example, with introducing slipware to Japan, which over time became a folk glazing technique in Shimane Prefecture. How Tunnard and Leach met is not recorded, but it could have been through the landscape architect's cousin, the painter John Tunnard, who, like Leach, was based in Cornwall.

From 1935 on, Tunnard became an intermittent contributor to the Institute of Landscape Architects' journal *Landscape and Garden*. Following in the wake of his writing on Japanese garden design, Tunnard published "Interplanting," an essay on the mixing of species that hinted at the depth of the author's horticultural knowledge.[57] In the article, Tunnard cautions that technical investigations, such as the analysis of soil composition, are needed before embarking on the selection of species. Though focused on botanical content, his repeated call to consider the aesthetics of the planting peppers the article. He followed this article with "Garden-Making on the Riviera," associating the selection of plants and layouts with the climate—a dry climate that makes achieving the beloved English lawn nearly impossible, and topography that demands terraces, retaining walls, and other construction. Given the heat and the sun, the pergola is a welcome feature, not only as a device for framing views but "when decorated with climbing and twining plants it provides grateful shade."[58] The temperate climate permits an abundance of species such as palms, cacti, agaves, araucarias, and even eucalyptus. Fortunately for the British expat or vacationer, "Rose gardens, paeony (the tree varieties), lavender (a native plant), and iris gardens can be layed [sic] out much as they are in England."[59] The following summer he reviewed the 1936 Chelsea Flower Show with a critical eye, condemning it as "fast approaching the moribund state of its prototype, [as] so little can be found of evolution, originality or evidence of a well-balanced sense of values among the exhibits."[60] Many of the displays were traditional and overly lavish, with crowd-pleasers such as "the same plant material jumbled together in chaotic masses, the same bunnies and babies, laughing boys and spouting dolphins...all as perennial as the gay impossible borders of plants, which flowering naturally at different seasons, are here shown together at the height of their beauty." He then asks, "What relation do these horticultural creations at Chelsea bear to everyday practical gardening?"[61] In reviewing the exhibition, Tunnard assumed the role of independent critic despite his having been educated by the Royal Horticultural Society, the sponsor of the annual exhibition. No doubt his disapproving stance ruffled a few feathers within the society. In the spring of 1937, a portfolio of photographs of St. Ann's Hill in Surrey appeared on the journal's pages, but little of his garden design was evident in the images.[62] Perhaps the landscape work was still too incomplete to be pictured. Other coeval projects received similarly spotty coverage. Tunnard illustrated his article on town gardens with his own project for the Schlesinger garden in Hampstead and another for the Isobar restaurant at Isokon Flats, the latter left unbuilt. Gardens may thrive and add to one's life in even the worst environments, Tunnard asserts, and as a genre, town gardens should differ from gardens in the country. In the article, he argues for the "business of providing lines and masses of colour to refresh the eye in the same fashion that one uses paint on a wall, or arrangement of stems and leaves to stimulate it, like the pattern of a wallpaper."[63] Moreover,

> it stands to reason that gardens in which the materials—the climbing, prostrate bushy and erect growing plants, the stones, gravel, grass and water—are calculated parts of a free and logical plan, design in three dimensions with allowances for growth and expansion, are more likely to be works of art than those in which plants are set out in containers on an unbroken surface of paving to be admired like trinkets in a show case, or, because unsuited for their purpose, are forced to languish in an uncongenial way.[64]

Although the values expressed are consistent with his other writings, perhaps it was the publication in a journal called *Decoration* that guided the author to focus so much on the ornamental aspects of the garden. Still in his twenties, by 1936 Tunnard had become an active and actively critical voice in advancing the cause of modern landscape architecture in Britain. The following year he took an even more active role, in his writings as well as through his own designs.

> As Author: *Gardens in the Modern Landscape*

The instigation for the essays that would become *Gardens in the Modern Landscape* is not clear, that is to say, whether they were solicited by the editor of the *Architectural Review* or proposed by Tunnard to the magazine. By 1936, Tunnard had established himself as one of the leaders in the movement for landscapes designed in accord with contemporary living, architecture, and the arts. The challenge: How precisely could this be accomplished, especially given the inherently conservative nature of plant forms? Space rather than form should be more significant; plants should be used not only for color and delight but also for their singular forms and space-defining capabilities. Hence the need, Tunnard believed, for writings that introduced, explained, and proselytized for the cause; and there is little doubt about the young landscape designer's conviction, confidence, and ambition in taking on the project. Tunnard's interest in a modern, if not modernist, landscape design had been growing steadily since his years at Wisley, and his contact with the leading voices in architecture and the arts could only have furthered his passion to shift the path of the landscape architecture profession to align with that of architecture and the arts. Hubert de Cronin Hastings, the publisher of the *Architectural Review*, and J. M. Richards, its editor, probably had their own reasons for wanting a book on the modern landscape as they shared an interest in expanding the modernist view to the outdoor environment. Certainly, the journal had been advancing architectural modernism for the better part of a decade, and its parent company, the Architectural Press, had already published F. R. S. Yorke's *The Modern House* in 1934 and *The Modern Flat* (Yorke with Frederick Gibberd) in 1937. Each of these compendiums presented work executed in the new manner, propelled by values that had squared off against British tradition.[65] In any event, Tunnard's essays began to appear in the *Architectural Review* in

October 1937, and continued through October 1938. In that same year the essays, with some revisions, appeared as *Gardens in the Modern Landscape* [figure 2-15]. The impact was almost immediate and would soon become widespread.

Read today, the book divides somewhat neatly into halves. The first half concerns the history of the garden—and to some degree, the greater landscape—in England; the second presents a series of thoughts, although less than a coherent thesis, for garden design today. A concern for the English agricultural and cultural landscapes, and the position of the garden within them, permeates the chapters of the book's second part. Hence the book's title, i.e., to conceive of and position the new garden in the greater landscape. For the first time, we discern in these later chapters Tunnard's ever-widening interests and his eventual turn to town and regional planning from more detailed landscape design.

In the book's introduction, Tunnard announces his thesis by telling the reader that to truly know the present and predict the future, one must first know the past, and he derides those architects who attack the styles of the past without truly understanding them. "These are the people who are defeating true modernism; they do not investigate sufficiently; they have discarded the older styles without bothering to understand what they represent or the demands placed upon them by the society that produced them."[66] He rejects the notion that a new manner derives only from a blanket dismissal of the old, and that in fact, the "style for our own times" will actually draw more upon history than we are often willing to admit. "In other words," he writes, "the modernist ought now to be broadening his range, not narrowing it, and trying his hand at all sorts of solutions."[67] There is no one style, no one way to approach design. Therefore, by extension, landscape design must embrace a conceptually wider sphere philosophically and spatially, by considering the landscape beyond the immediate plot. Apposite thinking is not a matter of style and form alone, but one of vision and accommodation. However, Tunnard firmly believed that landscape design was a cultural practice and an art, not just a technical practice, and this belief instigated his tackling the subject of the modern garden.

"A garden is a work of art," he wrote at the very opening of *Gardens in the Modern Landscape*. "It is also a number of other things, such as a place for rest and recreation, and for the pursuit of horticulture, but to be a garden in the true sense of the term it must first be an aesthetic composition."[68] Given his appreciation of England's naturalistic garden heritage, Tunnard's belief that landscape art should be discernible as the product of human intention and actions appears as a rejection of naturalism. To make his point, Tunnard cites André Le Nôtre as one of landscape history's most important figures despite the evident formality of his gardens. "Though bounded by innumerable sets of rules, an artist like Le Nôtre was at liberty to indulge his creative instincts without the necessity of producing a representational design."[69] This was a good thing. In Tunnard's eyes, however, the two manners were not irreconcilable. Of greater consequence were the shaping of the terrain and the informed and precise selection and planting of vegetation. He cautioned that "The painter's conception of landscape having by this time [in the eighteenth-century English landscape garden] become widely known, it was beginning to be recognized by a few as slightly artificial, selected, and untrue; though it was undoubtedly good art, there was just a possibility that it might be bad nature."[70] While the presence of artistic intent is more apparent in formal designs, it should be evident even in the most naturalistic landscapes. Capability Brown, though revered by the English landscape establishment, withered under Tunnard's denunciation; he was "far from being an artist, and his clients suffered for it."[71] On the other hand, the contradictions and vagueness that recur in Tunnard's thinking throughout the book troubled several reviewers.[72] Reginald Blomfield, who decades earlier had argued for a garden form sympathetic to the architecture of the house, sniffed at the very idea of modernism in England, purposefully titling his own book *Modernismus* to underline its relationship to German practices. In summation, Blomfield grunted that "what might be endurable in a suburb of Paris or Berlin is quite intolerable on the Chilterns and the English countryside."[73]

Art depends on science, Tunnard held, no less in the landscape than in the studio or laboratory. Art also follows economics: the great landscapes of eighteenth-century England would have been impossible without enclosure and the seigniorial system upon which the economy was based. In *Gardens in the Modern Landscape*, as in writings by modernist landscape architects such as James Rose and Garrett Eckbo in the succeeding generation, science is hailed as a source of design thinking. The particular nature of that source remained unspecified, however; the elevation of science was more a call to look at the world around you rather than the past. Tunnard became more specific in his citing of fertilizers, equipment, and technology, and hybridization as the gift of science to landscape architecture.

> The fairy ring has proved to be the work, not of fairies, but of fungi; and though science has restored in some measure that which she has taken away by giving us new and more substantial mythology, she is being beneficially ruthless with the old methods and styles. Just as the design of the locomotive, the aeroplane, and, for that matter, the modern house, is being changed by scientific invention, in a similar way science will transform the garden of the future.[74]

Tunnard's education and training at Wisley had embroiled him in the world of practice and his turn to theory was clearly by his own choice, gamely trying to balance the pragmatics that guide modern landscape-making with the aesthetic charge given its designers. Perhaps rehearsing Nikolaus Pevsner in his distinguishing of architecture from building, Tunnard states, "The fact that garden making is in part a science does not free it from the duty of performing an aesthetic function; it can no more be turned over to the horticulturist than architecture to the engineer."[75] Somehow, a balance must be struck; he proposes three potential models, which he terms "techniques."

> Toward a New Technique

After establishing a historical basis for this argument, and advancing his critique of picturesque landscape design, Tunnard proposed three "methods" by which to achieve a landscape design in accord with contemporary life. These he termed the functional, empathic, and artistic, although he admitted that there were other ways to approach the question; these three, however, were primary. "It would be a mistake," he reasoned, "to imagine that even the freest forms of planning are not based on unalterable laws and systems of values, and since we are faced with finding a new set to satisfy contemporary needs it can do no harm to suggest some obvious possibilities."[76] He then begins to search for these unalterable laws.

The functional approach derives to a large degree from architecture, where parameters such as circulation, structure, and environmental management are more easily measured. Here his concerns probably originate from his association with the MARS Group and in particular from his association with Raymond McGrath and Serge Chermayeff. But how does one measure function in landscape architecture? Today, at least to some degree, performance might be computed in terms of environmental sustainability, minimal earth movement, the capture of water on-site, and the like. But in the 1930s function in the landscape was not so easily defined. In addition, we could ask whether these considerations are true functions, rather than a sensible way by which to accommodate the demands placed on the land that more often fall under the jurisdiction of landscape planning. For Tunnard, "The functional garden avoids the extremes both of the sentimental expressionism of the wild garden and the intellectual classicism of the 'formal' garden; it embodies rather a spirit of rationalism and through an aesthetic and practical ordering of its units provides a friendly and hospitable milieu for rest and recreation. It is, in effect, the social conception of the garden."[77] He makes no mention of production as a garden function, however.

If the functional approach represented reason, the artistic approach embodied the pursuit of beauty, which Tunnard held to be "the by-product of the creative attitude to garden planning."[78] In the chapter entitled "Art and Ornament," Tunnard describes the role of art in the garden but avoids determining just how the garden itself gains status as a work of art. He noted that "although it is true that gardens, like buildings, can be complete in themselves without mural decoration or sculpture, it is necessary that the significant forces which find liberation in painting and carving or modeling shall also be expressed in the complex technical achievement which is the garden artist's manipulation of living and natural forms."[79] He derides the use of representational sculpture and reasons that if we still must have long vistas with focal points, "we shall find that they are better provided with simple terminals like stone columns or non-representational and geometrical forms in stone, concrete, metal or wood."[80] In all, though he advances the artistic approach as the equal to the functional and empathic, he is actually describing the role of art in the garden rather than the garden itself as art.

Perhaps the most fecund approach, the one offering the greatest potential richness and widespread application, was the final category, which Tunnard termed "empathic." Vague in Tunnard's definition, and in reality a resulting characteristic rather than a true category, the word is used to advance the role of the "Oriental" garden as a model for modern Western garden makers. Although the functional type has improved on the residue of the traditional garden, something more is required. Citing an unnamed source, Tunnard states that "the Japanese come by the beautiful by way of the necessary."[81] That is to say, the functional garden is but a stage along the way to achieve the artistic landscape. As we have seen, Tunnard's interest in Japan was long-standing and the subject of his first substantial article. In the chapter of the book titled "Asymmetrical Garden Planning," he contrasted the formality and geometric structure of Western gardens such as the Villa Lante in Italy and the Alcazar in Spain with the asymmetrical freedom—yet balance—of Japanese examples such as the Koho-an temple at Daitoku-ji in Kyoto, which in the book he presents in plan. The effect, he asserted, derives from an "occult balance," which is "essentially a relative quality depending on the interplay of background and foreground, height and depth, motion and rest, but as such it can be reduced to a science and obtains through all composition in art and nature."[82]

From Japanese history, like his distant colleague Sutemi Horiguchi, Tunnard found that "the neglected asymmetrical technique embraces the delicate nuance as well as the bold impression." Moreover, and more significantly, "It is symbolic of the plastic arts of our time."[83] Thus, from history we may derive a new present. In Japan the complete integration of house and garden has been achieved; trees are freely guided into desired shapes when planted, or later shaped manually when mature; color is used sparingly, in strong contrast to the English floral tradition. And unlike the Western garden, which has ossified over the last century, "All the important [Japanese] gardens are products of a highly stylized art in which experiment is encouraged and conventional repetition avoided."[84] In all, it is here in Japan that Tunnard found a model for the modern Western garden, and again used the landscape of Horiguchi's Kikkawa house as his illustration. It should be noted that at this point in his life Tunnard had never seen an authentic Japanese garden and would not for over two decades to come—and was instead relying for his knowledge on publication and his conversations with Bernard Leach.

Despite the course of action suggested in *Gardens in the Modern Landscape*, change was slow to come in England. The soil was more amenable in the United States where efforts toward modern landscape design were taking place at virtually the exact time of the book's publication. Tunnard received considerable notoriety in the wake of the book's launch and its celebrity positioned him at the forefront of efforts to formulate a modern landscape, not only in the English-speaking world, but eventually abroad.[85]

With the publication of *Gardens in the Modern Landscape* in 1938, his position as the leading voice in British landscape architecture was assured. The word "voice" here is well chosen given that his realized works were few in number, hardly remarkable in terms of formal innovation, and hardly "modern." As a group, they better demonstrated a keen rationale for functional planning and an expertise in the technical side of landscape design, that is, aspects such as grading, plant selection, and planned maintenance. This would not hold him back, however; his aspirations were international, exceeding the possibilities offered in England.

> **Early Practice**

Elizabeth Denby, "a writer, political advocate, and housing administrator," had worked as an administrator in social services until, in 1933, she met the architect Maxwell Fry, a fellow MARS member.[86] Denby soon became a major supporter not only of housing reform but of modern architecture as well. The commission for the 1934 Sassoon House apartments provided the opportunity for their first collaboration, Denby being primarily responsible for creating the program and Fry, the architecture that responded to it. Sponsored by the Gas Light and Coke Company, the project was intended to showcase the possibilities for using new technologies to live a more healthful, social, and pleasant life. Based on Denby's detailed investigations of community facilities, apartment configuration, and internal fittings, the 1937 Kensal apartments that resulted from the collaboration became a model widely emulated though rarely equaled.

Denby invited Tunnard to work with her on "The All-Europe House" to be displayed at the 1939 iteration of the *Daily Mail*'s Ideal Home Exhibition. She, alone, is credited with the planning and architectural design of the units while Tunnard received credit for the "Garden Layout and Planting" [figure 2-16]. The *Daily Mail* began the Ideal Home program in 1908 and over time it had become a major publicity vehicle for the newspaper. For the working- and middle-class visitor the exhibition stimulated both inspiration and aspiration. Traditionally mounted in the cavernous spaces of the Earls Court Exhibition Centre, the annual event introduced its audience to the newest

2-16
Elizabeth Denby.
All-Europe House.
1939.
Perspective by
H. F. Clark.

2-17
Christopher Tunnard.
All-Europe House.
1939.
Site plan.

2-18
Terrace houses,
Sweden.
Floor plan.
[*Europe Re-housed*]

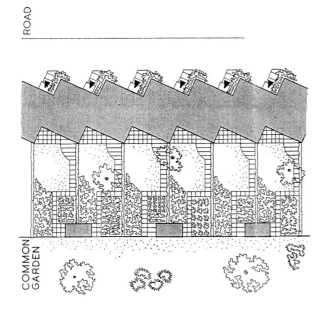

ROAD

COMMON GARDEN

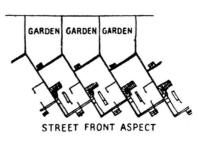

GARDEN GARDEN GARDEN

STREET FRONT ASPECT

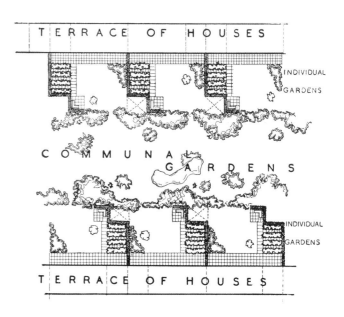

domestic technology, furnishings, and decorating, accompanied by live presentations of housekeeping and cooking. Periodically the shows also included an Ideal House competition, with the winning entry constructed for the following year's exhibition. Perhaps that competition was the origin of the Denby–Tunnard project; perhaps the organizers believed that dream of the single-family house would be more realistically achieved as a rowhouse, or even just a flat.

Thus, the Denby–Tunnard design proposed ideal housing rather than an ideal house—perhaps justified by the pressing interwar need for housing in Britain, or by a more inclusive interpretation of the term "ideal home." The design was described as "a scheme for mixed development with flats in central areas, at a density of twenty houses to the acre." Titled "The All-Europe House," it enfolded ideas from the Continent as well as Britain, no doubt with knowledge garnered from the research for Denby's book *Europe Re-housed*, published in 1938.[87] "It is a reflection on our ability to develop," the unnamed reviewer for the *RIBA Journal* dolefully admitted, "that in 1939 we look outside England for a rejuvenation of ideas, that we have to admit that the Continent can now contribute more to the solution of our housing problem than is comfortable for our self-esteem."[88] Although the terrace house was hardly an unknown building type in the British Isles, the scheme appears more reflective of recent housing in the Netherlands, Switzerland, and Scandinavia. In fact, the staggered units of the All-Europe home closely resemble those of an unidentified group of Swedish flats published in Denby's book [figures 2-17, 2-18].[89] One unit, with garden, of the Denby–Tunnard design was constructed on-site, but only photographs of two bedrooms were included in the single publication on the project located to date.

The exterior spaces, however, figured prominently in the article, if less so in the exhibition. The site plan shows units arranged as a sawtooth and aligned north–south to maximize solar exposure. While the apartments displayed greater unity and impact as a block, Tunnard's proposed gardens speak of individuality. Hedges divided the plots, each of which shared a common layout with paved walks and rear storage building. One perspective sketch suggests that over time greater individuality in the gardens would emerge, and that vegetables as well as ornamental plantings would be welcome [figure 2-19]. Beyond the limits of the private gardens was a common green area illustrated without much indication of the rationale behind its planting—it reads, in fact, more as generic green space. This pairing of individual garden and collective common space was hardly a novel idea at the time—it had become a common scheme in Scandinavian housing in the early 1900s and was a key ingredient in Eliel Saarinen's rowhouses and green spaces for the Munkkiniemi–Haaga suburb outside Helsinki designed as early as 1915. Here in Earls Court, however, the proposal spoke less of innovation than a furthering of Tunnard's idea of the "garden in the modern landscape" explained in the "Garden into Landscape" section of his book.

In the 1938 edition of *Gardens in the Modern Landscape* Tunnard illustrated the allotment gardens of Römerstadt in Germany and Neubühl in Zurich, both of which featured small individual plots connecting

2-19
Christopher Tunnard.
All-Europe House.
1939.
Collective garden.
Perspective by
H. F. Clark.

2-20
Haefeli Moser
Steiger, architects;
Gustav Ammann,
landscape architect.
Neubühl Siedlung.
Zurich, Switzerland,
1931–1940s.
[Marc Treib]

2-21
Christopher Tunnard.
Minimum Gardens.
[*Gardens in the
Modern Landscape*,
1948]

to larger communally held green space [figure 2-20]. In the 1948 edition of the book, Tunnard added a site plan based on the All-Europe House project under the rubric "The Minimum Garden," which he claimed is normally too large for its owners to maintain "yet never large enough to satisfy their need for space and exercise" [figure 2-21]. He regarded these gardens as extensions to the internal spaces of the rowhouse; they "contain a terrace under the house with windows, a rectangular lawn, a sheltered recess for tables and chairs, space for children's sandpit, play-room or tool shed, flower beds, and a screen planting of flowering trees and shrubs." By repeating the configuration of the garden lots a certain collective coherence was achieved—but sufficient opportunity remained for expressing individual tastes and idiosyncrasies, especially over time: "the garden need never become an impersonal thing or a mere copy of its neighbour."[90] In this context, the common green served as neutral territory in terms of both ownership and design, territory marked by shrubbery planted along the outer bounds of the private gardens used more to buffer than to define spaces.

Resulting from Denby's staggered building façades, the triangular spaces left between the front façades and the street received some landscape treatment; in the perspective drawing their planting appears quite anemic. The site plan and three perspectives were drawn by H. F. (Frank) Clark, who also had drafted plans for other of Tunnard's early projects. Like Tunnard, Clark had worked in the office of Percy Cane and it might have been there that they met. Clark would become, in time, the author of a small yet significant book on the English garden, a quite established landscape architect—his design for the York University landscape remains his best-known work, and teacher at the universities of Reading and Edinburgh.[91] It was Clark who tended Tunnard's projects after he departed for the United States in the late 1930s.

Transition: Leicester

In the mid-1930s, as his reputation as a progressive landscape architect was growing, Tunnard received the commission to design a garden to accompany a new house in Galby, some twelve miles northeast of Leicester, designed by the architect and fellow Martian Raymond McGrath. McGrath configured the plan for the C. R. Keene house as a bent east-facing bar with living spaces and garage below and bedroom area above. Although the plot was sizable, the house was tucked into its southwest corner [figure 2-22]. Presumably, by siting the house in this corner location, access road construction could be kept to a minimum while the area available for cultivation, development, or simply aesthetic pleasure would be maximized. The building's concavity sheltered an exterior living area to the southwest; a swimming pool, extensive terraces, and lawn areas completed the landscape adjacent to the house.

Although a complete file of McGrath's architectural drawings exists, only one Tunnard drawing remains among them, an early scheme curiously dated "3.6.94" [figure 2-23].[92] The sole surviving site plan by Tunnard shows the property carefully zoned, assigning the more public areas to the north and northeast, and those more private areas for family and entertaining to the southwest, where they could gather the warmth of sunlight. Hedges enclose the site to its full extent along its west and south borders. In form, we might compare the site plan to an American baseball diamond with the pool as home plate and the house positioned between first and third, opening outward like a megaphone to the "outfield" of the open landscape. The approach from the north terminated in an auto court defined by the canopies of six trees accompanied by a hedge running parallel to the north façade of the house. In this outer zone, Tunnard traced in greenery the line of the brick and wood façades of the house, using a curving hedge to effect the transition between the auto court and an enclosed garden for growing flowers and/or vegetables. Arranged as a checkerboard, this garden was to serve as a colorful parterre when viewed from the second-floor bedrooms of the house—particularly the master suite at the house's southern end. The living room that occupied the southeastern "bend" opened directly onto this garden.

A later McGrath site plan, dating from either late 1936 or early 1937, reflects an adjustment in thinking and a reduction in scope and required expense. From this plan, it is evident that the diminution of building volume for economy rippled into the outdoor planning. The intricacy of the southwest outdoor living area has been simplified: the pool is now kidney-shaped rather than rectangular, the massed shrubbery at the southwest corner has been reconfigured as a grid of square planting beds, and a circular "winter garden" now terminates the south end of the bar.

Along the southern property line, a turf walk sunken below the level of the lawn terraces serves as a formal promenade. In the sketch by Gordon Cullen, the species of shrubs and flowers planted between the walk and the boundary hedge cannot be identified with precision although the drawings suggest a variant of the vegetation used in the traditional herbaceous border [figure 2-24]. Overall, the scheme features a concentration of detail at the south-western corner of the site with hedges used architecturally to effect a transition between the house and the open parkland that lay beyond. As a result, the logic behind the planning of the landscape follows quite closely to Reginald Blomfield's notions of a "house-determined" garden rather than the freer wildness proselytized by William Robinson.[93] Yet—particularly in the faint checkerboards and grids—there appear touches of modern patterns that characterized certain French modernistic gardens of the prior decade. The house was ultimately built in a reduced form, alas, with little evidence of Tunnard's landscape design. Although it was not identified, Tunnard seems to have used a model of the house and site to illustrate an article in his *Architectural Review* "Garden and Landscape" installments titled "The Country Acre: A Typical Garden Problem." To make his point he tested various approaches to the planning of the site, and after four proposals that he found wanting, concluded with a plan remarkably similar to the Keene landscape. He notes that after dismissing the prior quartet of approaches, "the designer adopts a less formal plan which comprises, in effect, a series of independent gardens, each with its own character, arranged round the perimeter of the site, the centre being left free." In the last two images, he

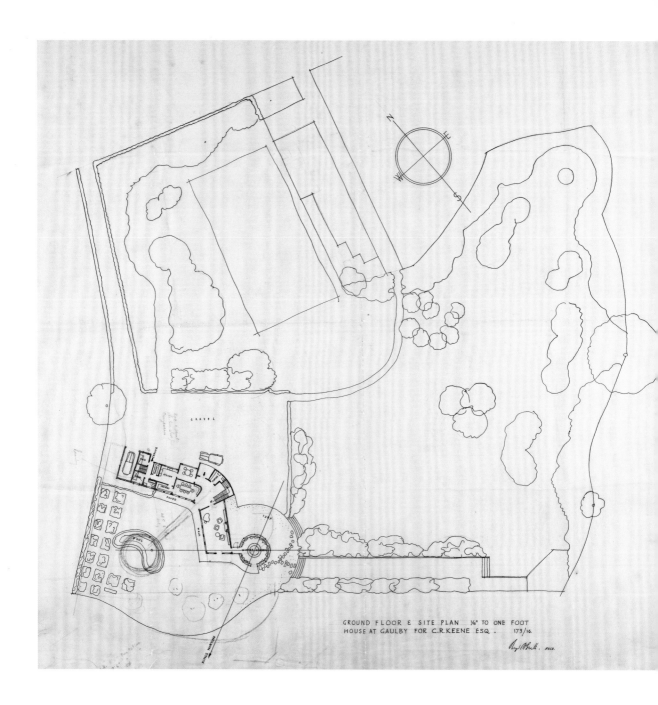

GROUND FLOOR & SITE PLAN ⅛" TO ONE FOOT
HOUSE AT GAULBY FOR C.R.KEENE ESQ . 173/16.

2-22
Raymond McGrath.
Keene house.
Galby, Leicestershire,
c. 1937.
Site plan.
［RIBA］

40 >

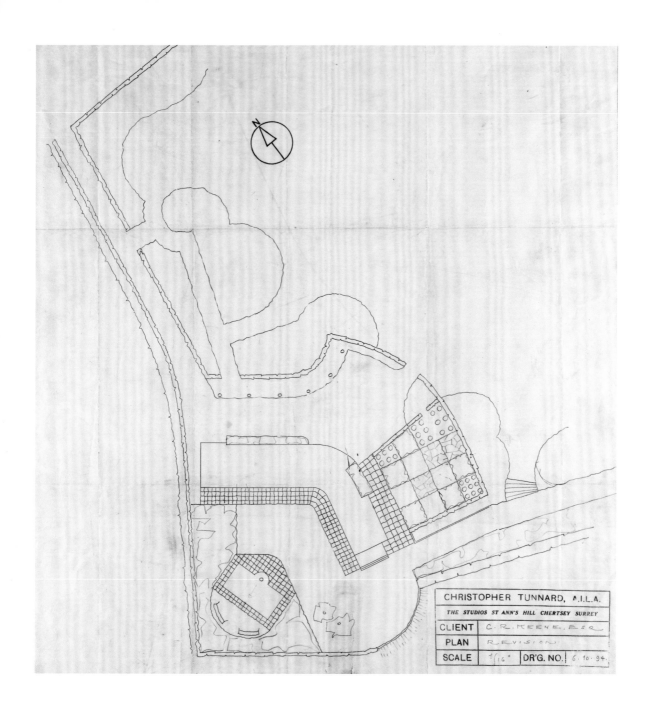

Within the plan's title block:

CHRISTOPHER TUNNARD, A.I.L.A.

THE STUDIOS ST ANN'S HILL CHERTSEY SURREY

CLIENT	C. R. KEENE, ESQ	
PLAN	REVISION	
SCALE	1/16"	DR'G. NO.	6.10.94

2-23
Christopher Tunnard.
Keene landscape.
Galby, Leicestershire,
c. 1937.
Site plan, c. 1934.
[RIBA]

describes the resulting design, noting that "The mound near the southeast corner is treated as an essay in scenic landscaping, as it is the most prominent object in the view from the house." It would be planted with rhododendrons. In all, the design comprised a central lawn surrounded by a series of gardens, each featuring a species such as the rose, or herbaceous plants.[94]

For the same family McGrath also designed a small, even minute (9' x 12' internal dimension), outdoor living pavilion. Just where on the Keene property the structure was to be sited is unknown, as McGrath's drawings show only the building, without any suggestion of its setting. This was to be a simple rectangular pavilion of wood complemented by a semicircular deck, the entirety raised above ground to avoid the damp and increase the visual pleasure that an elevated view provides. Regarded critically, we could say that the design tried to do too much with such limited square footage, although with its sloping roof and exposed beam ends, the building would have possessed a certain rustic charm. In a perspective sketch by Gordon Cullen, the house is shown before a small pond planted with flowers [figure 2-25]. In his caption to the drawing in *Gardens in the Modern Landscape*, Tunnard refers to the little cabin as recalling the Japanese teahouse, a comparison more easily made if one has never actually seen a real teahouse in Japan: "A modern garden in Leicestershire which adopts an aesthetic principle from the Japanese instead of merely borrowing the superficial style. Water, stones and planting are linked intelligibly to the small pavilion."[95] For those who have experienced the true Japanese structures, Tunnard's claim will appear highly hyperbolic. In any event, neither the building nor its garden were realized.

The mid- to late-1930s were Tunnard's most productive years in terms of landscape designs, with a flurry of commissions small and large, including the two major gardens and their landscapes for which he would be best known. Other, indeed most, gardens from these years followed a more traditional manner, following paths blazed decades before by the Edwin Lutyens–Gertrude Jekyll collaboration and British landscape architects thereafter, among them Percy Cane. This group of designs included the garden for Mrs. F. A. Dumoulin in Walton-on-Thames, with its by-then-common division into forecourt, lawn, terrace, roses, herbaceous plantings, and wild garden; the latter two were heavily gardens planted with a panoply of diverse species [figure 2-26]. The garden at Ravenhead in Leicestershire, also for the Keene family, was structured on a pair of long axial spaces, one dedicated to the entry drive, the other to a topiary walk [figure 2-27]. In a similar manner, the walk lined with herbaceous plantings at the 1936 Goldschmidt garden in Salcott, Cobham, recalled the Broad Walks of Kew and West Wycombe, another continuance of garden elements past [figure 2-28]. There were smaller projects as well, for example, the 1934 design for a garden to accompany the restaurant at the Lawn Road, or Isokon Flats by Wells Coates, one of the most innovative of the modern architects working in England in the 1930s.[96] The garden design was far less radical than the building it was to accompany, however [figure 2-29]. While its curves play against the rigor of the architecture, they appear as shapes rather than spaces, disposed on two levels—one planted to lawn, one lined in gravel. However, Tunnard proposed using the surrounding vegetation to shelter the lower garden area. In any event, like several other projects from this era the design was left unexecuted.

2-24
Christopher Tunnard.
Keene landscape.
Galby, Leicestershire,
c. 1937.
Drawing by
Gordon Cullen.
[*Gardens in the
Modern Landscape*]

2-25
Raymond McGrath,
architect;
Christopher Tunnard,
landscape architect.
Keene pavilion.
Galby, Leicestershire,
c. 1937.
Drawing by
Gordon Cullen.
[*Gardens in the
Modern Landscape*]

2-26

Christopher Tunnard.
Dumoulin garden.
Walton-on-Thames,
mid-1930s.
Site plan.
[H. F. Clark
Papers, Historic
Environment
Scotland, hereafter
HES]

2-27

Christopher Tunnard.
Keene garden.
Ravenhead, Ingarsby,
Leicestershire,
c. 1936.
[H. F. Clark Papers,
HES]

2-28

Christopher Tunnard.
Goldschmidt garden.
Salcott, Cobham,
1936.
[H. F. Clark Papers,
HES]

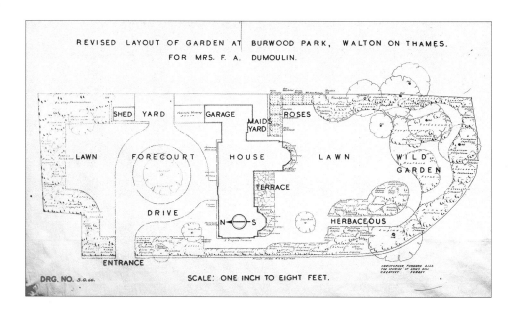

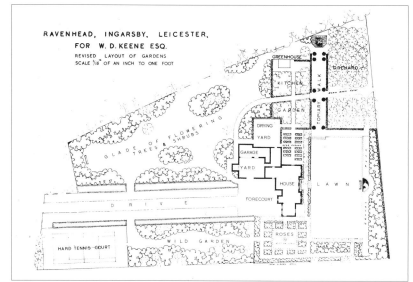

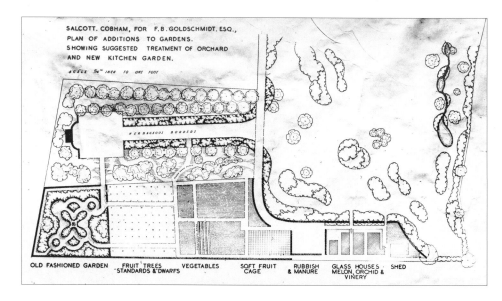

2-29
Christopher Tunnard.
Isokon Restaurant
Garden.
London, c. 1936.
Site plan.
[*Decoration*]

Bentley Wood

Following the Keene garden and other commissions Tunnard embarked on the two projects that would secure his professional reputation and bolster his status as a theoretician. The first was located in Sussex to the southeast of London, the second in Surrey, closer to the capital. Bentley Wood, set in the village of Halland, was designed by Serge Chermayeff for himself and his family. Born in the Caucasus but raised in England, Chermayeff was one of the consequential figures in British architectural modernism, and like Raymond McGrath a member of the MARS Group. This connection, or through the *Architectural Review*, seems to be the most plausible vehicle for linking the architect and landscape architect. The house, of slightly over 5,000 square feet, was configured as a rectangular block positioned east–west, whose primary orientation to the south supported a splendid vista over the Downs [figure 2-30]. Set to the northeast, perpendicular to the main block, a subsidiary wing accommodated services, storage, and auto-mobiles. Continuing the line—and width—of the service wing north of the house, a terrace extended southward into the meadow, its gentle enclosure suggesting a green forecourt set before the study and rooms destined for living and dining. Its construction relied on a frame of Australian jarrah wood and was prefabricated off-site.[97] A tan brick wall protected the terrace against wind and visual intrusion. West facing, its bricks also retained the heat of the afternoon sun, thereby extending the hours that could be comfortably spent outdoors.

A wooden lattice wall with glazed lower panels terminated the thrust of the Portland stone-paved terrace extending outward from the house [figure 2-31]. Indicative of the times, this pairing of frame and landscape also appeared in at least two of Paul Nash's enigmatic paintings: the 1929 *Landscape at Iden*, and more particularly the almost contemporaneous 1938 *Landscape from a Dream* [figure 2-32].[98] In this second painting, the frame of the transparent screen intensifies the elements of the landscape behind it; the wooden screen wall at Bentley Wood serves in just that same way, as both a spatial division and frame for the view of what lies beyond. In his plan for the terrace, Chermayeff inserted a linear planting bed between the wall and the paving, softening their intersection. Here Tunnard projected a mixed border of considerable intricacy. Heather, cotoneaster, juniper, and azaleas were to stand cheek by jowl with yucca, salvia, tulips, and phlox; *Sedum acre* occupied the cracks between the paving units and further softened the architectural assertiveness of the ground plane [figure 2-33]. Water lilies grew in the shallow pool on the terrace adjacent to the house. In contrast to the grand gestures played out in the meadow and woodland—massed plantings of trees and sweeps of flowers—this sedate garden sharing the terrace and plinth was restrained yet intricate.

Set before the screen wall and given pride of place adjacent to the six steps leading down to the meadow was *Recumbent Figure* (1938) by Henry Moore [figure 2-34]. In considering the project almost two decades after its origin, Moore noted the shift then occurring in the relationship between architecture and sculpture. At that time, that is, in the late 1930s, he claimed that some architects could be persuaded "not to have sculpture *on* a building, but *outside* it, in a spatial relation to it." Seen within the context of

2-30
Raymond McGrath, architect;
Christopher Tunnard, landscape architect.
Bentley Wood.
Halland, England, 1938.
General view with south façade.
[Dell & Wainwright, RIBA]

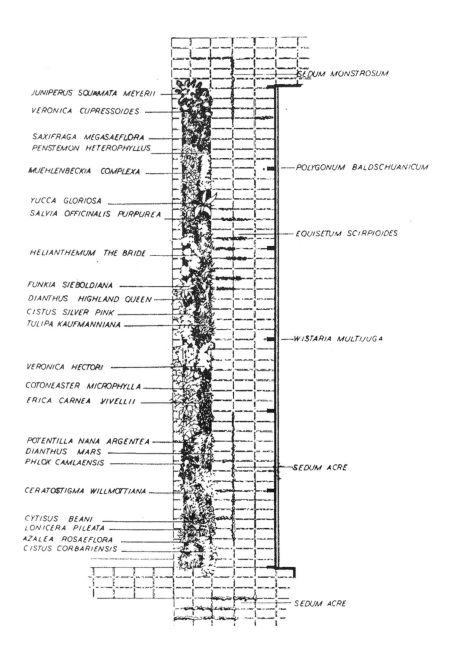

SEDUM MONSTROSUM

JUNIPERUS SQUAMATA MEYERII

VERONICA CUPRESSOIDES

SAXIFRAGA MEGASAEFLORA
PENSTEMON HETEROPHYLLUS

MUEHLENBECKIA COMPLEXA

POLYGONUM BALDSCHUANICUM

YUCCA GLORIOSA
SALVIA OFFICINALIS PURPUREA

EQUISETUM SCIRPIOIDES

HELIANTHEMUM THE BRIDE

FUNKIA SIEBOLDIANA
DIANTHUS HIGHLAND QUEEN
CISTUS SILVER PINK
TULIPA KAUFMANNIANA

WISTARIA MULTIJUGA

VERONICA HECTORI

COTONEASTER MICROPHYLLA

ERICA CARNEA VIVELLII

POTENTILLA NANA ARGENTEA
DIANTHUS MARS
PHLOX CAMLAENSIS

SEDUM ACRE

CERATOSTIGMA WILLMOTTIANA

CYTISUS BEANI
LONICERA PILEATA
AZALEA ROSAEFLORA
CISTUS CORBARIENSIS

SEDUM ACRE

Bentley Wood that observation is apposite, as the sculpture served as a figurative counterpoint to the latticed prism of the house. And as Alan Powers has suggested, the sculpture might also relate to the figures who periodically used the terrace for sunbathing, suggested by the deck chair that appeared in the iconic photograph looking out from the house across the terrace.[99]

Chermayeff had commissioned the work directly from the sculptor, having made an initial deposit of £50 against a total sum of £300. For Bentley Wood, Moore created *Recumbent Figure* from three laminated layers of green Haddon stone, carving a form that spoke of Mesoamerican sculpture, in particular the reclining stone sculptures of the Mexican god Chac-Mool. Despite its figuration, Moore's condensed organic forms and balance of void and solid—sharing with architecture the regard for space as well as mass—qualified the sculpture as firmly modern.[100] At Chermayeff's invitation, Moore had come to the site in 1936 to more fully understand the physical situation and to review the house design. "He wanted me to say whether I could visualise one of my figures standing at the intersection of terrace and garden," wrote Moore, and noted that it was "a long, low-lying building and there was an open view of the long sinuous lines of the Downs."[101] Responding to the prevalence of horizontal lines, he dismissed the idea of a standing figure, which "would have been more of a rebuff than a contrast, and might have induced needless drama." Instead, he conceived the sculpture as a focal point for the horizontal lines collecting at that point and a prostrate figure resulted. "My figure looked out across a great sweep of the Downs, and her gaze gathered in the horizon." The work, to Moore, existed independently. "It had its own identity," and it could be sited in other places. But to the sculptor the figure "enjoyed" being there at the end of the terrace—"introducing a humanising element; it became a mediator between modern house and ageless land."[102]

The classic photo of the terrace looking south, with Barbara Chermayeff reading in a chair as foreground, captured the informal modernity of the resulting setting; Moore's sculpture anchors the far end of the terrace while the vista is allowed to continue across the Downs [figure 2-35]. This was visual choreography of high caliber. Based on his writings about art and landscape, there is little doubt that Tunnard considered *Recumbent Figure* perfect for its setting and perfect in its setting. In placement, it echoed the relation of the Willi Soukop abstract sculpture to the house and garden at St. Ann's Hill, discussed below, constructed at roughly the same time.

Getting the house built was hardly an easy matter. Locals were unsympathetic to flat-roofed modern architecture in wood, and more or less insisted that all new construction in the area should follow the traditional pattern of stuccoed wall and pitched roof. Barbara Tilson has traced this "Battle of Bentley Wood," noting that after Chermayeff's scheme had at first been rejected, revised drawings and an intense campaign by favorable neighbors and well-known professionals were needed before a permit was finally issued.[103] In his own telling of the tale, Tunnard noted that the Uckfield Rural District Council rejected "the plans for this elegant building on the grounds that the design was 'unsuitable in the particular position chosen.'"[104] Today one wonders what the fuss was

2-33
Christopher Tunnard.
Bentley Wood.
Halland, England,
1938.
Terrace planting plan.
[*Landscape and Garden,* Spring 1939]

2-34
Henry Moore.
Recumbent Figure,
1938.
[© Tate, London,
2019.
Reproduced by
permission of the
Henry Moore
Foundation]

2-35
Raymond McGrath,
architect;
Christopher Tunnard,
landscape architect.
Bentley Wood.
Halland, 1938.
View from terrace
to the Downs.
[*Gardens in the
Modern Landscape*]

2-36

Christopher Tunnard,
landscape architect.
Bentley Wood.
Halland, England,
1938.
Perspective sketch
by Gordon Cullen
showing wildflower
plantings.
[*Gardens in the
Modern Landscape*]

2-37
Serge Chermayeff.
Bentley Wood.
Halland, England,
1938.
Survey Layout
Drainage plan
with vegetation
indicated.
[RIBA]

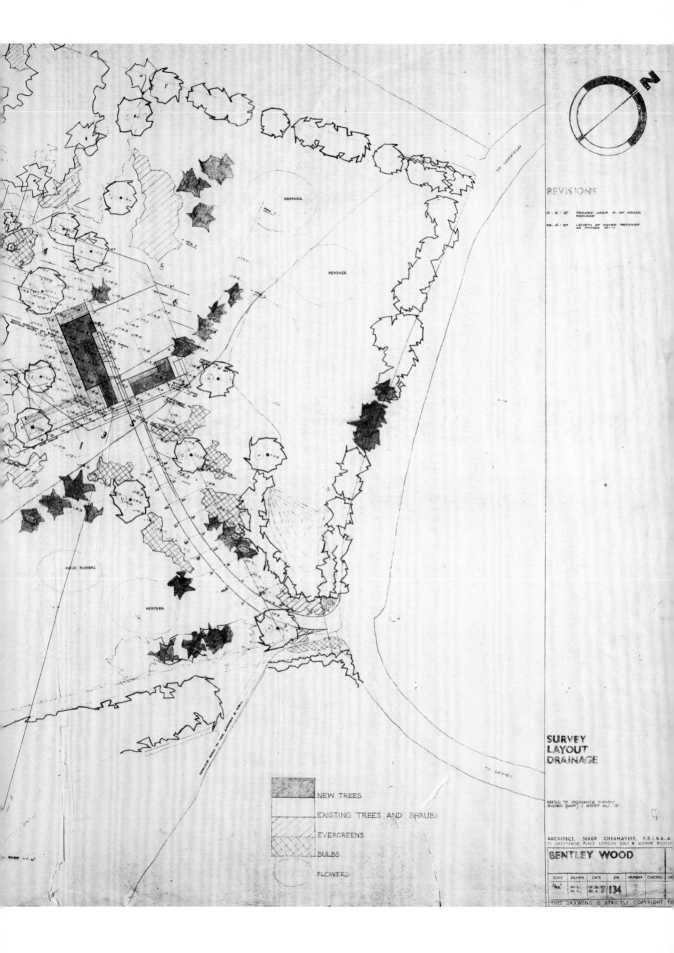

N

REVISIONS

2 : 4 : 37   DRAINED AREA W. OF HOUSE
            REDUCED

23 : 6 : 37 LENGTH OF HOUSE REDUCED
            AS PWNGS 10 - 11

TO UCKFIELD

HEATHER

HEATHER

WILD FLOWERS

HEATHER

TO LEWES

**SURVEY
LAYOUT
DRAINAGE**

REFER TO ORDNANCE SURVEY
SUSSEX [EAST] : SHEET XLI . 13

ARCHITECT.   SERGE CHERMAYEFF, F.R.I.B.A.
11 GROSVENOR PLACE LONDON S.W.1 ● SLOANE 9129/20

BENTLEY WOOD

SCALE	DRAWN	DATE	JOB NUMBER	CHECKED	
	W.L.	10:5:37	134		
	W.L.	24:6:37			

NEW TREES

EXISTING TREES AND SHRUBS

EVERGREENS

BULBS

FLOWERS

SCALE = 1:00?

about, especially considering the extensive acreage of the site and the small
footprint of the house, even including its appendages.

While the architecture of the house was uncom-
promisingly orthogonal, with the south terrace thrusting its geometry into
the meadow, the landscape itself remained pastoral, although it was obvious
that "the practices of agriculture, forestry, and even of industry had made the
pattern which we were to adapt to new use" [figure 2-36].[105] Indeed, parts of
the landscape had been shaped by years of use as sandpits while other parts
had been left neglected, for example, a coppice long untended. Rows of mature
trees marked the lot lines around the northwest and northeast edges of the site;
these are clearly demarcated on Chermayeff's site drainage plan of 24 May 1937
[figure 2-37]. To the northwest, the 84 acres of open fields joined 47 additional
acres of woodland. The landscape strategy, whether Tunnard's or Chermayeff's,
was to plant new trees where needed to complete the site boundaries or to
reinforce the presence of the existing trees that peppered the central part of
the site. Chermayeff's correspondence with Tunnard shows that his interest in
the relation of landscape and house, as well as in the selection of species to be
planted, was beyond the norm for architects of the time.

The approach road gently curved from the east and
entered the domestic zone through an opening in the long tan brick wall that
bounded the eastern side of the service wing to the north and the sun terrace
to the south. Along this road, new trees complemented the old; several were
specified to be evergreens. A proposed leitmotif for the landscape design was the
use of low coniferous shrubs to effect the transition between meadow and trees,
a strategy also evident in the swatches of heather, wildflowers, and bulbs such
as daffodils; in certain places bluebells were specified. The result was a meadow
visually vibrant in spring and green through the remainder of the year [see figure
2-36]. Tunnard also consulted on the trimming and thinning of the existing vegetation
to modulate the panorama viewed from the house and terraces.

As seen in early photographs the design of the
landscape was hardly startling in terms of innovative form [figure 2-38]. This was
by choice. In reporting on the collaborative design approach, Tunnard stated
that there were two ways to closely relate architecture to landscape. The first
is more formal, using hedges and geometry. The other is more natural, "which is
again a misleading term for a process which requires a high degree of conscious
art to be successful....Both can be subtle." Both were used at Bentley Wood. But
it seems clear the architect held the reins. Tunnard wrote,

> Chermayeff, who is a man of intellect, chose the method predominantly
> emotional in its appeal; but, with the eye of his profession, he declared
> in favour of atmospheric planting showing an architectural character; a
> free yet controlled scheme, related but in contrast to the formality of the
> building. It was a subjective and essentially pictorial approach which we
> eventually made.[106]

Several questions remain. For one, how much of the landscape in early photographs
already existed, how much of the executed design was the work of Christopher
Tunnard, and how much resulted from Chermayeff's initial scheme? In the spring
1939 issue of *Landscape and Garden*, Tunnard wrote about the Bentley Wood

project as "an experience in collaboration."[107] Before the landscape architect was invited to participate in the design, however, Chermayeff had already "fixed the position of the drive and started clearing the corner of the wood nearest the projected site of the house, leaving pleasant groups of trees in open glades."[108] The architect had also decided that timber from the woodland might have market value and that parts of the site could be let for sheep pasturage. Together they determined that the best approach would be to manage rather than form the landscape. "We decided," wrote Tunnard, "that our best work would be done by clearing existing shrubs and crowded trees on the west and north, leaving the shapeliest oaks and birches in the clear space round the building." The lawn would have "irregular but carefully planned boundaries." The shallow drainage ditch "running into the wood" would remain wet through most of the year by "the overflow of the house water supply from a windmill" and be transformed into a "planted dell" that would support the propagation of "primulas, water grasses, astilbes, and irises." These elements would comprise the frame while "colonies of scillas, crocus, and bluebells" would complement the "natural drifts of bluebells, primroses and foxgloves in the wood below."[109] A kitchen garden and orchard were sited some distance from the house and "screened by a line of gorse." All in all, Bentley Wood was an ambitious project—more a country estate than just a house in the country.

Documents that remained with his assistant H. F. Clark after Tunnard's departure for the United States reveal the extensive amount of work still to be achieved in autumn 1938, as well as the scope of Tunnard's contribution to the Bentley Wood landscape. These yet unexecuted tasks included transplanting certain existing trees and shrubs, but principally extensive new plantings that included major additions, such as twenty-four new Monterey cypresses (*Cupressus macrocarpa*), the white wisteria and magnolia (*Magnolia grandiflora*) at poolside, and a panoply of grasses, ivy, St. John's wort, climbing vines, and barberry. More functionally, the list cited the need for thickening the plantations of evergreens and cotoneasters to screen the septic tank.[110] Tunnard also replied at length to a letter from Chermayeff, presumably from 1938, answering the architect's numerous questions about planting a vegetable garden. He included advice on growing onions and potatoes, as well as tomatoes and herbs.[111]

In a 1989 telephone interview with the landscape historian Lance Neckar, Chermayeff claimed that although he himself was responsible for the landscape design he had consulted Tunnard only regarding species and selective pruning.[112] As many architects are less than forthcoming with credit or praise for their landscape architect collaborators, Chermayeff may have been guilty of some exaggeration. For one, we know that Tunnard had a masterful knowledge of the soils and vegetation of the English countryside gained from his education at Wisley, and that by this time his design sense had been honed by contact with the modern architectural community and through practice— admittedly with projects until then limited in scope and number. His aesthetic views had also developed from historical studies, and the basic idea of view and restricted planting squared well with his studies of the picturesque that would coalesce, at almost the same moment, in the publication of *Gardens in* the *Modern Landscape*. Art studies supported his landscape thinking, knowledge paired with a growing interest in things and landscapes Japanese. Therefore, it seems plausible to suggest—although it cannot be substantiated by the documentation that has come to light—that the site ("Survey Layout Drainage") plan, admittedly from the Chermayeff office, enfolded Tunnard's design ideas, although specifics like the exact positioning of trees may have been adjusted by the architect. Despite repeated attempts to ascertain just who did what and finding no definitive answer, we might best conclude by noting that the resulting ensemble of building and landscape was truly symbiotic and that Bentley Wood became iconic almost immediately. "It is not necessarily the use of local material," wrote Tunnard, "but the recognition and use of natural features on the site in any building scheme which make architecture a part of the countryside."[113] Note that he does not mention the word "modern" in this conclusion.

In the end, Bentley Wood became a modernized pastoral landscape, well-tempered for prospect, activity, and modulated seasonal color. Although the ideas behind its design were highly considered and developed, the final landscape looked to be fully in the English tradition rather than a landscape that smacked of innovation and modernity. This is not intended as a condemnation. If, at least during the brief period of the Chermayeffs' occupation, the garden resembled anything like Tunnard's description, it must have been an engaging place with a fascinating play of tree forms. "The frayed edges of the wood were bordered with evergreens, both rounded and columnar," wrote the landscape architect, "to mark the progress of a line starting from the house and receding to the farthest corner of the lawn. This chain of planting included diverse links—one of bright variegated subjects in the middle distance, one of red and purple foliage and one grey."[114] As we have seen, his planting plan for the slot between the terrace and its enclosing wall was rich in its number of species and squarely within the British mixed border tradition [see figure 2-33]. It is tragic that no color photos from these years remain, if any were ever taken. Unlike, for example, the cubistic experiments in France in the 1920s that accompanied houses by architects such as Robert Mallet-Stevens, the Bentley Wood landscape provided a quiet setting and matrix for Chermayeff's architecture, skilled in its manipulation of space and view but restrained in terms of form.[115] This would be a fair characteristic of virtually all of Tunnard's work, whether in England or the United States.

St. Ann's Hill

If Bentley Wood represented a lively exchange between architect and landscape architect, the project for the new house at St. Ann's Hill (also known as St. Ann's Court) in Chertsey, Surrey, brought Tunnard more closely into the design process as a potential client as well as landscape architect. Some few years before, Tunnard had designed a small urban garden in London for the same Schlesinger family to accompany their new house by the architect Oliver Hill in the city's Hampstead district.[116] While the scope of the work is difficult to ascertain, much of Tunnard's task seems to have been to sympathetically grade and plant the hillside and perhaps specify the vegetation for planting around the

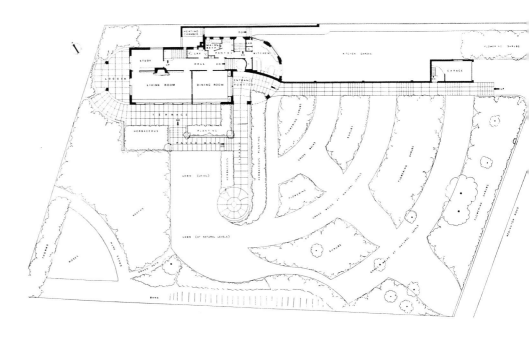

house and its terraces [figures 2-39, 2-40]. With the completion of the work at St. Ann's Hill, Tunnard joined Gerald Schlesinger in Chertsey. Although the precise nature of their relationship has not been revealed, it has been speculated it was sentimental as well as professional.[117] Although the landscape architect used The Studios at St. Ann's Hill as his address for almost four years, he lived in the remarkable new modernist house by Raymond McGrath only a part of that time.

The site had a long history, a history which Tunnard narrated in a series of drawings that form a subsection of *Gardens in the Modern Landscape* [figure 2-41]. Early development of the land had been minimal, given to cultivation within a protective walled enclosure; unpaved paths brought the site into contact with the greater landscape around it and the metropolis to the north. During the Renaissance period, a grander house had been built at the north end of the site with its volume having been further extended by the eighteenth century. At that time, much of the open land was under conversion to the ruling tastes of the naturalistic landscape garden and the planting of specimen trees. Additional modifications and extensions to the buildings were made in the nineteenth century—including the construction of service structures that included a greenhouse—but by then the landscape stood essentially fully shaped. At the time of the Schlesinger project the main house had stood in a condition unworthy of salvage; however, both a two-story block (probably called The Studios, where Tunnard worked during and after construction) and the greenhouses remained. In response to this classic, if not classical, setting McGrath devised a building of a shape and nature completely alien to both the existing architecture and landscape: a round structure executed in concrete, painted white—a full-tilt exercise in the International Style [figure 2-42]. One can only speculate about the rationale behind the design's circular and radial organization. Perhaps in the circle McGrath found a geometry that gathered in the site's disperate fragments of construction and history while opening the principal spaces to long prospects over the historical landscape. The architectural form became the lynchpin, an abstractly contextual design bearing no formal relation to anything that had come before—whether natural or constructed.

A circular motor court announced the theme. Passing through a transitional foyer the convex outer wall of the living room led the eye outward to a splendid panoramic view of the near garden and distant terrain. The bedrooms on the second floor echoed the plan of the floor below. On either side, the rooms on the upper floor opened to terraces framed by the structure—a neat opposition of a rectangular frame to the irregularity of the planted and agricultural landscapes beyond: architectonic frames that literally rendered the landscape picturesque. The remainder of the spaces embraced these two rooms in a series of arcs on both floors. Despite the willful nature of the circle as the primary design concept, McGrath's skill produced a design almost free of awkward moments.

In a preliminary plan, McGrath extended the central core radially with a wing used to shelter an indoor swimming pool. In time, the swimming pool would be constructed outdoors, set in the garden and away from the house, but vestiges of the original idea remain as a glazed conservatory and

2-39
Oliver Hill, architect;
Christopher Tunnard,
landscape architect.
Hill House and
garden.
Hampstead, London,
1938.
Perspective.
[*Decoration*]

2-40
Hill House and
garden.
Hampstead, London.
Site plan.
[*Oliver Hill*]

2-41
Raymond McGrath,
architect;
Christopher Tunnard,
landscape architect.
St. Ann's Hill.
Chertsey, Surrey,
1938.
Site plan.
[*Gardens in the
Modern Landscape*]

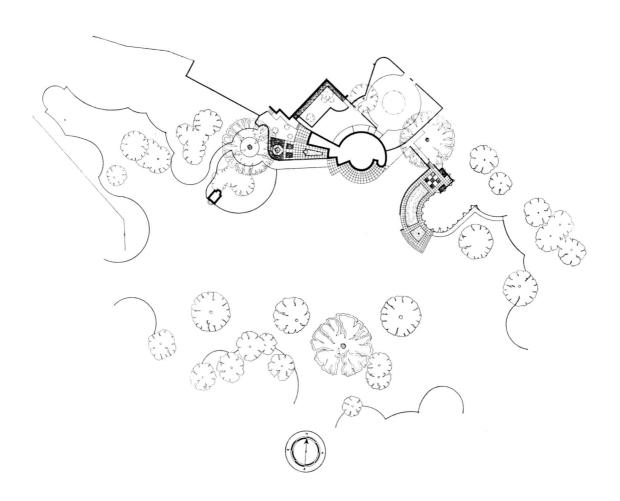

2-43
Raymond McGrath,
architect;
Christopher Tunnard,
landscape architect.
St. Ann's Hill.
Chertsey, Surrey,
1938.
Courtyard sketch
by Gordon Cullen.
[*Gardens in the
Modern Landscape*]

2-44
St. Ann's Hill.
Chertsey, Surrey.
Courtyard looking
to the conservatory.
[Marc Treib]

outdoor court traced along the same radial geometry [figures 2-43, 2-44].[118] Here one senses Tunnard's influence on the planning as it shares a disposition he had proposed for the Keene garden several years before. As an architectural device the court joins the new house with the historic structures, while the aperture in its southern wall recalls Le Corbusier's *fênetre en longeur*—the ribbon windows, glazed or open—he used so successfully in his 1931 Villa Savoye in Poissy, France.

Lance Sieveking, a writer and television producer for the British Broadcasting Corporation, visited St. Ann's Hill with the painter Paul Nash shortly after construction was completed. McGrath had designed the interiors for the new offices of the BBC in London in 1932 and Sieveking had become a "great friend" of the architect.[119] A visit to this uncompromisingly modern work was therefore in order. "We were invited to luncheon by the owners," Sieveking wrote. "Christopher Tunnard was a Canadian landscape gardener, a tall, fair, elegant young man of about twenty-six. Mr. Schlesinger was a short, rather burly, black-haired man of forty-five or so." The owners knew Nash by reputation and were "proud to be able to show him their wonderful new house." To the producer, "it seemed to be all window, and what was not window was pink concrete."[120] Nash was "enchanted," running up and down the "circular flight of steps made of feathery openwork metal...exclaiming all the time his admiration" after quitting the flat roof where he had gazed across the landscape.[121] "The enormous eighteenth-century garden had been preserved with here and there stalactited grottoes and follies in stone," noted Sieveking. Despite his pleasurable experience as he toured the house, Sieveking's keen eye noticed that the only "true innovation...was a swimming pool in the shape of an elongated S"—here he missed the crescent shape of the pool. "The garden through all these changes [the demolition of the existing house] had been left as it was."[122]

The luncheon became a humorous episode given that "the whole of one wall of the airy dining-room consisted of a vast aviary in which more than a hundred budgerigars [common parakeets] disported themselves." At one key point in the group's conversation, the birds "began to shriek, squeak, and chatter all together," creating an enormous din. Nash, humorously rising to the occasion and "recovering momentarily from a coughing fit, gasped into my [Sieveking's] ear: 'No wonder they're called buggery-gars.'" Try as he might, Tunnard was unable to quiet the birds, and the remainder of the lunch passed "in the deafening uproar of the budgerigar tumult," causing the group to converse in "pantomime."[123]

Once again, Tunnard's precise contribution to the landscape's design is undocumented and thus at least to some degree mystifying. David Jacques and Jan Woudstra found that during the course of the garden's design, Tunnard borrowed a number of books from the Royal Horticultural Society's Lindley Library, among them Henry Hubbard and Theodora Kimball's *Introduction to the Study of Landscape Design*—against which the young modernist students at Harvard were then rebelling, Madeline Agar's *Garden Design in Theory and Practice,* and G. C. Taylor's *The Modern Garden.*[124] It seems likely that the placement and configuration of the swimming pool, with its appended pool for aquatic plants, followed designs by the landscape architect. Its curving form, like that of the house, shaped an entry to the lawn while embracing a mass of rhododendrons whose origins probably dated to the nineteenth century [figure 2-45]. Having been long left unconstrained, the vegetation was vastly overgrown at the time of construction. In response, Tunnard directed the pruning of the trees and massed shrubbery to open views and increase the richness of on-site movement. The courtyard planting softened the constriction of its bounding walls, and leapt through the long window opening to join the courtyard vegetation with the lawn and meadow outside it. In some places, Tunnard played lacey vegetal forms against the flatness of the concrete surfaces, using them more "sculpturally"— an idea he would advance in several essays after the war. The view from the house, however, revealed a landscape far less modern in aspect, given that much of the eighteenth-century vegetation remained [figure 2-46]. Again, Tunnard's landscape modernity was tenuous and incomplete.

As a result of its planting and spatial configuration, the court became a pleasant space that flowed with equal ease from living room or conservatory, protected from the wind and oriented toward the sun. At its flared far end, a shallow linear pool led the eye outward to a doorlike aperture in the wall to link the house with the woods beyond. To create a centerpiece within this architectural frame Willi Soukop was commissioned to create an abstract sculpture. Soukop's tapered egg resonated with the boundary wall and its breach, the void within the sculpture echoing in miniature a similar opening in the frame [figure 2-47]. Soukop and Tunnard may have met through a landscape project at Dartington Hall in Devon when Tunnard was working for Percy Cane shortly after completing his studies. Wilhelm Josef Soukop (1907–1995) had emigrated from Austria to England in 1934, and through the gracious efforts of a sponsor was given a position at Dartington, where he taught from 1935 to 1945. In style his works varied considerably, ranging from simplified figurative forms, to those more geometric and abstract, like the piece commissioned for St. Ann's Hill.[125]

Ironically perhaps, the untitled piece Soukop created for St. Ann's Hill was probably the most abstract work he ever produced: executed in cast concrete, possibly with some degree of carving thereafter. Its geometric severity fully fitted the architecture of the house and its courtyards.[126] In the "Art in the Landscape" chapter of *Gardens in the Modern Landscape* Tunnard established the need for collaboration with artists despite his belief that garden design itself was an art. Certainly his associations with at least some of the architects and artists in the MARS Group and the authors of *Circle*—and of course his cousin John Tunnard—made him aware of the most advanced artistic ideas floating around England at that time. He seems to have made active efforts to keep abreast of the currents and to be a part of the discussions.

Art in the Landscape

Given that Tunnard considered the landscape a work of art in itself, it is somewhat peculiar that he became such a strong proponent for the inclusion of sculpture in its composition. One might interpret this simply as the continued legacy of the classical and Arts and Crafts garden traditions in which the sundial, the relief, or the statue provided the terminus to an axis, physical or visual. But for Tunnard

2-45 (*overleaf*)
Raymond McGrath, architect;
Christopher Tunnard, landscape architect.
St. Ann's Hill.
Chertsey, Surrey, 1938.
View over the pool toward the house.
[Marc Treib]

2-46
Raymond McGrath,
architect;
Christopher Tunnard,
landscape architect.
St. Ann's Hill,
Chertsey, Surrey,
1938.
View from the upper
terrace.
［Marc Treib］

sculpture was, perhaps more critically, a symbol of a new era within a setting that was essentially timeless—constrained by the inherent conservative forms of plants and trees. To be understood as art, landscape design must be recognized as a contribution *to* the arts. Early in the chapter, he noted that "the seventeenth-century formal style, degenerate and cluttered with absurdities of decoration as it became, was an art in a sense that the landscape style was not." Moreover, "Though bound by innumerable sets of rules, an artist like Le Nôtre was at liberty to indulge his creative instincts without the necessity of producing a representational design."[127] Tunnard's appreciation of the formal garden seemingly contradicts his continued involvement with the English picturesque tradition, in both his writings and his design projects. For Tunnard, however, to rank as art the landscape must have a noticeable form; that is to say, its artifice must be apparent, however subtle. As we have seen at Bentley Wood and St. Ann's Hill, the landscape was treated so lightly that the designer's contribution took some effort to discern. Yet the planting of selected species, their combination and composition, their pruning managed to enhance a view, the shaping of more complex spaces, and even the modeling of the terrain—however softly—nonetheless constituted efforts toward creating an artwork. In defining a new landscape art, Tunnard's task became how to formulate a modern landscape while accepting and reworking history in accord with contemporary needs and values. Obviously, this goal could be accomplished not only through an innovative structuring of landscape space but also through the use of architectural elements such as walls and paving—and finally, by collaborating with artists.

Henry Moore's contribution to Bentley Wood and Willi Soukop to St. Ann's Hill underscored the values of adding art to architecture that itself was becoming increasingly abstract. Each of these modern sculptures remained a singular object within the new landscape—focal points to terminate vistas—and in the end, their function did not considerably differ from that of classical statuary in historical formal gardens. It was their forms rather than their role that had evolved. A closer collaboration between artist and landscape architect was required for making the modern garden. "The sculptor and the painter once participated in gardens," Tunnard wrote, "in spite of the fact that the best of modern sculptors are designing for open spaces and the painter's conception of form and colour is essential to a modern appreciation of garden planning."[128] Almost contradicting his own approach to the making of the landscapes at Bentley Wood and St. Ann's Hill, he claimed that "The modern house requires modern surroundings, and in most respects the garden of today does not fulfill this need." Statements such as these provided the foundation for looking to modern art for a vocabulary for the new garden. The goal, at least in England, would only be achieved in degrees, and not by leaps and bounds.

> A Modern Landscape Manifesto

In 1937, the Société Française des Architectes de Jardins sponsored the first International Congress of Garden Architects in Paris, an event linked to the international exposition then occupying sites on and around the Champ de Mars and others on the Trocadéro hill across the Seine. Under the leadership of

2-47 *(opposite below)* Willi Soukop. Abstract sculpture. St. Ann's Hill. Chertsey, Surrey, 1938. [*Gardens in the Modern Landscape*]

Achille Duchêne, known more for his restorations of *Grand Siècle* gardens than modern designs, the meeting of landscape architects featured presentations from Europe and Scandinavia—the Americans and Russians, among others, declined the invitation to participate in the meeting due to its political undercurrents. Tunnard reviewed the meeting for *Landscape and Garden*, assessing the presentations country by country.[129] The French, as hosts, should be discussed first, Tunnard reasoned. Although mildly impressed with Duchêne's visions of a future utopia, he found the French too bound up with history, reason, and the return to order that had followed the devastation of the Great War. In his review, Tunnard quoted André Vera's pronouncement that "The aim of the modern garden is explicit in the provision of regularity and order, by means of formal symmetry, as an antidote to the shifting sands of political change."[130] Such a theoretical stance troubled the young Canadian: he dismissed formalism of this type in his essays for the *Architectural Review*, later collected as *Gardens in the Modern Landscape*, asserting that the move toward a modern manner was marked by the incremental shift from symmetry to asymmetry, culminating in "occult balance," a term coined by Fletcher Steele in his classic 1930 article, "New Pioneering in Garden Design."[131]

Tunnard was more sympathetic with Teutonic landscape trends, those in Switzerland, for example, where recent gardens were "extremely well merged into their surroundings and the[ir] liberal use of indigenous plants ensures that they shall not seem incongruous in the magnificent scenery which is the nation's chief pride."[132] While he was cautious about commenting too positively on a Germany already within the nasty grip of National Socialism, Tunnard had praise for the country's use of landscape as an instrument for public and personal health: "a wholly estimable ideal for the individual even if its obvious primary aim may be only part of a wider and less commendable militarisation programme." No mention of recent German landscape architecture could avoid discussing the landscape of the new "trunk roads" such as the Reichsautobahn. There was little to say about Italy and far more to say about Scandinavia, while, once again, formal issues were somewhat marginalized. Tunnard had affinities, and thus special praise, for the contribution of Swedish landscape architect and professor Sven Hermelin. "He considered that the garden of the future would be simple in design," wrote Tunnard of Hermelin's presentation, "and a mere framework for the display of plants and for the provision of health-giving amenities such as swimming pools, sand pits for children, tennis courts and arbours for rest. Swedish landscape architects prefer to group their plants in simple natural arrangements," he continued, "rather than confine them to severe geometrical patterns."[133] That pronouncement could have described Tunnard's own work until that time, and much of what was to follow.

In summarizing the presentations at the meeting, Tunnard was diplomatic.

> It says something for the vitality of the art of landscape design that the theories already outlined exist in Europe today, enriching rather than destroying the fabric of our garden tapestries. We may quarrel in some cases with the method of approach—with the lack of imaginative or intellectual ideal in German planning, perhaps, or with the narrow limits set themselves by French designers—but we dare not say that any one national scheme of planning is less consistent than our own.[134]

When all was said and done, however, "there remains a technique which is international, which rejects the old ways and looks forward to the new, unfettered by restrictions of fashion or of academic theory, yet adapting itself to the conditions of the day by the use of logic and sanity and a poetic interpretation of the needs of civilisation." Easy to say, especially when statements such as these border on platitudes and their author provides no concrete examples from which we might glean an understanding of the relation of the landscape's program to its resulting form. In closing his review, Tunnard paraphrased "the words of a modern artist" who went unnamed: "In landscape design, as in thought, music, science, there is only one road that will take us anywhere and that is the road between to-day and to-morrow and the great discoveries of the future."[135] Amen.

Tunnard's commentary on Belgian landscape design provides the link to the organizational project that followed in the wake of the Paris conference. In his review, Tunnard said little about Holland and Belgium, other than that the latter "treats the plant as a means to an end, and avoiding experiments in colour, concentrates almost wholly on form."[136] He then mentioned, for the first time, the Belgian Jean Canneel-Claes, but only to present his ideas on the education of the garden architect.[137] By this time, Canneel had clearly departed from Belgian garden traditions, for example, those maintained by more conservative landscape architects such as René Pechère who would dominate the country's landscape profession in the postwar years. Working with modernist architects such as Huib Hoste and Herman de Koninck, Canneel produced a series of gardens with highly rationalized plans whose vertical dimension employed rows of trees as green planes to distinguish the various areas of activity, channel views, or screen unwanted visual elements: "the tendency towards simplicity which identifies this type of garden with the modern house."[138] Using orthogonal compositions, at times populated with rectangular beds planted in tulips, Canneel's plans reflected the influence of Low Countries Neo-Plasticism as formulated by artists such as Theo van Doesburg and Piet Mondrian. On other, larger sites, however, existing vegetation, landform, and convention were of greater consequence in shaping the design.

Canneel's frequent use of modular concrete pavers lent structure and rhythm to both the design and the ensuing promenade, and it was probably this rationalizing element, above all, that attracted Tunnard's attention when he first saw the gardens in photographs. The de Koninck garden later appeared in *Gardens in the Modern Landscape*, possibly another byproduct of Tunnard's and Canneel's encounter in Paris. In the caption accompanying a photo of the model for the Heeremans garden in Liedekerke (c. 1938) in *Gardens in the Modern Landscape*, Tunnard wrote, "It shows an appreciation of the sculptural quality of plant material and an asymmetrical arrangement of the plan units which are distinguishing characters of the few sympathetic gardens for modern houses" [figure 2-48].[139] In addition, as landscape historian Dorothée Imbert has determined, certain aspects of Canneel's writings from the early 1930s shared spooky resemblances to phrasing later appearing in Tunnard's *Architectural Review* articles.[140] These correspondences suggest he may have been familiar with Canneel's work at a much earlier date, or at least had been provided with copies of his publications at an early meeting.[141]

2-48
Jean Canneel-Claes.
Heeremans garden.
Liedekerke, Belgium,
1938.
[Marc Treib]

In all probability, the two men first met at the Paris congress, although they may have shared correspondence before that time. Mutually displeased with either, or both, the presentations at the meeting and the direction in which the profession was headed, they jointly formulated a plan for creating the International Association of Modernist Garden Architects (or in short form, the AIAJM, derived from the French version of the organization's name, Association Internationale des Architectes de Jardins Modernistes). As Tunnard later reflected on the state of landscape architecture in the 1930s, and the reason for assembling a group of like-minded landscape architects, he wrote, "They had come upon the end of a movement, which had grown tired, recondite, and introspective, and was as much exercised by its position in a world which very largely ignored its definite contribution to the study of architecture and planning."[142] To advance their effort Tunnard and Canneel forged a manifesto ultimately issued in three languages. In their declaration's opening lines, the authors announced their support for the network of existing associations and that their intention was to supplement, rather than replace, these national efforts "as an active movement concerned with the problem of gardens and landscapes of the 20th century." While the criticism of contemporary practice was only implicit in the manifesto, it was nonetheless evident—especially in the context of the highly elaborate floral displays that characterized most exhibits in the landscape section of the exposition. The AIAJM would not restrict membership to garden or landscape architects but would fully welcome architects, town planners, sculptors, painters, writers, and "all those actively engaged in the study of contemporary problems and familiar with current developments in landscape architecture." Theirs was a broad regard.

The co-conspirators enumerated five objectives:
1. To promote rationally planned gardens in accordance with the physical and mental needs of contemporary life—these are the functional considerations.
2. To study and develop connections between gardens, architecture, and town planning.
3. To foster collaboration among design professionals.
4. To encourage a regard for the historical development of garden art "and the part played by scientific materials and methods in these evolutions."
5. To defend the interests of members and their work "where defence is not organized or is insufficient."
Other than the last point, which aimed at protecting the profession, the manifesto rehearsed Tunnard's personal project as expressed in *Gardens in the Modern Landscape*. The "objectives" were followed by seven "resolutions":
1. Garden art is not about decoration; it is a branch of architecture and as such must address contemporary problems like housing.
2. Rational planning should be based on the idea that "the function determines the form."
3. Landscape architecture involves artistic creation and not the "servile imitation of natural phenomena."
4. Design begins with a full understanding of the nature of the site.
5. "Simplicity of structure and concision in means of expression" will produce the best examples of garden art.

6. The plan lies at the root of all good designs.

7. "Finally we believe in the probity of the creative act...the reliance of the designer on his own knowledge and experience and not on the academic symbolism of the styles or outworn systems of aesthetics, to create by experiment and invention new forms which are significant of the age from which they spring."[143]

While the manifesto was issued in French and German as well as English, with conviction, goodwill, and an acceptance of all nations, the efforts toward creating a society of modern garden architects never-theless arrived stillborn. For one, and above all, the traditionalists were too firmly entrenched in positions of power. In addition, only a handful of European designers were then working in, or even aspiring to, a modern garden form. Most practitioners were instead content to continue tradition, following academic norms or simply executing what the client requested. In any event, the outbreak of hostilities within two years after the Paris meeting ended most efforts in private practice across the Continent. Interest in the association evaporated in the wake of war.

In 1938, the Germans played host to a second congress, but given the bellicose nature of the National Socialist regime and the reduced resources at the organizers' disposal, the meeting had far fewer attendees. For his part, on moral grounds, Tunnard refused to even submit his work for display.[144] After Belgium's capitulation and occupation by Germany, Canneel worked with the Committee for the Reconstruction of the Country. Although this unit designed only benign projects such as sports fields and cemeteries, Canneel's name was nevertheless tarnished by charges of collaboration. All thoughts of an international association of landscape architects were put on hold. It would be a decade later that renewed efforts for forming such an international society gathered steam. Spearheaded by other British landscape architects such as Geoffrey Jellicoe, Sylvia Crowe, and Brenda Colvin, the International Federation of Landscape Architects (IFLA) was founded in Cambridge on 14 August 1948. The formation of IFLA completed the project first proposed by Tunnard and Canneel ten years and a global holocaust before.[145] Neither landscape architect played a part in the birth of the new organization, whose purview would not be restricted to any one manner such as modernism. Only in a talk some years later did Tunnard reflect on the "abortive attempt on the part of the writer and the Belgian modernist Jean Canneel-Claes to form an international group of landscape architects" based on "the probity of the creative act" rather than "academic symbolism." That effort had foundered, he admitted, because "at that time the landscape architects who were willing to join were too few and too scattered."[146] Like so many other noble initiatives, the time and place for its formation were not conducive to success. When a decade later IFLA was finally established, there was no mention of modern-ism; rather than focusing on the approach or manner, the organization focused on practice and the profession.

Tunnard's return to North America in the early 1940s brought him additional recognition and commissions. On the one hand, he was regarded as the English-speaking world's foremost theorist on modern landscape architecture; on the other, he was now also known as a Harvard professor with an ever-growing knowledge and comprehension of the making and historical evolution of the designed environment. His interests spanned from the singular art object to the region, and he argued persuasively for each in its respective place and at its appropriate scale.

> Return to North America

By 1939 Tunnard's reputation as the leading light in modern landscape architecture in the Anglophone world was assured. He had issued a clarion call that would inspire practitioners on both sides of the Atlantic for decades to come. His landscape designs—if small in number—had been well received and influential, and he had become an *intime* among the avant-garde in British arts and design. His associations with this group would support his move to the United States and an academic rather than professional career.

The 1936 appointment of Joseph Hudnut (1886–1968) as dean of Harvard University's new Graduate School of Design signaled an almost complete overhaul of the school's existing programs in architecture, landscape architecture, and planning. Although offering independent curricula, both architecture and landscape architecture were still very much under the sway of Beaux-Arts classicism and its teaching methods. Under Hudnut's leadership, these programs would be revamped to be more in tune with contemporary society and its needs, and would be recast as the Graduate School of Design in 1936, shortly after his arrival. Hudnut had begun his professional life as an architect, himself working in a traditional mode, but over time had converted to modernism in both thinking and design idiom. To implement his academic ideas, he hired Walter Gropius, an émigré architect who had fled Nazi Germany for England. Living and working there in a short-term partnership with Maxwell Fry, he was also a member of the MARS circle and had become familiar with Tunnard's writings and work. As the founding director of the celebrated Bauhaus, first in Weimar and thereafter Dessau, he was lauded as much for his innovations in pedagogy as for his architectural production. Gropius seemed the right man for the Harvard job and his arrival in Cambridge brought fresh ideas and enthusiasm to a school that had long ago settled into complacency.

In time, Hudnut would oppose Gropius' increasing focus on prefabrication and housing with only a subsequent regard for the neighborhood or the city. Gropius believed in continuing a more formalistic program similar to that of the Bauhaus he had once directed, including the famous introductory *Vorkurs*. Hudnut, on his part, held a more humanistic view of modernism that included a deeper regard for people at the individual level as well as their part in the greater society.[147] Though fully converted to modern architectural thought and practice, Hudnut remained resolutely humanistic, regarding the modernist approach as a means to an end rather than an end in itself. As their tenures at Harvard progressed, the breach between the two men widened, and as Jill Pearlman convincingly establishes in *Inventing American Modernism*, Hudnut and Gropius became increasingly at odds.[148]

Harvard's landscape architecture program was then under the direction of Bremer Pond (1884–1959), who was not easily cajoled into new ways of thinking; as a result, the curriculum had suffered from a certain degree of ossification. As a student, the landscape architect James Rose was told that a tree was always a tree; trees weren't produced in factories and therefore would not be affected by any new—read: modernist—way of doing things. Interestingly, Henry Hubbard, co-author with Theodora Kimball of *An Introduction to the Study of Landscape Design*, published first in 1917 and thereafter the standard text on the subject, chaired the program in planning rather than landscape architecture. Clearly, the landscape architecture program needed new blood and a new vision. Gropius suggested to Hudnut that Christopher Tunnard was the most able candidate for the job. When, in the spring of 1936 Hudnut traveled to England to finalize the terms of the Gropius appointment, he met Tunnard for the first time. He found that they held sympathetic design values and a shared vision for Harvard's landscape program.

Tunnard arrived in Cambridge, Massachusetts, three years later, for the fall 1939 term, with the title of lecturer, and soon became part of the multidisciplinary teams responsible for teaching the school's integrated courses—an idea Hudnut shared with Gropius in accord with his revised vision for the school.[149] Tunnard quickly became the leading light of the landscape architecture program among the students and a source for those students seeking modernist thinking similar to the ideas then floating in the architecture studios.[150] From the school catalogs, we can gauge Tunnard's contributions at both the graduate and undergraduate levels. Most of Tunnard's assignments placed him within a team of instructors, for example, "Architectural Sciences 2b" and "Architectural Sciences 10," which he taught with four other faculty members. These were omnibus courses that began by addressing "utilitarian function, the selection of materials and techniques, the evolution from these of a form to meet both useful and aesthetic needs."[151] The factors became more complex as the term progressed, and architecture studios included the design of the landscape as well. The 23 April 1940 "register" of the Graduate School of Design lists Tunnard as teaching "Practice in Landscape Design," the introduction to landscape architecture taught both semesters with Norman Newton, then an assistant professor, and other members of the faculty.[152] In the 1940 summer session, Tunnard oversaw "Landscape Architecture S2a," although it was taught "in collaboration with the instructors in Architectural Design." The purview of this course was broad: "A study of the cultural patterns of American landscape design and its relation to the contemporary scene, applied to specific problems in planning....Opportunity for work on specialized units including the private garden, housing developments, and public areas will be provided by collaborative effort on actual site problems."[153] Unfortunately, no student projects from these courses have been located.

Among the Tunnard papers, however, remains a syllabus for "Site Planning," a course taught in fall 1940. The industrial towns of New England were its subject, with students investigating "existing natural resources, materials, and power; growth cycles of industrial development," and "speculation and taxes." Successive class meetings delved more deeply into the study of these factors. It is to Tunnard's credit that although only two years or so had passed since he wrote *Gardens in the Modern Landscape*, his knowledge had broadened markedly and his interests had become sweepingly comprehensive. Although listed as a site-planning course, there seems to have been little content focused on that particular aspect of the built environment or landscape practice.[154] The subject of the studio was a new landscape for New England, based to a large degree on the resuscitation of farming in the region, and in his course description Tunnard is careful to point out the reasons for the decline of agriculture in the Northeast and the need to farm in larger units to maintain financial viability.[155]

The final examination in "Architecture 1c" in January 1942 seems to have been written by Norman Newton, although perhaps with input from Tunnard. The examination was both specific and tough, with questions asking the "required density for 2-story row-houses in defense housing projects," "the maximum percentage of slope allowed on driveways and project streets," and "the advantages of the co-operative farm."[156] In the summer 1942 term, Tunnard returned to landscape architecture, once again teaching the introductory course.[157] The content centered on the study of form in relation to topography applied to the design of "A Picnic Area in a Large Park." The following project introduced traffic circulation, parking, and the design of a city park.[158] For beginning students, the education was rigorous. An unidentified course project for "Architecture 37b" shows Tunnard developing student creativity rather than the factual education more characteristic of Newton and Bremer Pond. For "Free Design Using Earth, Water and Trees," the project encouraged the modeling of topography and strategic planting of trees. "The area should not encompass too many elements," Tunnard cautioned, "but should take in enough land to enable a study of tree groupings to be undertaken." While the design project could include structures such as "shelters and pavilions," the intention of the course was to utilize trees and vegetation rather than construction.[159] One can only wonder why Tunnard had been relegated to instructing entering students and never received any assignment to teach more advanced courses. Perhaps the established figures in the landscape department were less impressed with Tunnard's accomplishments and thinking than Hudnut and Gropius and therefore offered some resistance.

From their later interviews and writings, we know that the graduate students in landscape architecture regarded Tunnard very highly and saw him as a beacon that signaled a new day. *Gardens in the Modern Landscape* became their bible, replacing Hubbard and Kimball's *An Introduction to the Study of Landscape Design*, which had reigned supreme for almost two decades.[160] No doubt Tunnard's presence was less appreciated by the more conservative factions of the faculty, for example, Lester Collins who critically reviewed the 1948 edition of *Gardens in the Modern Landscape* in *Landscape Architecture* magazine.[161]

Having completed their studies before Tunnard's arrival, the trio of James Rose, Garrett Eckbo, and Dan Kiley bristled at a curriculum mired in tradition. Each member of the trio, in his own way, struck out in the search for a modern landscape architecture. While influenced by the garden design experiments in France during the 1920s, Eckbo found in Tunnard's writings a more comprehensive way of thinking about landscape, especially because he was able to position the private garden within the context of the greater environment. In fact, it was only the publication of Eckbo's own *Landscape for Living* in 1950 that finally superseded *Gardens in the Modern Landscape* as the primary English-language source for modern landscape architecture thinking.[162] Like Tunnard, Eckbo addressed both the micro- and megascales, while considering social as well as environmental issues. His landscapes for the Farm Security Administration during the 1930s and the work by Eckbo, Royston and Williams thereafter yielded a much more impressive portfolio than the handful of Tunnard projects presented in either the 1938 or the 1948 editions of *Gardens in the Modern Landscape* [see figure 2-51]. Inspired by reading the book, Lawrence Halprin turned conclusively to landscape architecture and credited Tunnard alone for his decision.[163] Halprin was not alone.

The last record of a landscape course taught by Tunnard, dating some time after 1948 and postdating his transfer to Yale University, was "Modern Landscape Design."[164] The topics for the proposed lectures demark Tunnard's vision for landscape architecture: History, Aesthetics, Social Aspects, Planting, Water, Sculpture, Gardens, and Parks. With this move to Yale in 1945, Tunnard's teaching in landscape architecture withered and his interest shifted more consequently to city and regional planning and historic preservation. In terms of landscape architecture, Tunnard had not moved far from the vision first presented in the 1938 edition of *Gardens in the Modern Landscape*, or even in the revised 1948 edition, for that matter.

The outbreak of war drew Tunnard back to Canada where he enlisted in the Royal Canadian Engineers. His resignation from Harvard stimulated a reply on 22 December 1942 from Dean Hudnut, who was naturally disappointed by the loss of such a noted and well-regarded faculty member. "You may be sure you will be missed at Robinson Hall, and of course we expect you to take your job back and carry on as soon as the war is ended."[165] Overly optimistic, like so many, he foresaw the hostilities as lasting only several months. Poor eyesight led to Tunnard's medical discharge from Officer Candidate School in 1943 after only several weeks. He treated this unfortunate event—unfortunate in light of the upswell of patriotism and stampede for military service at the time—with some degree of acceptance and humor. Writing to the landscape architect and then-president of the Institute of Landscape Architects, Geoffrey Jellicoe from Ste. Anne's Military Hospital in Quebec he reported, "After a week at Officer Candidate School they sent me here for tests on a blind right eye. I was hoping they wouldn't notice, but when I couldn't hit the ball they got suspicious."[166] Jellicoe responded the following month, commiserating on Tunnard's discharge and noting that efforts were afoot to finally create one or more true landscape architecture programs in British schools of architecture.[167] This was evidently an issue of mutual concern and interest, and it would be the subject of many letters between the two men in the coming decade.

Perhaps written while convalescing or awaiting

discharge, "Modern Gardens for Modern Houses: Reflections on Current Trends in Landscape Design" is arguably Tunnard's most straightforward, coherent, and persuasive reasoning toward the making of the modern garden. Unlike *Gardens in the Modern Landscape*, which like Le Corbusier's epochal 1923 *Towards a New Architecture* suffers from its origins as disparate essays, here Tunnard's discussions of historical and traditional garden forms were kept to a minimum. Instead, he spoke more about the current condition. Modern architecture and art have triumphed: Why not a modern garden truly in accord with the modern house?

Forget the plans and photographs in garden magazines; the garden need not match the style of the house. More critical was understanding that garden design at root was "space division for use."[168] Point by point Tunnard dismisses or demolishes all stereotypes then governing American garden design, among them the axis and the use of plants for display rather than practical purpose. In their stead, he stresses the need for design that employs an economy of means, and somewhat curiously, "a return to a vigorous folk art." In this case, however, the term "folk" should not be conflated with naïve, but instead "a poetic appreciation of plants [that] would be preferable to the historical attitude that now prevails."[169] His closing paragraph begins by listing what not to do: "Do not go to fashionable gardens for design inspiration"; instead, "study the design of orchards, of truck gardens and experimental grounds, where plants are grown scientifically." He also directs the makers of gardens to study the grand projects of infrastructure: "new forms of shelter, the gigantic sculptures of the oil derrick, the simple pattern of a fish hatchery."[170] In seeking inspiration from these works, Tunnard was clearly ahead of his time, not only in landscape design but also in the arts. However, he seems to contradict what he himself had written some five years earlier when he claims that "Gardening is not a fine art: it is an art of the people." Perhaps most potently, he encapsulates his thinking with a catchy phrase: "The right style for the twentieth century is no style at all, but a new conception of planning the human environment." In the right style, the garden is a key building block.[171]

The result of Tunnard's optical disability was his return to Harvard in 1943, not to teach but as the recipient of a fellowship for study and travel. Following the termination of hostilities Tunnard planned to visit England, writing ahead to Jellicoe in 4 March 1946 and telling him about his move to New Haven and Yale University, and his evolution of interests from landscape architecture to town and regional planning. His first appointment had been as a lecturer within the architecture department, but in 1945 he was appointed assistant professor of city planning, and promoted thereafter to associate professor in 1948.[172] Learning of Tunnard's impending voyage, Jellicoe invited him to lecture to the Institute of Landscape Architects on the subject of recent developments in American landscape architecture.[173] In his reply, written on Yale University Department of Architecture letterhead, Tunnard explained that the choice of venue and his broadened interests would lead to a talk covering topics other than landscape design alone. "Since the lecture is to be at the R.I.B.A.," he wrote, "and since my file now includes town planning as well as landscape architecture, I would like to make the approach rather broad and show the relationship between the arts of architecture, landscape architecture, and town planning." He proposed a title on the lines of "The American Scene."[174] At Jellicoe's suggestion, the title became "Town and Country Landscape USA."[175] In the talk Tunnard reviewed the history of American settlement, noting the English contribution to that effort, but also citing the differences occasioned by the American democracy that—at least in Tunnard's view—contrasted vividly with the situation in England.[176] The lecture, delivered in July 1947, was presumably well received.

Tunnard was chronically in arrears in paying his Institute of Landscape Architects dues, but fortunately for researchers, the apologetic letters that accompanied his late payments provide rare fragments of biographical information. For example, in a letter written 2 December 1949 to Mrs. Gordon Browne, the executive secretary of the institute, he announced the recent birth of his son, Christopher Russell Tunnard, who, "Of course...looks just like his proud papa." It has been his involvement with the "Institute of Planners and Institute of Architects," he explains, that has prevented better communication with "his first love," the Institute of Landscape Architects.[177] In a subsequent letter he announced with pride that he had been promoted from a lecturer to an assistant professor for city planning.[178] Although Tunnard's interests and research now lay with planning, he continued to accept a handful of landscape commissions, almost all of which would remain as proposals. These include a design for the sculpture garden of the Museum of Modern Art in New York, consulting on the sculpture garden for the Yale University Art Gallery (Douglas Orr and Louis I. Kahn, architects, 1951–1953), and even a mysterious project for a garden at the new United Nations headquarters in New York City. Yet despite any new work, or even his projects in England and the Boston area, he remained best known for his writings, in particular *Gardens in the Modern Landscape*.[179]

The invitations Tunnard received to speak at prestigious events testify to the high regard in which he was held as a spokesman for the garden and greater landscape. In several of the papers he delivered or published at the close of the 1940s, Tunnard again returned to the subject of the design professions and art, although his purview also included architecture. In a 1948 issue of *Task*, he admits that architecture includes social, scientific, and aesthetic functions, but claims that the first two categories have received too much attention, as has sociology. As a result, the concern for aesthetics has waned. "We cannot afford to wince at the words 'beauty' and 'proportion'.... If we continue to hope for beauty as a by-product of design, good building will not be the result. A positive approach to aesthetics," he asserts, "is essential if architecture is to survive as a useful profession."[180] In April 1948, at the Ann Arbor Conference on Esthetic Evaluation held at the University of Michigan, Tunnard questioned whether the landscape is the setting for a building or is the building only "incidental to a comprehensive landscape design."[181] Gardens and landscape possess their own characteristics, concerns, and qualities. Landscape "has aesthetic rules which apply to it alone," and include "the rule of color," which differs from the "role" of color in architecture, and "the rule of planes, which is guided by optical considerations and the effect of patterns on extending horizontal surfaces."[182] These were techniques requiring development and application in twentieth-century landscapes. "We need now a positive drive toward the creation of beauty, not as a by-product, but as an integral part of our design."[183]

Tunnard renewed his call for beauty at the symposium "What Is Happening to Modern Architecture?" held at the Museum of Modern Art in 1948 and moderated by cultural and architectural historian Lewis Mumford. In his 11 October 1947 "Skyline" column in the *New Yorker*, Mumford had questioned the validity of an "international style" and instead argued that architecture should respond to local conditions: topographic, environmental, social, and aesthetic.[184] In response to this salvo in support of regionalism, the museum mounted a symposium the following February and invited a group of architectural luminaries to proffer their opinions. As the single landscape representative among the speakers—a validation of the high regard in which he was held—Tunnard avoided any discussion that pitted regional modernism (which Alfred Barr referred to as an "ingratiating kind of wooden domestic building") to the MoMA-favored International Style (whose supporters Mumford termed "mechanical rigorists").[185] Instead, Tunnard questioned the current emphasis in architectural circles on sociological and functional concerns, and questioned the absence of beauty from most of the presentations. "If we don't make the latest thing in architectural magazines our exclusive diet, perhaps we shall be able to create again buildings which receive the approbation of all good critics."[186] In some ways Tunnard's position aided the Mumford cause by ranking the aesthetic dimension of construction over any formulaic slavery to function and engineering, and by granting higher status to the local rather than the international.

Other art museums played an active role in promoting discussions and presenting exhibitions about modern landscape architecture in addition to art and architecture. The San Francisco Museum of Art, in fact, had mounted the first international exhibition of contemporary landscape as early as 1937, a project organized by an association of Bay Area landscape architects. A decade later, the same group reprised their initial effort with *Landscape Design*, displayed at the museum in 1948. Contributors to the catalog included landscape architects Thomas Church and Garrett Eckbo, the sculptor Claire Falkenstein, and the architect William Wurster; Tunnard's essay "Landscape Design and City Planning" was a natural assignment, considering his background and contemporary academic position. In his text Tunnard condemned the state of the American city as characterized by "deserts of stone and concrete," lacking comprehensive planning, and devoting too little attention to its green spaces. While Americans might be successful in what he termed "landscape engineering," Tunnard questioned the absence of art in the making of cities and the low quality of the nation's open spaces. How does this happen, Tunnard asked, and chided the reader by claiming that "We talk vaguely of introducing new parks into cities, but should actually be thinking of a city set in a park."[187]

> A Revised Edition

The first edition of *Gardens in the Modern Landscape* had been a major critical success in both England and the United States; a second edition followed a decade later with several subsequent reprintings.[188] As the book was essentially a compilation of essays originally published serially in the *Architectural Review*, the second edition was essentially a reprinting of the first edition, with several notable exceptions. The first was the tone of the preface, which is softer in its assertions, the author noting that ten years of writing, research, and practice had tempered his thinking, for example, in a reconsidered appreciation of the nineteenth century and the belief that "creative art has a firmer foundation when based on accumulation of acquired knowledge rather than on intuitiveness alone." While more openly asserted here, that stance merely reinforced Tunnard's original premise that one must know history to create modern work. As a closing shot, the book reprints a 1940 essay on the modern garden by Joseph Hudnut—who, of course, as dean of the Graduate School of Design had brought Tunnard to Harvard at the start of his American academic career.

In the preface to the second edition, Tunnard also noted that although his views had evolved, the basic premise of the book remained the same—a common stance taken by those who would like to see the return of an earlier work to print without having to undertake numerous revisions. Despite this proviso, there are some noticeable differences, in particular a softening of tone and an increased interest in larger landscapes beyond the scale of the garden. The illustrations remain essentially the same, as does the book's layout. Although the text has undergone minor revisions, among the principal changes were the addition of a portfolio of planting schemes and a presentation of American gardens that included four of Tunnard's own projects. Among these works were photographic presentations of Frank Lloyd Wright's Taliesin West in Paradise Valley, Arizona, and Thomas Church's gardens for the Golden Gate International Exposition from 1939.

In the first edition, Tunnard clearly had taken issue with all that was sentimental and unquestioned in the English landscape, although his own designs more closely resembled historical landscapes than any that might be read as "modern." Despite the argument for a landscape in accord with contemporary life, Tunnard nonetheless stressed—as in the first edition— that one must understand what has come before. If one is to react against or ultimately even rebuff historical manners, one should at least know what is being rejected and why. He reproached the reader:

> May one say with fairness that there are too many architects and others who adopt a "modern" style without regard to its origins or philosophy? These are the people who are defeating true modernism; they do not investigate enough; they have discarded the older styles without bothering to find out what they represent or the demands of the society which produced them.[189]

After railing against the persistence of entrenched ways of thinking about landscape architecture, he somewhat curiously concluded that the future landscape would probably resemble what has already been. "'A style for our own times' may not be anything like what we imagined a few years ago: perhaps it should, in fact, be more like what was current a hundred years ago—a meshing of several styles or idioms with entirely dissimilar physical results. In other words, "the modernist ought now to be broadening his range, not narrowing it, and trying his hand at all sorts of solutions."[190] As we have seen, his philosophical stance expressed in the 1942 article "Modern Gardens for Modern Houses" contradicted this assertion, when he proposed that "the modern style in gardening may be no style at all."[191]

Apparently in response to requests for specifics by which to realize his more theoretical discussions, Tunnard included a portfolio of planting schemes—identified with scientific and common names—by which the modern garden could be enacted. For these drawings Tunnard again turned to Gordon Cullen, who had by this time acquired his own identity as not only a delineator graced with enviable skill but also as a town planner and important personage in the "townscape" movement.[192] In some ways, one could view townscape as the urban parallel to Tunnard's thoughts for the landscape. Each looked to what had been good in the past, each attempted to retain their positive characteristics and use them against the forces of rampant urbanization and escalating traffic. Moreover, each had roots in the English picturesque tradition.[193]

Of the eight planting situations illustrated, let us look at only one. The scheme portrayed in Cullen's illustration for "Plants with grey foliage" is dominated by three species, two of which are set in a shallow pool: Matilija poppy, Plantain lily (*Hosta*), and ornamental onions (*Allium*) [figure 2-49]. In the caption, Tunnard explains the concerns that inform their procurement and care, although he gives no aesthetic rationale for their selection and mixture. The undercurrent of the writing suggests that the species have been selected for their formal properties rather than their native origins, horticultural rarity, or even their color. Form reigns.

At the time of its second edition, *Gardens in the Modern Landscape* still had no serious rival in the English-speaking landscape world as the subject's leading theoretical tract. Yet to some degree, its moment had passed and it had already become a historical text. As Harvard professor Lester Collins wrote in his review of the second edition in *Landscape Architecture* magazine, the conditions affecting landscape had changed considerably since the first edition of the prewar years; as a result, the book was hardly radical in contemporary discourse. In addition, Collins continued, much of the text did not apply to the American situation and its particular landscape history, which lacked the burden of tradition, unlike England. By 1948, the publication date of the second edition, experiments for the new garden by Thomas Church, with park designs and site plans by Garrett Eckbo for the Farm Security Administration, had already surpassed in originality the landscapes that Tunnard had actually realized [figures 2-50, 2-51]. Despite Collins' criticisms—which were apt—the book nonetheless remained the lone call for the new garden; at least in the United States, it would occupy that position until it was superseded in 1950 by Eckbo's *Landscape for Living*, a more comprehensive investigation of the subject illustrated with a far more impressive portfolio of work by Eckbo, Royston, and Williams. Yet despite any of the book's or its author's limitations, *Gardens in the Modern Landscape* represented the opening call for a turn from traditional forms and a search for something vibrant and vital—something new in the garden and the greater landscape. It remains a classic.

> American Projects

Although now a member of the Yale planning faculty, with a turn to more research and teaching in preservation and planning, Tunnard continued to accept residential

2-49
Christopher Tunnard.
"Plants with grey
foliage."
Drawing by
Gordon Cullen.
[*Gardens in the*
Modern Landscape,
1948]

2-50
Thomas Church.
Donnell garden.
Sonoma County,
California, 1947.
[Marc Treib]

2-51
Garrett Eckbo.
Farm Security
Administration
Community Park.
California,
late 1930s.
[Marc Treib
Collection]

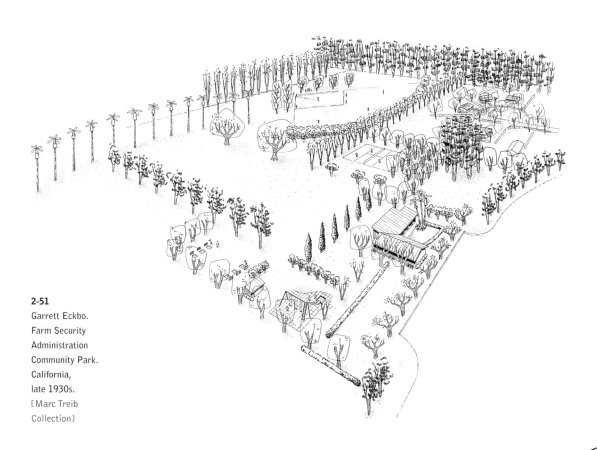

commissions and gradually those of slightly increased scale. In all, the American projects tended to be small in size, limited in number, vague in scope, and as a group, displayed no major departures from his design work undertaken prior to his return to North America. If his associations with the editorial staff of the *Architectural Review* and English modern architects such as Serge Chermayeff and Raymond McGrath had brought him commissions for both writing and landscape designs, his teaching position at Harvard introduced him to a new rank of design professionals that brought corresponding opportunities. Although they were no longer his primary concern, Tunnard continued to accept a handful of design commissions in the greater Boston and Tri-state regions.

In the late 1930s, the village of Lincoln, Massachusetts, located about fourteen miles from downtown Boston, became a center for modern architecture. Given its location on the periphery of the metropolis, land at that time was available and relatively affordable. In collaboration with Marcel Breuer, Walter Gropius built his own house there in 1938, with land and funds provided by the philanthropist Helen Storrow, a fervent supporter of modern design. The Gropius house has been hailed by some writers as a hybrid of modernism and the American vernacular tradition, but in fact, the vernacular influences are most obvious only in its wooden construction [figure 2-52]. Whether the choice of material was a response to a Colonial vernacular or merely a pragmatic response to budget is open for debate. The house took form as a two-story block with a section of its rear upper floor held back to create an open terrace. White walls, single-pane windows without mullions, and a blocky mass announced its modernity and signaled the design's departure from the more prevalent Cape Cod style heralded by architects such as Royal Barry Wills.[194]

Following in the wake of the Gropius house, more modern homes were constructed in Lincoln by several Harvard faculty and clients who supported the modernist cause. Among them were designs by Bauhaus colleague Marcel Breuer (again collaborating with Walter Gropius, 1939), Walter Bogner (1939), Constantin Pertzhoff (1938), and Gropius and Breuer's residence for the husband-and-wife team James and Katherine Morrow Ford, who authored two early albums of residential designs made in the modern manner: *The Modern House in America* (1940) and *Design of Modern Interiors* (1942).[195] Almost all the houses clearly represented the new idiom, marked by flat or softly sloping roofs, compact masses, and planar walls of wood or natural stone. Around 1940, the Monks house joined this modernist enclave in the Boston suburbs.

Its architect was G. Holmes Perkins, a Harvard graduate, who joined the architecture faculty of his alma mater in 1930.[196] Perkins had accompanied Dean Joseph Hudnut on his trip to England in 1936 and assisted in the negotiations with Gropius about his appointment as head of the architecture department; Perkins met Tunnard for the first time in London on the same trip.[197] At their meeting, Perkins was impressed with the young landscape architect, found him interesting and personable, and even invited him to stay with his family on a subsequent trip to Boston.[198] From England, Perkins traveled to Finland and visited Alvar and Aino Aalto at their 1934 home on Riihitie, a house that would have a major influence on the residence he was then designing for his family in Brookline.

Perkins, then an emerging architectural talent,
designed and built the Monks house in Lincoln and added to the town's growing
number of modernist works; construction was completed in 1940. The plan of
the house was configured as a pinwheel with the living-dining room wing—with
bedrooms above—as its dominant volume. The entrance vestibule served as the
pivot of the plan: upon entry, through the dining room's floor-to-ceiling windows,
the garden was revealed almost immediately. Exactly when Tunnard entered the
project is not known and his contribution is difficult to determine with precision—
a sadly familiar story. In an interview in 1994, Perkins explained that Tunnard
was the consultant for the landscape design but that all the construction drawings
and details for the walls, terrace, and pergola were prepared by the Perkins
office.[199] Tunnard's principal contributions, both of which were executed without
drawings, were suggesting a visual axis to be created by cutting a channel through
the trees, and thinning the woods to reduce their density. The majority of the
site was treated as softly modeled lawn of a naturalistic demeanor articulated by
some specimen planting. These areas around the house may have stemmed from
Tunnard's interventions or may just have resulted from following local patterns.
For his part, Tunnard only reproduced photographs of the terrace, stone retaining
walls, and pergola in the 1948 edition of *Gardens in the Modern Landscape*.

      The landscape's design gestures were soft and
hardly radical in any way. Collectively they show that in the ten years since the
original publication of *Gardens in the Modern Landscape*, many of Tunnard's

ideas had already become common practice on both sides of the Atlantic. The terrace, graded to manage the slope and to facilitate access from the living and dining rooms, was paved with flagstones set in grass, more a durable lawn than an architectonic surface. The low retaining wall was built of fieldstone laid dry, that is, without mortar. Some authors have assigned this construction method to the American tradition, but the practice was equally characteristic of British residential designs by Gropius and other émigrés as well as English architects themselves. In fact, in the first edition of *Gardens in the Modern Landscape*, Tunnard published a photograph of a house in England designed by the German architect Peter Behrens that featured a wall of similar construction. By the mid-1930s, the dry stone retaining wall had become the common solution for modern British residential landscapes that required regrading. With its constituent natural units, in addition to its architectonic function as a vertical plane, the dry stone wall formed the perfect transition between terrain and the white-walled building that rose from it. Despite the efficacy of such a solution, Tunnard derided the stone wall in the first edition of *Gardens in the Modern Landscape*, noting that the fieldstone steps and walls are "left-overs from the vernacular period and fail entirely to harmonize with the character of the house."[200] By the time he collaborated on the Monks garden, he seems to have changed his mind.

The Monks landscape, probably dating from around 1941, is almost completely green, except in autumn, of course, when scarlet and yellow leaves visually energize the New England landscape and dazzle the eye [figure 2-53]. Flower planting was concentrated in one corner of the terrace and along the edge of the retaining wall on its upper side. In presenting another small residential garden design of the same date—the Terzaghi house in nearby Winchester —Tunnard described the design by saying that "here there is very little planting— just earth moving, terraces, and lawns." The same characterization aptly characterized the Monks landscape.[201]

The Terzaghi garden, accompanying a house also designed by G. Holmes Perkins, appears as a near sibling to the Monks landscape. The fall of the land was more severe along the lakeside in Winchester, however, and creating level terrain was necessary both for the construction of the house and for creating useful outdoor space adjacent to the living-dining room. The pattern was familiar: near the house, flagstones provided support and thwarted erosion by rain and snow. A dry stone wall retained the soil to create a terrace for the family's outdoor activities, while at the opposite end of the house a series of steps gracefully descended the slope. Between them the earth was banked, the resulting effect being similar to that of the eighteenth-century English ha-ha. A part of Tunnard's charge was to reveal and maintain views of Mystic Lake nearby; trees were kept at a distance from the house and thinned and pruned to create a visually permeable screen that appears to be of deciduous trees whose bare winter state would allow long views over the frozen lake surface.

A garden in Cambridge, Massachusetts, completed the design of a house by the architect Carl Koch for his parents. Koch received his master of architecture degree from the Graduate School of Design in 1937 and it was probably through the Harvard connection that Tunnard came to know the

2-53
Christopher Tunnard.
Monks garden.
Lincoln,
Massachusetts,
c. 1941.
[Marc Treib]

2-54

Christopher Tunnard.
A. C. Koch garden.
Cambridge,
Massachusetts,
c. 1937.
Axonometric.
[*Gardens in the
Modern Landscape*,
1948]

2-55

Carl Koch.
Snake Hill houses.
Belmont,
Massachusetts,
late 1940s.
Site plan.
[*Gardens in the
Modern Landscape*,
1948]

know the architect. William Wurster, who became dean of the School of Architecture at the Massachusetts Institute of Technology in 1945, hired Koch, whom he regarded as an emerging design talent. Perhaps Koch was not yet registered to practice, however, as credit for the design of the house, built in 1934, was shared with Edward Durell Stone, for whom Koch had worked in New York after graduation from college.[202]

The site in central Cambridge was tight and there was little space for a garden. In plans of the house published as late as 1940 there is no evidence of Tunnard's design, suggesting that the garden design came sometime after the house's occupation, though possibly as early as 1941 [figure 2-54].[203] In a caption to images of the garden in the second edition of *Gardens in the Modern Landscape*, Tunnard wrote that the design tried to maximize the perception of a limited space by creating several zones defined by a wooden screen and stone platform cocked at an angle to the boundary wall. Flagstone, sharing the qualities and texture of the garden walls, was used within the house as a transition to similarly paved areas outdoors.

Upon the terrace Tunnard placed a piece of driftwood as sculpture, a gesture learned from the English painter Paul Nash with whom, as we have seen, Tunnard was friendly.[204] Nash had painted a series of works that shared parallels with the metaphysical paintings of Giorgio de Chirico, including at least one painting that bore the title *Metaphysical Landscape*. In this work, the element of the stump and haystack, through placement and scale, became surreal objects in the landscape. Nash's regard, or relooking, at common objects such as a piece of driftwood—the surrealist *objet trouvé*—seems to have had an effect on Tunnard. "Paul Nash was unique among English modern painters in depicting the most minute details of natural objects," wrote Tunnard late in life, "along with a command of the sweep of the sky over broad planes, seascapes, and country parks." Nash, like Tunnard, had become a proponent for preserving the English countryside. The artist, however, looked at the landscape and its elements with a different regard: "his house in Hampstead was crammed with 'found objects' mostly given him by the postman and other friends."[205] While walking along a riverbank on one of his frequent stays outside London, Nash encountered a tree trunk he would soon title *Marsh Personage*. "Yesterday," he wrote, "I found a superb piece of wood sculpture (salvaged from a stream) like a very fine Henry Moore. It is now dominating the sitting room waiting for a bright sun to be photographed." The found object became a turning point in his artistic direction: "Henceforth Nature became endowed for me with a new life. The landscape, too, seemed possessed of a different animation."[206] Nash's influence remained with the landscape architect long after his move to America: "It was my privilege in the 1930s to know an artist who could paint and write so sensitively of the natural world."[207]

It is difficult to characterize the style of the garden at the Koch house, and in the few available photos the design appears overly complicated by too many elements. While articulated to maximize the potentials of a small and visually bounded space, the resulting design suffers from fragmentation and a lost sense of the whole—unlike the more expansive designs achieved

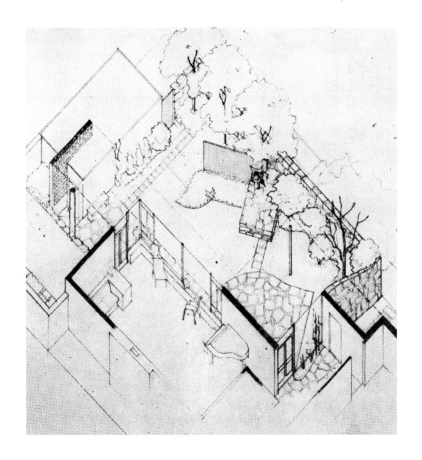

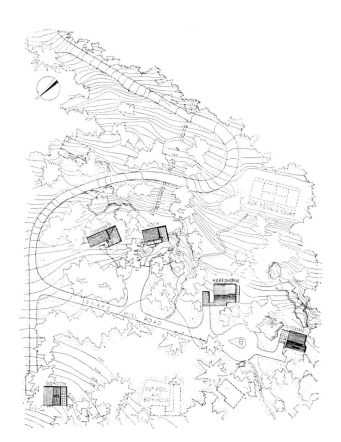

before Tunnard left England. Even the number of ground materials—"grass, marble chips, purple granite, concrete paving blocks and bluestone"— seems excessive for such a small space.[208] The planting plan shows a street front and court filled with vegetation, carefully selected and massed as a foil to the architecture. The success of the garden's planning, in contrast, results from the continuation of the house's geometry and coordination of views from the interior to the garden—for example, the way in which the view from the living room falls on the angled screen wall, stone platform, and driftwood sculpture.

Tunnard also cites his participation in the landscape design for Koch's cooperative house community at Snake Hill in Belmont, outside Boston [figure 2-55]. Sadly, once again we have no precise information on the nature of Tunnard's contribution, although the project probably dates from around 1940 when he was teaching at Harvard. Given the steep terrain, he may have consulted on grading the site for the access road and single-family house sites. For the most part the landscape around the houses was treated as natural woodland, perhaps due to the very limited flat land available for planting gardens.

A related New England project involved the terrace and garden for the Soby house in Farmington, Connecticut, executed some time shortly before the 1948 edition of *Gardens in the Modern Landscape*. The house, in the Greek Revival style, was purchased in 1935 by the art historian and curator James Thrall Soby, then working at the Wadsworth Atheneum in nearby Hartford. Soby knew from "the moment I saw the 'for sale' sign out front" that he would purchase the property—though it had been vacant for some time and was badly in need of repair. The grounds were greatly overgrown.[209] Because the extent and the dimensions of works in his art collection made spatial demands far beyond those the old house could satisfy, a new wing would be required. For its design, Soby turned to his friend, the architectural historian Henry-Russell Hitchcock, then teaching at nearby Wesleyan University, and who in 1932 had co-curated the landmark International Style exhibition at the Museum of Modern Art. As Hitchcock had no formal architectural training, he must have directed the project by working directly with the builders. But the construction of the modern addition—with its sizeable living room below, and bedroom and bath above— progressed smoothly and construction was completed in January 1936.[210]

As in his earlier collaborations with Chermayeff, McGrath, and Perkins, it is difficult to determine the exact extent of Tunnard's input. In the caption to the sole illustration of the project published in the 1948 *Gardens in the Modern Landscape*, Tunnard wrote, "View of a terrace in the garden of James Thrall Soby at Farmington, Connecticut, designed by the author. The wing to the right is a gallery for modern paintings by the architect Henry-Russell Hitchcock. There is a swimming pool and a large free-standing mobile by Alexander Calder" [figure 2-56].[211] The published photograph features the laid stone retaining walls that support two terraces. The upper terrace, which extends the dining room, was probably the work of Hitchcock, configured to match the stone base upon which rest the white walls of the new wing.[212] Gracious broad stairs, also in stone, flowed from the upper terrace through the intermediate level to the expansive lawn that surrounds the house [figure 2-57]. Perhaps this

constituted Tunnard's contribution, perhaps not. Masses of shrubbery defined the outer edge of the upper terrace; planting along the perimeter seems to have been restricted to flowers, employing a design strategy similar to that used at the Monks house. It should be noted that given the venerable age of the original house, the stands of mature trees that surrounded the building were quite grand. Tunnard acknowledged their presence and restricted the number of new plantings by adopting the features of the existing landscape, as he had done on St. Ann's Hill. Over the years a swimming pool has been added and other changes in grading and planting have been implemented and today it is virtually impossible to uncover the nature and extent of Tunnard's involvement.

For Tunnard the 1947 Jefferson National Expansion Memorial Competition in St. Louis, Missouri, occasioned a major departure in scale and approach, and provided an opportunity to intertwine his co-interests in landscape architecture and urban planning. In contrast to the residential projects that had comprised the bulk of Tunnard's practice through his move to the United States, here was a project of suitably heroic New World scale. The idea for the memorial to Western expansion dates from 1935, but realization of that idea had been postponed until after World War II. The venture was the brainchild of Luther Ely Smith, a leading St. Louis citizen and booster, who contributed a substantial sum toward funding the instigation and design of the memorial. Urban renewal was another stimulus for the project; rejoining the St. Louis downtown with the Mississippi River would be a fortuitous byproduct of the memorial's construction. By the end of 1942, several blocks of nineteenth-century commercial structures had been demolished through eminent domain, the authorities firmly believing that work on the memorial would certainly proceed as soon as peace returned. The demolition of the district did not receive universal applause, however: "A lot of people felt that it was the heart of St. Louis and it was being ripped out."[213]

The competition for the memorial's design opened at the end of May 1947; the year before, the Philadelphia architect George Howe had been named as its professional adviser. That appointment, with its responsibility for selecting the members of the jury, tilted the outcome of the competition toward a more modern solution—the precise antithesis of the contest that had yielded John Russell Pope's 1943 Pantheon-like Jefferson Memorial in Washington, DC. The jury was evenhandedly constituted, however, balancing modernist Californians Richard Neutra and William Wurster—who chaired the jury—with the more traditional Fiske Kimball and the St. Louis architect Louis LaBeaume. The competition program called for the memorial itself, a Museum of Westward Expansion celebrating the Louisiana Purchase, restaurants, an outdoor theater, reconstruction of several historical buildings, an auditorium, parking, and recreational land on both sides of the Mississippi. Luther Ely Smith himself desired a memorial "transcending in spiritual and aesthetic values" that would attract people of all nations.[214] The competitors were given only three months to prepare their entries; the deadline was 1 September 1947.

Tunnard was but one member of a team of eight. Led by the architects William N. Breger, Caleb Hornbostel, and George S. Lewis, it included the painters Allan Gould and Andre Schwob, and the sculptor Ralph

Menconi, as well as landscape architects Donald L. Kline and Christopher Tunnard.[215] All the members of the team except Tunnard were then based in New York, leading to questions about how active was Tunnard in the memorial's design. On the other hand, Tunnard's planning expertise might also have entered into play given his rise to prominence in that field following his recent transfer from Harvard to Yale. The Tunnard team's entry was one of five to advance to the competition's second stage, due in February 1948. Their revised scheme received third prize.

 The submission drawings show the memorial first and foremost as a park with an open center; structures, including the memorial itself, played a subsidiary role [figure 2-58]. Extending laterally along the riverfront, the plan acknowledged the old courthouse—a set piece for the competition— with only an understated grassed mall joining the historic structure with the new park, and ultimately to the Mississippi River. Thus, grass replaced the brick and mortar that had previously occupied the site. In accord with the competition brief, Tunnard's group retained several historic structures, including the old cathedral and its dependencies, and the Manuel Lisa warehouse on the riverbank; the design team also proposed reconstructing several other buildings in the manner of Colonial Williamsburg. All these structures were minor players in the overall scheme, however, resembling chess pieces set on a sea of green, whose isolation precluded any collective benefits [figure 2-59]. The museum, a light structure capped by an umbrellalike roof, anchored the northwest corner of the site and extended southward as a terrace set at the level of the road. An appendage of the museum occupied the space below the terrace—an adroit profiting from the difference in land elevation. A new pedestrian footbridge over the river would link the memorial site with a corresponding park on the opposite bank where the recreational facilities would be concentrated. Curiously, or perhaps interestingly, the memorial did not align with the old courthouse but left it with a direct view to the river. In contrast, the winning scheme by Eero Saarinen centered the void of the great arch on axis with the courthouse.

 In the revised scheme, as in the preliminary, the central area of the landscape was left as a great greensward, with vegetation concentrated along Memorial Drive, which bordered the site on the east—and which was soon to be transformed into an interstate highway. Here the landscape architects positioned several rigorous allées of trees that marched virtually nonstop from one end of the two-thirds-mile-long site to the other. The procession paused only briefly before the cathedral and the courthouse mall before terminating at the museum. In the tradition of the grand boulevards of Paris, the allées mediated between the orthogonal city and the more naturalistic memorial landscape, while buffering the park from the adjacent buildings. By depressing the highway, the team sought to still the effect of traffic and gain a better bond with the urban fabric on its other side.

 The drawings show little planting within the linear arboreal frame except as clustered clumps used to situate and protect architectural elements such as an architectural museum, the reconstructed village structures, a campfire theater, and a restaurant. The text accompanying the proposal described the landscape in this way: "The planting consists of ornamental and shade trees

2-58
Christopher Tunnard
et al.
Jefferson National
Expansion Memorial.
St. Louis, Missouri,
1949.
Site plan.
［National Park
Service］

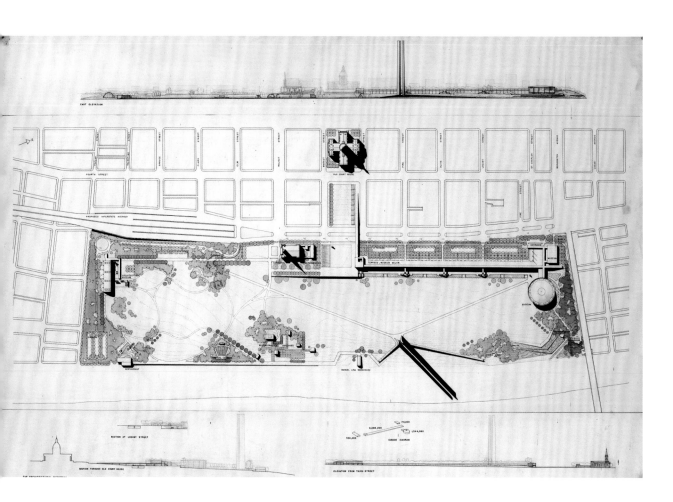

2-59
Jefferson National
Expansion Memorial.
St. Louis, Missouri.
Aerial perspective.
［National Park
Service］

of several types, grass and occasional ground cover." Flowering shrubs and other vegetation requiring continued maintenance were not precluded. "The trees are deciduous and variously conical, pyramidal or void in form." No specific selections were given: "appropriate species" might include oak, maple, elm, ginkgo, linden, and poplar.[216] Other than several fountains, there would be no water features: "With the river visually so close," their statement reads, "it seems unsuitable to introduce any large area of artificial water."

While formed in the tradition of the colonial common, or green, ultimately there is something suburban about the Tunnard team's design. The two-pronged shaft of the memorial proper appears to float, untethered, in space, anchored only by diagonal walkways tying it to the corners of the site and retaining walls that from the memorial play outward to the river. In addition to the overall impression of a landscape of objects floating in space, one wonders about the effects of climate on the visitor experience. Given the city's cold, windy, and nasty winters—especially where exposed to the river— and its hot, humid summers, vast expanses of lawn were probably not the best solution. In any event, it was the majesty of Saarinen's grand stainless-steel arch, set in the forested park by Dan Kiley, that won out and was constructed.[217] Time has confirmed the wisdom of the jury's decision.

> Three Last Landscapes

If, in fact, the Warren garden in Newport, Rhode Island, was the last realized landscape design by Christopher Tunnard, it offers a curious and puzzling terminus, perhaps relating to landscape architecture what Marcel Duchamp's *Étant donnés* (1946–1966) was to art—an enigma. In idiom the garden appears highly baroque, with its twisting hedges and planting beds. Spatially, however, it is quite classical, with a central lawn surrounded by beds and shrubbery, enclosed by walls and the masses of tree canopies. At first glance, Tunnard seems to have turned his back on all he had argued for in *Gardens in the Modern Landscape*. A more careful review, however, can situate the design comfortably within Tunnard's precepts for a modern garden, especially in its relation to the artwork that would be its central feature.

The precise date of the commission for the Warren garden has not been found but the garden does not appear in the 1948 edition of Tunnard's classic, suggesting a completion date somewhere around 1949 [figure 2-60].[218] The clients were George Henry Warren, a stockbroker and former director of the Metropolitan Opera, and Katherine Urquhart Warren, a founding member and president of the Preservation Society of Newport County, art collector and donor, and a trustee of the Museum of Modern Art.[219] Tunnard may have met her through his project for the Museum of Modern Art's sculpture garden or his preservation efforts in New England after he shifted base from Cambridge to New Haven.[220]

The three-story Warren house, built in a Federal style and dating from the opening decades of the nineteenth century, is a nearly solid block of brick punctuated politely by ranks of windows on each floor. A modest portico engages the street. The garden, which was adjacent to the house rather than connected to it, is thus urban—and small, measuring only some 45 by 65 feet. One of Tunnard's tasks, no doubt, was to facilitate a stronger bond between the ground floor of the house and the garden level some three feet below it. In the remodeling, a wide door replaced small windows, and a new terrace eased movement from inside to outside, and from the house above to the garden below. Steps extending the full width of the terrace facilitated this transition. Both terrace and steps were set slightly askew to the façade of the house to compensate for the off-center location of the door. Tunnard used this diversion from the orthogonal to create a diagonal visual line that extended the reading of the space toward the southwestern corner, psychically expanding the dimensions of the garden within the concrete-block boundary walls [figure 2-61].

      The set piece for the garden was the 1947 bronze sculpture *Chimerical Font* by Hans (Jean) Arp. Positioned as the focal terminus to the diagonal axis, the polished bronze sculpture was set on a base in a pool painted black to increase the reflections [figure 2-62].[221] The sculpture generates multiple readings, among them a bulbous treatment of the human figure, or more abstractly, as smaller biomorphic forms set against a central egg-shaped volume. Tunnard seems to have used this biomorphism as his point of departure for the design, although one could read the forms with equal merit as derived from baroque classicism. The wiggly shapes of the hedges, most apparent in plan and from above, relate clearly to this biomorphic idiom used by Arp in his sculptures, and Joan Miró in his paintings [see figure 2-61]. Contradicting such a contemporary reading are two circular pools set within the irregular waves of yew (*Taxus*), their inner surfaces painted white—said to attract birds—each half-enclosed by a low hedge: in all, a scheme setting formal geometric elements against the row of small-leaf lindens and the wall behind.[222] The planting palette is suitably restricted. In addition to the lindens on the garden's street side is a dense planting of arborvitae (*Thuja*) used to screen the garage to the north, and rows of poplars beyond the western wall—for privacy, and perhaps as a screen against the strong summer afternoon sun. Ivy (*Hedera helix*), boxwood (*Buxus sempervirens*), and flowers completed the plant list. This was essentially a green garden with sheared shrubs and shaped flower beds offering controlled splashes of color.

      Essentially meant to be viewed from the ground in the manner of a baroque green theater, the prevailing mood generated was one of calm and order in which visually active elements enlivened a simple scheme. No conflict troubled the pairing of visual delight and quotidian use: the central lawn supported social gatherings, both neighborly and familial, while a shaded, gravel-lined space tucked into the northwest corner fostered shaded solitude. In *Gardens in the Modern Landscape* Tunnard called for gardens that addressed function, included art, and produced empathy; in the Warren garden he successfully addressed them all, a skilled departure from many of his other landscape designs.

      About this same year—no document establishing the precise date has been located—Tunnard produced a vision for a garden for the new United Nations headquarters in Manhattan under construction at that time. Whether this design responded to a suggestion from someone at the organization

2-60
Christopher Tunnard.
Warren garden.
Newport,
Rhode Island,
c. 1949.
Replica of original
sculpture by Hans
Arp as visual
terminus.
［Marc Treib］

2-61
Warren garden.
Newport,
Rhode Island.
Plan.
［*Modern Gardens*］

2-62
Warren garden.
Newport,
Rhode Island.
［Marc Treib］

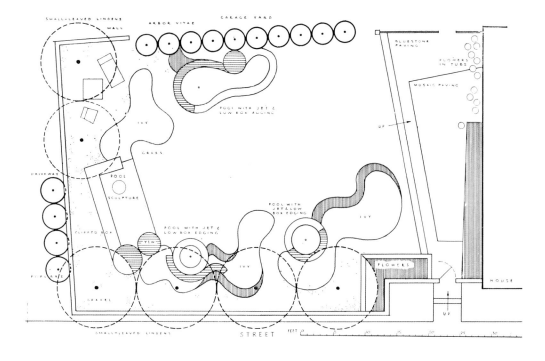

2-63
Christopher Tunnard.
Garden for the
United Nations.
New York, 1949.
Perspective by
Charles Prentice
Thompson.
[*Architectural
Review*]

2-64
John McAndrew
and Alfred Barr, Jr.
Sculpture Garden.
Museum of Modern
Art, New York, 1939.
Plan.
[*Museum of
Modern Art Studies
in Modern Art 6*]

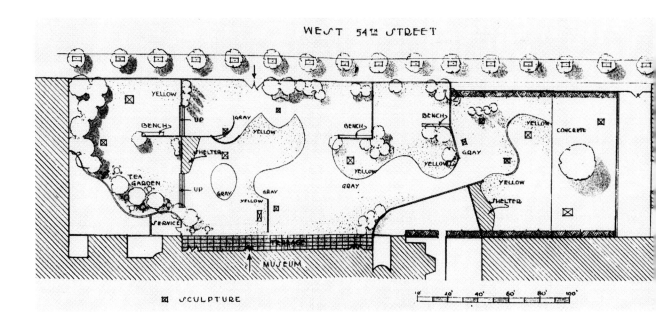

or was self-generated is unknown, though the latter is more probable. In fact, virtually nothing is known about the project except for information given in a news brief in the *Architectural Review*'s "Marginalia" section and in one other unidentified publication. The sole illustration, an aerial perspective executed by Charles Prentice Thompson, a young architect or possibly a Yale architecture student, shows trees surrounding an open central area [figure 2-63].[223] Tunnard's scheme eschewed any truly axial planning, and the published description stressed that "the strong directional lines...are softened by the weaving of the tree pattern, which, with its irregular bays and openings, provides a setting for sculpture not always immediately seen." From the complex's 47th Street entrance on First Avenue, the public would be allowed to pass directly to the edge of the East River. In contrast, the garden for the delegates would be more private, "with quiet places and a good deal more colour in the flowers, mosaic pavements and mural paintings on the walls." Screen walls were situated to dampen the winds coming off the river; a set of circular pools at the public garden's center would "churn and bubble in the warmer months," while becoming "ice fountain[s]" in winter. Despite the schematic nature of the design, Tunnard nonetheless mentioned specific plants, a wide variety that would span from "birch to rhododendron to bearberry and ivy." Nothing became of the Tunnard proposal.

Philip Johnson and James Fanning's handsome design for the Museum of Modern Art Abby Aldrich Rockefeller Sculpture Garden in New York City is so established as a masterwork of modern landscape design—and as a model for the outdoor display of sculpture in urban conditions—that it comes as a surprise to find that Tunnard too had prepared more than one proposal for the garden.[224] Designed by Philip Goodwin and Edward Durell Stone, the new home for the museum opened in 1939. The strikingly modernist building occupied only about half its site between West 53rd and 54th Streets, allowing sufficient outdoor space for the display of sculpture drawn from the museum's holdings, and loans from trustees and other collectors. Since the nineteenth century, the scale of sculpture had been growing, but at the time of the first sculpture garden—quickly designed by the architecture and design curator John McAndrew in consultation with museum director Alfred Barr, Jr., to accompany the opening of the building—most of the works were no larger than the human body. The McAndrew design was provisory and used waving walls of woven wood to fashion a series of suitably modern biomorphic spaces displaying the works sympathetically and to advantage [figure 2-64]. It was an expedient solution and served for about a decade. By 1942, however, a movement was afoot for a more permanent garden, a site for events such as openings and concerts in addition to its more quotidian purpose of outdoor sculpture display. A café might also be in order.

On 16 September 1943, architecture and design curator Elizabeth Mock responded to the exhibitions director Monroe Wheeler's request for names of possible landscape architects for the project. Christopher Tunnard topped her list. "A young Englishman [*sic*] who came to this country in the summer of 1939," she wrote, "and taught landscape architecture at the Harvard Graduate School of Design until he joined the Canadian army in December 1942." He had recently received a medical discharge, she wrote, and is now at work on a second book with a fellowship from Harvard, "and plans to work as much in New York as in Cambridge during the coming year."[225] Tunnard, she stressed, already had extensive design experience and "wrote the authoritative book on the subject." Before listing his completed design projects in England and the United States, she closed with, "He is reputed to know northeastern plant materials thoroughly and would do a fresh, sound job of design." Mock also named Michael Rapuano, who was "recommended by Howard Myers as a landscape architect of ability and wide experience. Has evidently done some work for Ed Stone."[226] She then cautioned that "It is doubtful whether he would produce as interesting a plan as Tunnard." Nothing came from the Mock initiative, but by 1946 a project by Tunnard, collaborating with the museum's architect Philip Goodwin, was in progress to accompany a new wing of the museum [figure 2-65]. To date, only two photos of the model that document the scheme have been found. Tunnard used walls and plants set diagonally to counter the orthogonal geometry of the site, perhaps taking cues from contemporary work by Garrett Eckbo and James Rose, and perhaps also influenced by the earlier experiments in France during the 1920s.[227] Nothing issued from the proposal.

The project for a sculpture garden was resurrected several years later, and in September 1949 Tunnard submitted a new design for which he was the sole author. The illustration boards, executed in ink and gouache, were probably drawn by a Yale architecture student, as Tunnard seems to have displayed little talent for or interest in drawing or rendering. The design of the sculpture garden is competent and complete, but unremarkable, certainly lagging behind the innovations currently underway in California. In many ways, the design would have more successfully displayed plants and trees than sculpture, although the siting of each artwork had obviously been considered carefully. Tunnard paved the ground plane with stone along the edges of the building—as it had been in what he identified as the "Old Garden"; the remainder of the garden surface would be gravel, perhaps for economy. A bosk of trees, possibly salvaged from the prior sculpture garden, filled the northwest corner of the site. The low lines of an elongated pool animated with jets, and a linear planter bed, would confront visitors entering the garden from the museum [figure 2-66]. The low wall of the planter played against a higher wall to its rear; both were set against the mass of trees arranged as a formal bosk. A row of shrubs and trees outlined the bed, its line reinforced by a second flank set along the façade of the museum in the garden's southeast corner. Diagonally opposite, a circular pool echoed a circular display area partially defined by low walls. The free placement of the vegetation in this area confronted the geometry of the lines and grid used along the building. It appears that Tunnard was consciously using trees and shrubs architectonically in proximity to the museum structure and more freely toward the garden's northern boundary on 54th Street.

Tunnard's plan proposed a play of planes pairing those set vertically against horizontal beds and pools, a strategy that suggests the influence of Mies van der Rohe, in particular his German Pavilion at the 1929 Barcelona Exhibition [figure 2-67]. However, the tops of the majority of the walls were low, well below eye level. As a result, the zones within the garden read as soft

2-65
Christopher Tunnard.
Sculpture Garden,
Museum of
Modern Art.
New York, 1946.
Model.
[Museum of
Modern Art]

2-66
Christopher Tunnard.
Sculpture Garden,
Museum of
Modern Art.
New York, 1949.
View from the
museum to the linear
pool with water jets.
[© The Museum
of Modern Art, ,
Licensed by SCALA/
Art Resource, NY]

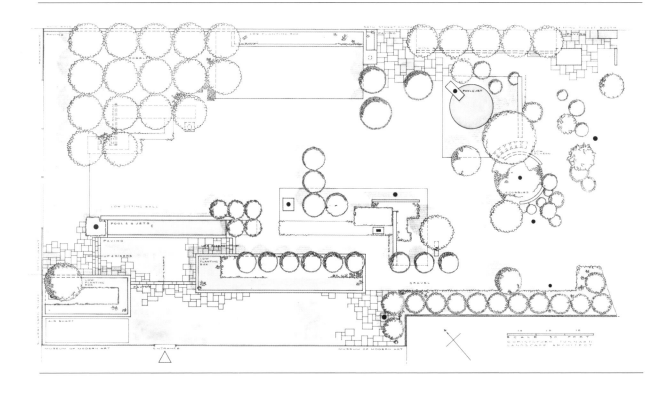

2-67
Christopher Tunnard.
Sculpture Garden,
Museum of
Modern Art.
New York, 1949.
Plan.
[Museum of
Modern Art]

2-68
Sculpture Garden,
Museum of
Modern Art.
New York.
View toward
the northeast.
[© The Museum
of Modern Art, ,
Licensed by SCALA/
Art Resource, NY]

2-69
Sculpture Garden,
Museum of
Modern Art.
New York.
Planting plan.
[Museum of
Modern Art]

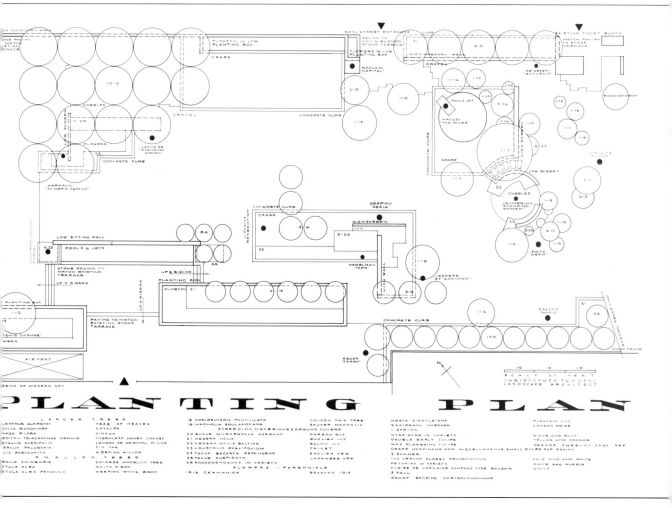

modulations of the overall space rather than as discrete subdivisions. The trees in rows, bosk, or clusters—rather than constructed walls—provided the primary spatial divisions [figure 2-68].

In the planting plan, Tunnard introduced a significant mixture of trees, shrubs, and flowers, and proposed variations in ground covers to distinguish the upper surfaces of beds whose constructed outlines appear quite similar [figure 2-69]. English (*Hedera helix*) and Baltic ivy (*Hedera helix baltica*) would stand against areas of lawn and the gravel used throughout the garden. Golden rain trees (*Koelreuteria paniculata*) comprised the bosk in the southeast corner of the garden, which would have added a spectacular splash of yellow when in bloom. To the right of the exit door a row of saucer magnolias (*Magnolia soulangeana*), which flower a creamy pink, traced the line of the museum's north façade. One can only imagine the composite effect of all these species blooming in spring, especially if the golden rain trees and saucer magnolias flowered at the same time. Against the museum's northern façade, further west, toward Fifth Avenue, Tunnard set a dense row of Chinese angelica trees (*Aralia chinensis*) to soften the impact of the wall. The tree's delicate palmate leaf would have ensured a more complex visual texture within the garden although the nature and amount of debris generated in autumn might have been troublesome. In the zone of the circular forms the planting was less homogenous, with additional plantings of Chinese angelica tree, interspersed somewhat curiously with the large-leafed *Catalpa bignonioides*, and more sympathetically with a *Ginkgo biloba*, whose yellow autumn hue would chromatically echo the Chinese angelicas. Along the north wall a line of London plane trees (*Platanus acerifolia*) shielded the garden from the traffic of 54th Street and provided an arboreal background for the variety of plantings in the circular zone.

If Tunnard took great care with the planting design and positioning, heights, and lengths of the walls that partitioned the garden, his plan displays an equal concern for the placement of the sculpture. The list of the works to be placed on show was no doubt provided by the curators. These included Alexander Calder's *Whale*, Jacques Lipchitz's *Figure*, Gaston Lachaise's *Standing Woman*, Aristide Maillol's *The River*—sympathetically set on the edge of the circular pool—and Isamu Noguchi's softly modeled *Capital*. Although the Calder and Noguchi sculptures were more "modern" in their forms, their small scale was sympathetic to the human figure represented by most of the other sculptures projected for display. In all, Tunnard's plan suggested a richly planted garden with sculptures to a greater degree than a garden dominated by them. Certainly he did not need to contend with the large-scale works such as monumental pieces by Mark di Suvero that are common in today's sculpture parks.[228] For whatever reason, the Tunnard project was not adopted, and about three years later the design by Johnson and Fanning was constructed to both professional and popular acclaim. Although the garden has been modified several times since its completion, that judgment has endured, despite renovations and additions to the museum buildings over the ensuing half-century.[229] With the proposal for the Museum of Modern Art sculpture garden and the completion of the Warren garden, Christopher Tunnard's career as a landscape architect was essentially completed.

2-70
Isamu Noguchi.
The Family,
1957.
Connecticut General
Life Insurance,
Bloomfield,
Connecticut.
[Marc Treib]

For his part, Tunnard never lost his interest in art, especially art in the garden. In 1957, when the new suburban campus for Connecticut General Life Insurance was reaching completion outside Hartford, Tunnard was commissioned to spend a day on-site to critique the proposed siting of a sculptural group by Isamu Noguchi. For this modernist curtain-walled office complex designed by Gordon Bunshaft of Skidmore, Owings & Merrill, Noguchi had designed three of the courtyards and the employees' terrace. He also had created a cluster of monumental stone sculptures he called *The Family* [figure 2-70]. The sculptor first proposed that the stone grouping be sited adjacent to the building on the employees' terrace, but after some deliberation a site on the gently modeled landscape designed by Joanna Diman was judged a better location.[230] That Tunnard's aesthetic judgments were highly regarded is evident in his having been solicited to review the placement of sculptures by the corporate administration. In his opinion, "The new location suggested for the big sculptural group is more satisfactory than a position on the terrace, where...the figures would be too insistent. On the rising ground at a distance from the building and with the background of trees, I think they will be quite striking and will evoke some of the feeling that stone age monuments give rise to in Europe."[231] Tunnard's verdict was accepted, suggesting that even Noguchi himself considered the judgment a good one, and *The Family* remained in that location until the vacating of the buildings in the 1990s.

Tunnard's scale of interest continued to expand, shifting from the garden and landscape to the city and region, accompanied by

interest in the urban landscape in between. The title *Gardens in the Modern Landscape* and the book's later chapters on the cultural landscape, of which the garden was only a part, testify to these interests even in his early years. From this point, he would be known as an educator, planner, and preservationist—but always with references to and reliance upon his formation and experience as a landscape architect. Ian McHarg, in 1958 chair of the Department of Landscape Architecture at the University of Pennsylvania, wrote to Tunnard soliciting his suggestions for a reading list for his students. He noted that "your book is still the best in the field." As noted above, Lawrence Halprin claimed after reading *Gardens in the Modern Landscape* in 1943 he immediately made up his mind to become a landscape architect. Over the years, long after these last design works, Tunnard was invited to lecture or speak at symposia addressing planning or aesthetic issues, almost always with some indication that his invitation was predicated on his work in landscape architecture.

> **Epilogue**

Although the focus of this book ends before 1950, by which time Christopher Tunnard had moved conclusively from landscape architecture to city planning, let us at least outline his accomplishments in the succeeding decades. Tunnard's thinking continued to be informed by his earlier training and practice in landscape architecture [figure 2-71].[232] While some authors have regarded his move to planning with a renewed interest in historical patterns as being a "renunciation" of modernism, it may be more instructive to see these shifts merely as an evolution from small-scale to large-scale thinking.[233] In addition, as we have seen in regard to his realized designs, we can question whether Tunnard ever achieved any truly modernist landscapes. He did remain a modernist in many ways, however, at least in his writing. But now, rather than concentrating on the garden, he addressed issues such as the city, its skyline, and the roads, agricultural fields, and industrial plants of the American landscape. He no longer produced gardens or other landscape designs, but he actively continued to write, lecture, and consult, in addition to teaching at Yale.

Tunnard's advancement up Yale's academic ladder—achieving the rank of professor of city planning in 1962 while serving as director of the department's graduate program—paralleled the expansion of his fields of operation. He became instrumental in the workings of preservation groups in Newport, Rhode Island, and his current hometown, New Haven, Connecticut. With Henry Hope Reed, Tunnard authored *American Skyline*, published in 1953, a comprehensive survey of the history of American cities and their architecture that was graced by a narrative free of academic jargon, supported by considerable detail, and enlivened by numerous quotations from novels and other literary forms. It is true that Reed himself was a classicist, evident in his book *The Golden City*, and that Tunnard did contribute to the *Ars in Urbe* exhibition of civic art held at Yale in April 1953.[234] But I cannot agree that Tunnard truly shared Reed's classical sympathies. It is true, as we have seen, that Tunnard's landscape designs never equaled the ambition of his writing, and that he never conclusively discarded the picturesque in his work and writings. However, if we cannot agree that Tunnard

2-71
Christopher Tunnard with the Monroe Planning Study, c. 1955.
[Charles Alburtus, Yale University Archives]

remained a modernist, perhaps we can agree that he did remain modern—at least in aspiration—but as always, his modernism was viewed through an understanding of the past. And yet the arena of his inquiry had widened, now encompassing an ever-greater section of the landscape, now the region rather than the garden or even the city.

No matter the dimensions of the surface area of the landscape in question, to Tunnard its design and management always presented an opportunity. "A regional landscape when recognized," he announced in the 1953 Gulf States Regional Conference, "is a most exciting thing—and it comes very close to affording the esthetic satisfaction of a work of art. It may be the product of ecological succession or largely the result of man's intrusion on nature—How it has come about is not always important in our appreciation of its qualities." Yes, it is a question of how we perceive the landscape before or around us rather than the factors that shaped it. We should not fear the future but embrace the potentials offered by mechanization and regard it as a "tool to increase well-being and not a menace."[235] These investigations and observations would coalesce in the book *Man-Made America: Chaos or Control?*, co-authored with Boris Pushkarev and published in 1963.

In the book, the discussion of topics such as the road and the grand landscape makes evident that Tunnard had acquired an understanding of human movement and visual perception; these complement the more practical knowledge of subjects such as grading and road building contributed by his co-author. That said, we could also note that at root, Tunnard's ideas about the land and landscape still recalled earlier ideas about the English landscape park, the relation of form to topography, and of vegetation to structures. By the 1960s, Tunnard's interest had turned far from the garden in the modern landscape to the modern landscape itself. That definition of landscape was predicated on higher population densities, reliance on the car and truck, urban sprawl, and what was generally regarded as rampant ugliness.

During the 1960s a movement to improve the beauty of America had gathered considerable steam, propelled by the passage of the 1965 Highway Beautification Act and the publication of books such as Peter Blake's *God's Own Junkyard*, in 1964, and *Street Graphics: A Concept and a System* by William Ewald, whose publication in 1971 was supported by the American Society of Landscape Architects. Although one might interpret this war against ugliness as a rebirth of the City Beautiful efforts made in the opening years of the twentieth century, its doctrine made references to neither classical architecture nor functional planning. Instead, one might trace the origin of the new beautification movement to Ian Nairn's 1955 issue of the *Architecture Review* entitled "Outrage!" Given this forum Nairn, an architectural and cultural critic, attacked the despoliation of British cities, their choking traffic, advertising clutter, and rampant disrepair. While Nairn focused his gaze on Britain, his commentary had repercussions across the ocean. Curiously, unlike the other Tunnard books, *Man-Made America* is less a polemic against ugliness than a handbook about what can be done to mitigate it. The intention of the authors was to

> deal with the visual as well as the non-visual side of urban design. The
> esthetic ideas presented are offered within a planning framework; they

are not necessarily the ideas of an architect, a landscape architect, or an engineer, but deal with spatial and structural characteristics in general terms. ... [W]e *are* concerned with the position of man-made objects in space and in the values of scale in the landscape: with streets, open spaces, and large-scale industrial and commercial facilities—in other words the esthetic values of man-made elements which have received very little attention in the recent past.[236]

Tunnard is credited with the sections on open space and historic preservation, and in those chapters he provides analysis and insight into the problems plaguing these fields but also proposes thoughtful resolutions to alleviate them. If you are not a road engineer or a regional planner you may be bored by the mechanical specificity of certain parts of the text, but the arguments about how to proceed are convincing. All of this is to say that *Man-Made America* is less a manifesto—or only a very soft one—and more a manual on how to remediate the problems troubling the contemporary landscape. While the book's technical detail—much of it provided by Pushkarev—is impressive, behind it lies the analytical approach of a landscape architect, who like a doctor is trying to improve the health and appearance of his patient. "[T]he physical and economic realities of our large-scale man-made environment, in spite of their inherent order," cautions Tunnard, "are incapable of producing beauty by themselves. Here, beauty can only emerge from a deliberate effort to express the encounter between society and environment in significant form."[237] Echoes of *Garden in the Modern Landscape.*

Tunnard's final major publication, *A World with a View: An Inquiry into the Nature of Scenic Values*, was published by Yale University Press in 1978, a year before its author's passing [figure 2-72].[244] In the text, he reprised themes that had meandered through his writings from the very start, although the stress to some extent now lay in his plea for visual pleasure. "Our surroundings are being destroyed and we are losing all the qualities of what used to be called 'scenery,'" Tunnard laments. "When a landscape is considered to be 'scenic,' its esthetic qualities are somehow better served. Only when a proper appreciation of scenery returns can destruction be halted and the esthetic content restored to our cities and countryside, to what we build and to what we plan."[245] In some ways, the book rehearses continued interests while serving as a memoir of ideas treated in prior writings, some of which even harken back to his earliest essays—although now viewed with a perspective broadened and graced by forty years of travel, study, teaching, practice, and writing. Chapters such as "Landscape and Science" and "Landscape as Art" faintly echo themes first explored in *Gardens in the Modern Landscape.* Another focuses squarely on the garden and curiously rehearses the story of the historical European and British landscapes through the filter of China and the vague aesthetic concept of *sharawaggi,* or "graceful disorder." The detail in this section is extensive, in contrast to the other chapters of the book, which are narrated with a looser, more avuncular tone. The content of the chapter is puzzling given Tunnard's experience in the modern landscape—yet explicable in terms of his longstanding interest in the history of the English landscape garden. In a letter to the editor of the *Architects' Journal* in 1946 Tunnard tried to explain *sharawaggi* in considerable detail.[246] We need recall that Nikolaus Pevsner, among his own essays published in the *Architectural Review,* also weighed in on this supposedly Chinese aesthetic idea at a time when Tunnard was part of the journal's circle. Perhaps it was just expedient to use an essay already conceived or even already written.

Illustrations in *A World with a View* ranged from sketches by John Ruskin, to paintings by William Gilpin, Paul Nash, and Hans Memling, to photos of the Padua botanical garden and the Villa Cicogna in Italy, and the Villa Vizcaya in Miami. Throughout the text, yet again, Tunnard examined the pitting of technology and progress against social values and aesthetic effects. He ends the book optimistically, stating that "A beginning has been made to bridge...the yawning chasm between the unbridled exploitation of technology on the one side and full development of the cultural patrimony on the other. The gap will only be bridged when the esthetic values of society are properly understood."[247]

That Tunnard argued for beauty and landscape preservation in his last major publication is less a retreat from modernism, as some have proposed, than a repositioning of ever-evolving ideas within an ever-broadening field of concern. His interest in the historical English landscape, as we have seen, occupied nearly half of *Gardens in the Modern Landscape*, accompanied by a belief in the importance of art—such as sculpture—in the landscape, at the same time asserting that the garden was itself a work of art. Thus, though less convincing as an argument, I see *A World with a View* as an amplification of thoughts long held rather than their abandonment. He instructs us that "Nothing takes the place of the insight of truly humanistic observers who are moved by the forces of nature and who can invest even a humble forest trail with mythic and classical imagery."[248]

In 1960 Tunnard finally got to travel to and in Japan, having been invited to participate in the World Design Conference held that year in Tokyo. Today the meeting is known in architectural circles primarily for its launch of the Metabolist group and its use of the organic metaphor as a means for generating urban form. Tunnard responded to the initial invitation enthusiastically, suggesting that he could "perhaps contribut[e] a paper on Problems Common to the Design of Cities East and West."[238] The glitch was that Yale would not fund his attendance. Perhaps the U.S. government could fund his travel and participation. Apparently the funding was eventually secured, as on 13 May 1960 Tunnard presented a talk titled "Design & Environment." In the lecture he "discuss[ed] settlement patterns and technological change in the modern world, showing good and bad design solutions in urban and rural landscapes, and generally presenting a picture of the new challenges to all types of designers which the population explosion presents."[239] The talk was broadly sketched and lacked specifics. Despite its many generalizations, Tunnard's lecture nonetheless demonstrated a comprehensive understanding of urban patterns and the issues facing the city in the second half of the twentieth century.

After the conference Tunnard traveled to the Kansai region to visit Kyoto gardens such as Shugaku-in, Katsura, and the Heian Shrine.

2-72
Christopher Tunnard.
*A Word with a View:
An Inquiry into the
Nature of Scenic
Values,* 1978.
Dust Jacket.

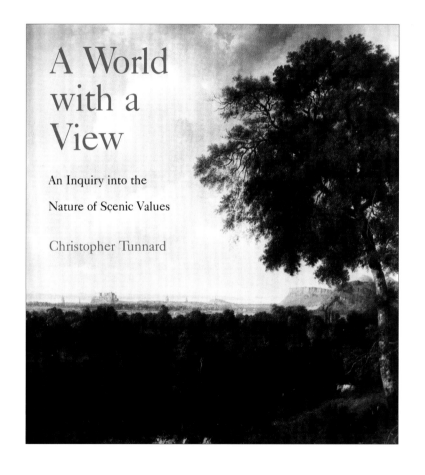

A World
with a
View

An Inquiry into the
Nature of Scenic Values

Christopher Tunnard

Among these, his favorite was the garden at Ginkaku-ji, the Silver Pavilion.[240] In a paper destined to be published in the *Garden Club of America Bulletin*, he described his experience in that garden—the formal entry between high green walls and the irregular pond—and he questioned the origin and reasons for the two mounds of sand that fill the central part of the garden: the Sea of Silver Sand and the Moon-Viewing Height [figure 2-73].[241] While any of the several reasons for the mounds he offered were "plausible...their main interest today is that they are unique in the world of gardening and probably irreplaceable."[242] As he had written in his very first article, Tunnard linked the forms of the Japanese garden to its culture: "The careful and symbolic arrangement of lanterns, basins, fences, and gateways in a tea garden has very little meaning in countries where the tea ceremony is not practiced....But, gardening the world over would undoubtedly improve if the Japanese art of relating natural material were properly studied."[243] True, he admits, garden form follows specific cultural norms. However, in terms of syntax, its lessons are universally applicable.

In all, how should we regard Christopher Tunnard's contribution to landscape architecture, and specifically a *modern* landscape architecture? As we have seen, rather few, if any, of his landscape designs advanced practice in a remarkable and truly progressive way; he remained a transitional figure whose aesthetic was rooted firmly in the past, in the golden age of the English landscape. Instead, it is in his writings where his principal contribution lies. "Do as I say and not as I do," parents frequently tell their children. The dictum comfortably applies to Christopher Tunnard as well. What he called for, and the sources from which he acquired such ideas—the need for and use of art in landscape design, the lessons that Japanese garden art may provide—remain valid today, as do the continuing needs for informed site planning and the denunciation and amelioration of ugliness. "You may, like the farmer, know the land," he instructs us, "but not the landscape. It may take an artist to provide this knowledge."[249] And not the least of his contributions was the inspiration he provided for a group of students and landscape architects who sought a way beyond the classical and naturalistic traditions. He provided the call and suggested the means, if not the realized landscape models that fully embodied the innovation and depth of his thinking.

Tunnard's contribution to the making of a modern landscape architecture was pivotal, if inconclusive. At the time of their publication his writings were fresh, inspiring, and perhaps even convincing, although read today we may question just how modern his ideas ultimately were. The inherently conservative nature of plants, whose forms remain virtually unchanged through the ages, seems to always dampen the most vibrant spirits of innovation. Nature tempers the extreme idea. Yet in the creation of space, the implication of artworks, and in overall spirit, Christopher Tunnard's writings and certain of his landscapes rightly occupy a key position in the development of modern landscape architecture in the twentieth-century West. In the East, Sutemi Horiguchi was pursuing similar goals, similarly burdened by tradition, but a tradition of a far different kind.

2-73
Yoshimasa Ashikaga.
Ginkaku-ji
(Garden of the
Silver Pavilion).
Kyoto, 1480.
The Moon Viewing
Height.
[Marc Treib]

3. > Sutemi Horiguchi: Ahead Through the Past

Although Christopher Tunnard visited Japan for the first time only in 1960, from his earliest writings he had lauded the work of historical Japanese garden makers and argued for the relevance of their work to contemporary landscape architecture practice in the West. These gardens of centuries past, Tunnard asserted, provided lucid models for balancing design with process, form with space, and equilibrium with dynamism. Modern Japanese landscapes, in turn, demonstrated that enduring principles could assume new forms in sympathy with evolving modern architectural practices, including the highly alien vocabulary of the imported International Style. The gardens designed by Sutemi Horiguchi—architect, landscape architect, literary figure, aesthete, and educator—confirm Tunnard's position [figure 3-1]. Building and landscape, Horiguchi believed, were inextricably linked, and their design should result in a unity of architecture and garden. Any discussion of Horiguchi's search for a contemporary expression for the garden therefore necessarily requires a discussion of his architecture, even though at different stages of his career, or in different situations, either building or landscape might prevail.

Born in 1895, the fifth son of an agricultural and landowning family, Sutemi Horiguchi's turning to architecture was hardly preordained. His father's visions assigned him to the military or perhaps to medicine, as his elder brothers would inherit the principal share of their father's estate. Their location in Gifu Prefecture was not at a great remove from the culture of the tea ceremony centered in Kyoto, and the Horiguchi family actively embraced the precepts and practice of *cha-no-yu* (literally, hot water for tea). Its values

3-0
Sutemi Horiguchi.
Okada garden.
Tokyo, 1934.
[*Architectural Beauty in Japan*]

and prominence would only increase during the life of the Horiguchi family's fifth child.[1] A chance encounter with an architect friend of the family catalyzed the choice of career the young Horiguchi would pursue. In 1917, aged twenty-two, he enrolled in the architectural engineering program of the prestigious Tokyo Imperial University. The school's curriculum was largely rooted in structural engineering and academic neoclassicism, the official style adopted for government buildings during the Taisho period (1912–1925). Architecture was not taught independently of engineering, however, and the courses and stylistic biases of the faculty troubled Horiguchi and several of his classmates. Garden design, not taught in the schools and in any case influenced less by foreign importation, had for the most part ceased to evolve since its codification during the Edo period (1603–1867). In any event, residential and temple landscapes remained the province of the Kyoto gardener families that had dominated garden design for several generations. Rehearsals of idioms and practices that had held sway for literally centuries had almost completely stifled innovation, except to a minor degree.

> Precedents

The gardens of the early Edo era are normally regarded today as a high point in Japanese landscape design. In contrast to the selection, reduction, and minimalism of the older *kare-sansui*, or dry garden style, these were instead lush landscapes heavily planted, at times intended to evoke memories of the Golden Age of the Heian period (795–1182) when aristocratic cultural life in Kyoto reigned supreme. The *kaiyu-shiki*, or stroll garden, characteristic of larger aristocratic estates, utilized compositions that were aesthetically pleasing from any vantage point along the route. Of greater consequence were the composite views that could be mentally assembled from successive station points, while walking, perhaps, along the path that shadowed the shoreline of a pond: that is, wherever terrain and economic resources allowed. Aristocratic projects such as the seventeenth-century Katsura and Shugaku-in Imperial Villas, occupying sites at the diagonally opposite ends of Kyoto, reshaped the land in accord with both the social and aesthetic dicta of the day [figure 3-2]. In the former case, the low-lying lands adjacent to the Katsura River were sculpted to fashion a meandering water body that drained the marshy land on which the villa and its garden were constructed; the *tatami* and wood floors were raised abnormally high to elevate buildings and their occupants above potential flood surges. In the case of Shugaku-in, set in northeastern Kyoto, a colossal earthen dike was constructed to retain seepage, rain, and water from hillside streams and thereby create a pond of impressive dimensions [figure 3-3].

In these gardens, mediating the movement of eye and body was paramount. Using techniques such as "hide-and-reveal" (*miegakure*), a relatively small site might be rendered magnificent by multiplying, through artifice and composition, the actual dimensions of the garden plot; the resulting perceptions of the space were correspondingly increased. Curving pathways traced the contours of hills and swales, while adroitly positioned stepping-stones traversed streams and ponds—each element choreographed a shift in the visitor's pace, direction, and gaze. Adding to the original conception the intense urge to

3-1
Sutemi Horiguchi,
1971.
[Horiguchi Archives,
Meiji University,
Tokyo, hereafter
HA, MU]

3-2
Prince Hachijō
Toshihito.
Katsura Imperial Villa.
Kyoto, 1620–1670s.
[Marc Treib]

3-3
Emperor Gomizunô.
Shugaku-in Imperial
Villa.
Kyoto, 1660s+.
The vista revealed.
［Marc Treib］

perfection characteristic of Japanese maintenance, these were in all, landscapes of elaborate sophistication and aesthetic pleasure.

The waning power of the imperial house under the pressure of successive shoguns, paired with the restricted aesthetic display allowed the merchant class, led to an increased ossification of garden design over the course of the eighteenth and nineteenth centuries. Without doubt, gardens of great beauty were nevertheless created in this period, but gardeners and their clients seem to have been content with revisiting existing manners, materials, and methods rather than attempting to innovate in any significant way. By the end of the nineteenth century, garden-making patterns had become fixed, with small ponds, artificial hills, clipped shrubs, the ubiquitous rockwork, and gravel as the principal elements; in many instances, these were employed to grace sites of very modest dimensions with visions of grandeur [figure 3-4].[2]

With the forced opening of Japan to the Western powers in the mid-nineteenth century and the subsequent establishment of treaty ports in Shimoda, Yokohama, Hakodate, Kobe, Nagasaki, Niigata, and Osaka, foreigners and foreign ideas began to trickle into a country that had been cloistered for most of its modern-period history. Early Meiji-era imports from the West were primarily technological and military, but were accompanied in time by practices in the cultural spheres that included architecture and eventually landscape design. Based in Kyoto, Jihei Ogawa (1860–1933) designed gardens for the grand estates of Kyoto merchant families after the sumptuary restriction of materials and expenditure had been removed by a government edict that followed the Meiji Restoration of 1867 and the promulgation of a new constitution some few years thereafter.[3] Bolstered by the construction of a brick aqueduct that brought much-needed water for the growing city from Lake Biwa over Kyoto's eastern hills, the features and plants in these gardens bordered on the extravagant. For his design sources, Ogawa looked to the present as well as the past.

The elements of Ogawa's landscapes derived from the gardens of the Edo period and had therefore existed for centuries, but gradually a new sensibility became evident in his designs. For one, expanses of lawn began to increase in surface area and prominence, paired in many cases with ponds of considerably enlarged dimensions [figure 3-5]. The garden for the Heian Shrine, laid out in 1895 to commemorate the 1,000th anniversary of the founding of Kyoto, accompanied shrine buildings designed by Chuta Itô, who would soon become Horiguchi's professor at the Tokyo Imperial University. The elements of this garden were neo-traditional, with winding paths, a pond, stands of cherry trees, and a wooden bridge roofed by a pavilion that recalled the fifteenth-century Silver Pavilion in Kyoto. These were conventional elements; it was in the handling of the space and selection of forms that Ogawa moved beyond the past. More personal to him were cylindrical stone posts used as stepping-stones to traverse the pond. Set nearly level with the water, they appear as a play of stone circles that visually animate its surface [figure 3-6]. In all, the garden was traditional, yet to some degree modern, foreshadowing Horiguchi's own works of the 1930s. Ogawa's garden for the Furukawa residence

3-4
Josiah Conder.
"Hill Garden–
Rough Style."
[*Landscape*
Gardening
in Japan]

3-5
Jihei Ogawa.
Tairyu-san-so.
Kyoto, Japan, 1917.
Stream and clipped
plant forms.
[Marc Treib]

3-6
Jihei Ogawa.
Garden of the
Heian Shrine.
Kyoto, 1896.
Cylindrical
stepping-stones
traverse the pond.
[Marc Treib]

(1917), built at the northern edge of the Yamanote in Tokyo by Josiah Conder, signaled the direction in which Japanese garden design was moving. This course acknowledged the past while accepting the future, as evidenced by the former Meiji-period slogan: *Wakon yôsai*—"Japanese spirit, Western knowledge."

The architect Josiah Conder (1852–1920) was a young Englishman who arrived in Japan in 1877; in time, he became the first professor of architecture at the Tokyo Imperial University. At twenty-four years of age, and thus only slightly older than his first pupils and with little if any practical experience, Conder himself was less master than apprentice. However, he quickly grew into his responsibilities, although he was no innovator.[4] His design for the Furukawa residence is undistinguished—a bland, if credible, essay in an English stockbroker style, built of brick, faced with a ruddy *shin-komatsu* andesite. Unlike houses of Japanese tradition, solid walls rather than paper screens separated inside from outside, replacing the minimal and elevated spatial transition between those that had belonged equally to the *sukiya* and *minka* styles of the past.

To mitigate the effect of the slope, Conder terraced the terrain in three levels in a somewhat eighteenth-century Western manner, but replaced the more commonly used boxwood with evergreen yew and potentially gaudy azaleas—whose blooms would nevertheless have been selectively plucked to avoid any too garish display of color [figure 3-7]. The effect was that of a hybrid, not quite Western but far from Japan's own practice of *karikomi* (topiary), said to have derived from the aesthetic transformation of the tight pruning used on tea plantations to stimulate new growth.

To accompany, or possibly as antidote to, this alien environment, Ogawa created a pond garden at the bottom of the hill entered through a wooded transitional zone that separated the new world of European architecture from the timeless calm of the Japanese garden [figure 3-8]. Though the garden's design displays little innovation, the outsized rocks and overscaled lantern proclaim a near-Mannerist exaggeration of historical practice, as if hyperversions of tradition were deemed necessary to confront the new methods and alien forms found in the mansion on the summit of the hill.

Conder's designs in Tokyo for the first Imperial Museum (1881) in Ueno Park, the Rokumeikan (1883) in Hibiya, and the Iwasaki Villa (1889) at Shinagawa in southern Tokyo, amount to an imposition of almost-English architectural styles upon a vast urban agglomeration in the midst of rapid transformation. Increasingly concerned with the practice of Japanese art as well as landscape design, however, Conder also undertook a study of Japanese gardens that resulted in his handsome two-volume *Landscape Gardening in Japan*, first published in 1893.[5] Drawing on Japanese studies, some published as early as 1633, its author first traced the history of the garden and thereafter developed his own lexicon of garden types and elements. Long the only major study of the subject in English, the book has enjoyed numerous republications and remains in print in several different editions.

Foreign-influenced construction in brick and stone, each graced with a neoclassical or Queen Anne vocabulary, transformed the central districts of the capital such as Ginza and Marunouchi.[6] The departure from

3-7
Josiah Conder.
Furukawa-tei.
Tokyo, 1917.
[Marc Treib]

3-8
Jihei Ogawa.
Garden for the
Furukawa-tei.
Tokyo, c. 1917.
[Marc Treib]

conventional construction in wood, paper, and earth was cataclysmic; the new buildings wore styles that appear as if from another planet. There were also imperfect essays in the new mode by untrained, at least as seen by Westerners, Japanese master carpenters. They created amalgams—curious to the Western eye—that merged two of the Japanese building types that relied on solid wall construction: the fortified castle and the *kura*, or storehouse. As integrated works of architecture, their efforts were a good deal less successful than Ogawa's gardens, which achieved an unquestionable unity and integrity as fully-fledged works of garden art.

In the early years of the Meiji era, then, we first encounter both foreign works by non-Japanese architects and works in a foreign style by native designers. In the years that followed, Japanese architects trained by Conder began to play a more evident and influential role in the making of Japanese architecture and the nation's cities. Katayama Tôkuma and Tatsuno Kingo were responsible, respectively, for major works such as the 1895 Kyoto National Museum and the 1914 Tokyo Central Station. Their brand of ponderous neo-academicism, more Teutonic than British in figure and feeling, came to dominate construction for government and major businesses well into the twentieth century. For the most part, residential *minka* (folk house) architecture remained as it long had been: single story, perhaps with a second level where demanded; constructed of wood with interiors divided by *shoji*, translucent paper sliding screens, hence spatially flexible; deficient in internal plumbing and

3-9
Sutemi Horiguchi.
Crematorium
(student project).
Tokyo, 1920.
Elevation.
[HA, MU]

lacking comprehensive heating; with roofs of thatch, or if in an urban context, unglazed ceramic tile. Such was the architectural and gardening context in which the young Sutemi Horiguchi completed his architectural studies at the Tokyo Imperial University and then, after an interrupted *Wanderjahr* in Europe, took up independent practice.

> Bunriha Kenchiku-kai

Early in his architectural education, Horiguchi demonstrated uneasiness with the doctrine informing the curriculum's emphasis on engineering and structure, that is to say, the very manner in which architecture was conceived at Tokyo Imperial University. Moreover, to Horiguchi and a number of his classmates, the Greco-Roman classicism that dominated the design of governmental structures was a Western import with little relevance in an Asian context; even in the West, academic neoclassicism was rapidly going out of fashion. In reaction to these views, a small cohort of Horiguchi's fellow architecture students sought to envisage a modern Japanese architecture that might somehow merge native tradition with the evolving modern lifestyle, what in other words might be called a "New Architecture." This group named itself the Bunriha Kenchiku-kai (Architects Secessionist Group, often termed the Japanese Secession Group in English). The 1924 catalog accompanying the third of its exhibitions asserted, "From this moment forward we shall endeavor to prevent the spread of small, narrow, anti-cultural functionalist thinking that we have so ardently resisted

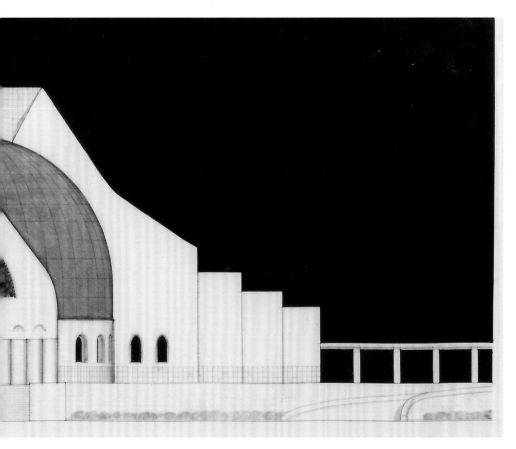

from the very beginning."[7] If idealistic, the students were not naïve in declaring that a building of wood, earth, and pantile was no solution for the industrialized city—especially when quickly evolving techniques of construction in steel and reinforced concrete offered remarkable opportunities for new architectural expression. Despite these lofty pronouncements, Horiguchi's 1920 student project for a crematorium looked to pre-World War I Germany for its stylistic sources, its design attempting to induce monumentality by joining the bulbous form of a great hall with subsidiary wings staggered in their arrangement [figure 3-9]. More an unresolved utterance than a coherent statement, this project nonetheless signaled the path Horiguchi would follow in the early years of the 1920s.

In 1919, with fellow students Mamoru Yamada and Mayumi Takizawa, Horiguchi had traveled to Tsingtao (today Qingdao) in China, where the three were greatly taken by buildings in the German colony designed in an interpretation of *Jugendstil* that in some instances bordered on expressionism. Augmented by four additional students, who included Kikuji Ishimoto, they formed the core group of the Bunriha.[8] Among all the several German-language revisionist groups, their main reference, of course, was the Viennese Secession, which itself had withdrawn from the Academy of Fine Arts in Vienna to found an artistic movement centered on the expressive, symbolic, and psychological aspects of art and architecture—in contradistinction to the sentimental or historical themes still perpetuated by the Academy.[9] Ironically, while adopting the name of its Austrian predecessor, the young Bunriha under-graduates either did not accept, or were unaware of, the language of its more recent buildings. Instead, they proposed a more plastic architecture that in no way resembled the celebrated 1897 Secession Pavilion in Vienna designed by Josef Maria Olbrich, a cubic structure of planar white surfaces famously crowned by a gilded latticework globe, whose internal spaces were all orthogonal [figure 3-10].[10] In contrast, the Bunriha members proposed bulky buildings with curving surfaces, whose designs echoed prewar works by German architects such as Hermann Finsterlin and Bruno Taut, in particular, the latter's 1917 proposals for an Alpine architecture resonant with its dramatic mountain setting. Bunriha architecture, in contrast, was intended to disrupt and innovate, with buildings primarily used as exhibition material that would remain unbuilt [figure 3-11]. Following its rather intense undergraduate beginnings and initial years, the life of the group waned over time; its exhibitions, however, persisted until 1928. Aspects of the Bunriha projects would nonetheless remain and reappear in Horiguchi's designs executed well after his return to Japan from a European sojourn undertaken shortly after graduation.

Although in no way responsible for its overall planning, Horiguchi submitted designs for several temporary buildings for the 1922 Taisho Peace Exposition held in Tokyo's Ueno Park. These, such as the Forestry Pavilion, were essentially long, rambling utilitarian sheds with expressionist and *Jugendstil* dressings positioned at their centers and other points of entry. In his preliminary studies Horiguchi experimented with two alternate architectural styles for the same plan, one employing the English Arts and Crafts style—drawing rather directly from a project by Mackay Hugh Baillie Scott published in *The*

3-10
Josef Maria Olbrich.
Secession Pavilion.
Vienna, Austria,
1897.
[Marc Treib]

3-11
Sutemi Horiguchi.
Project for
a museum.
Location unknown,
c. 1920.
Elevation.
[HA, MU]

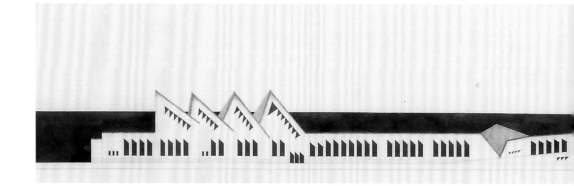

Studio, the other an ensemble of jagged forms that would have been extreme even in Germany [figure 3-12]. In the end, the fair's supervising architects opted for a more sedate architecture. The plans of the buildings as realized were simple in the extreme: single-space pavilions devoted to the display of forestry and mining, aviation and transportation, and culture. Horiguchi's most noteworthy contribution was not these pavilions, however, but, the fair's theme tower, based on Olbrich's final work, the Hochzeitsturm (Wedding Tower, 1908) at the Mathildenhöhe artists' colony outside Darmstadt, Germany [figures 3-13, 3-14]. Presumably funded by the fees received for his work at the fair, Horiguchi set out for Europe in 1923 to expand his cultural horizons and experience the architecture he had hitherto known only from published photographs.

> Abroad

Horiguchi's first actual exposure to European architecture was to have a major impact on his thinking as well as his future architectural designs. His travels included visits to France, Belgium, Austria, and England. With his somewhat unfocused enthusiasm for expressionist architecture as a guide, Horiguchi spent considerable time in Germany, including a visit to Darmstadt, as far as we know to visit the artists' colony, several buildings of which had been designed by Josef Maria Olbrich. In Berlin, Horiguchi purchased a hefty number of German books and magazines on architecture and interior design, including a bound set of *Deutsche Kunst und Dekoration* comprising issues from 1914 to 1921. While impressed overall with architecture in all the countries he visited, it was the Netherlands and recent social housing by J. J. P. Oud in Rotterdam, and the latest manifestation of the so-called Amsterdam School, that would exert the greatest influence on Horiguchi's design practice in the next decade.

Dutch architecture in the first decades of the twentieth century incorporated influences as wide-ranging as Frank Lloyd Wright in America, the English Arts and Crafts movement, the German *Jugendstil*, and innovative works by Hendrik Petrus Berlage in the Netherlands itself. It was a heavy architecture of brick walls and tile roofs, and yet in the hands of such architects as Michel de Klerk, Piet Kramer, and J. F. Staal these buildings acquired a smooth plasticity. In any event, orthogonal city blocks did not necessarily yield strictly orthogonal building units. Instead, walls of Amsterdam School buildings were softened by curves, while roofs received picturesque treatment.

3-12
Sutemi Horiguchi.
Exhibition pavilions.
Taisho Peace
Exhibition.
Tokyo, 1922.
[HA, MU]

3-13
Sutemi Horiguchi.
Theme tower.
Taisho Peace
Exhibition.
Tokyo, 1922.
[HA, MU]

3-14
Josef Maria Olbrich.
Wedding Tower.
Mathildenhöhe.
Darmstadt, Germany,
1908.
[Marc Treib]

136 >

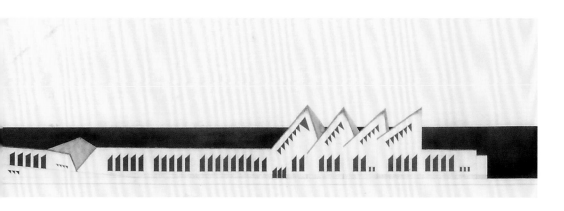

Although massive in aspect, a basic intimacy of scale nonetheless pervaded work such as the 1920 Eigen Haard housing estate in Amsterdam by Michel de Klerk [figure 3-15]. A number of these housing projects were commissioned by cooperative housing societies, associations that did not yet exist in Japan and were only conceived there after the Great Kantô Earthquake of 1923.

The Amsterdam School seemed to have been able to realize, at least in part, the dreams that the Bunriha had achieved only in drawings and plans, and Horiguchi was understandably taken with the Dutch work. Here were lessons to be learned. However, the catastrophic earthquake of 1923 forced Horiguchi to return home—rumor has it that he had considered staying in Europe to study at the Bauhaus in Weimar.[11] Whether or not this is true, upon returning to Japan the young architect was soon given the opportunity to apply his European experience, visual and formal, to the design of a small house and its garden in Tokyo.

> Early Practice

The Koide house (1925) was small and thus necessarily intimate, more traditionally Japanese than international modernist. The ground level had mostly wooden flooring and appeared contemporary in comparison with the upper floor that was completely given over to *tatami* mats—although not strictly following the conventions of the so-called *sukiya* style [figure 3-16]. Only the more or less rigidly planar wall surfaces of the south (garden) façade, an unusually gracious use of glass, a few minor interior details, and the dominant, obliquely patterned tile roof that seems to sit awkwardly on its support displayed any inkling of the insights garnered from foreign travel. The site was so restricted that it precluded any real garden of note.[12] Horiguchi's achievement with the Koide house was meager and undigested, but he had finally built and by this means announced his return to Japan to fellow members of the architecture profession.

A greater opportunity came at about this same time, the commission for a more dramatic villa called the Shien-sô, located north of Tokyo at Warabi in Saitama Prefecture, and completed in 1926 [figure 3-17]. In the Netherlands, Horiguchi may have visited—or at least seen images of—the villas of Park Meerwijk, built around 1916 in the seaside town of Bergen in North Holland. This was an engaging group of houses that paired vernacular Dutch *boerderij* (farmstead) roof forms shaped by expressionist angles and window shapes with a notably eccentric treatment of traditional thatching. The Villa Meershoek (1918) by Cornelis Jouke Blaauw is today among the best known of these buildings [figure 3-18]. The experience garnered in the Netherlands was not lost on Horiguchi; he applied its ideas directly, first tentatively in designing the Koide house and more emphatically to the Shien-sô shortly thereafter.

Horiguchi's design for this exurban "Villa of Purple Haze" was willful—an approach typical of many young architects who apply what they have just seen to a first or early work. This was especially true in Japan where at that time there was little if any stigma attached to imitation. For Horiguchi the design was a determined attempt to emulate and reinterpret Dutch architecture within the context of a modern Japan. He was aware that thatch was common as

3-17
Sutemi Horiguchi.
Shien-sô.
Warabi, Saitama
Prefecture, 1926.
[*Making a Modern
Japanese
Architecture*]

3-18
Cornelis Jouke
Blaauw.
Villa Meerhoek.
Bergen, Netherlands,
1918.
[Marc Treib]

a roof material for rural structures in both countries and thus appropriate for this relatively remote site in Saitama Prefecture. Here he could procure a local species of rush that had been used to roof riding stables in the immediate neighborhood, as well as a teahouse adjacent to the Shien-sô site.[13] From most angles, the roof of the little villa reads in photographs as a substantial cone or pyramid of thatch—one with a definite vertical thrust sitting somewhat uncomfortably on a modest architectonic base. Because the interiors all had false ceilings, this expressive external roof form had no internal consequences and served little purpose other than as an emblem of something novel. Although most traditional Japanese urban dwellings also made use of interposed horizontal ceilings, the prominently sculpted roof forms at Shien-sô would seem to promise more varied and dynamic spaces within, something in the nature of certain Japanese farmhouses with exposed roof structure. In the living room of the Shien-sô, this expectation was met only in a space of gracious, if slightly unwieldy, height. The plan of the house, a square with external projections, arranged the rooms using neither symmetry nor formal structure, at least as measured by Western standards [figure 3-19]. Overall, a simplified logic appears to have determined the disposition of the internal spaces, with each room treated independently—a possible reflection of the balanced asymmetry of Dutch De Stijl compositions. As in much of Horiguchi's work from this early period, one can interpret the Shien-sô in two ways: first, as an inclusive architecture of innovation that relied on Japanese tradition while hesitantly infused with Western modernism to invigorate the native norm; or viewed more critically, as an incomplete understanding and appropriation of non-Japanese ideas and compositional methods.

While the exterior of the building intentionally paired outer walls of a modern feel with a distinctly rustic if well-wrought thatch roof, the main reception room exuded a modish, if slightly lugubrious, Art Deco ambiance. Existing photographs (the villa had a very short life, destroyed by fire the year after its occupation) show a living room with dark walls and softly tinted upholstered chairs, enlivened by papered porthole windows that provided limited light and little formal interest; French doors facilitated access to the garden that extended to the east. The four circular windows, ganged as a quadrant to form a transom above the pair of muslin-hung French doors, effected a play of solid and void. While these windows, together with a larger round, papered window, created intrigue as a formal investigation within the room and from the exterior as elements of the façade, the resulting interior light quality appears to have been harsh and marred by considerable glare. Other rooms, at least as seen isolated within their photographic frames, sport a look of European modernism, with elegant internal furnishings simply set against plain wall surfaces. Various details demonstrate a fusion of East and West, old and new—such as panels of glass approximately the dimensions of standard *shoji*.

Announcing the rear, or garden, entrance to the house was a shallow and nearly square pool, whose stepping-stones recalled those at Jihei Ogawa's 1896 Heian Shrine in Kyoto [figure 3-20; see figure 3-6], but here rectangular in shape. Thus, where Ogawa had arranged a series of stone cylinders to serve as steps traversing a deep pond, Horiguchi used rectilinear stone planks to resonate with the villa's orthogonal plan. Unfortunately, the nature and quality of any landscape on other sides of the site has gone undocumented. But based on more or less contemporary urban projects by Horiguchi, we can assume that the surroundings were given to lawn, with shrubs massed along the lot lines for privacy, if privacy were required here. The mature trees that appear in several photographs suggest that that the new house may have replaced a prior construction.

Horiguchi's borrowing of a Dutch architectural idiom isolated the garden from the house and vice versa, a dilemma posed by the insertion of a foreign building style into a Japanese milieu. The architect would attempt to resolve these problems in succeeding projects, either by extending elements of the building into the landscape or by dividing the house and garden into two distinct zones—one Japanese, one Western. In all, the Shien-sô was a fascinating hybrid, a tour de force of ideas acquired on his European travels or garnered earlier from publications. Several of its elements remained to some degree undigested, like Meiji-period architecture executed by artisan-carpenters with an incomplete grasp of their foreign models. Horiguchi would later propose few projects or works in this same style, and none as thoroughgoing as the Shien-sô in intent and execution.

By the end of the 1920s, Horiguchi had moved cautiously but decisively from *Jugendstil* and expressionism to a pursuit of high European modernism. Given Horiguchi's linguistic proclivity, the books in his library, and his earlier travels, it is unsurprising that his sources were more often German than French. Regardless of any particular precedent, however, rarely do Horiguchi's plans evince the strength or clarity found in coeval European work. In his plans, each room looks to have been planned independently and thereafter assembled as a group to form a whole—as opposed to a single figure in which the constituent spaces are subservient, that is to say, planned in the manner of much Western classical architecture. The 1930 Kikkawa (in some publications referred to as Kichikawa or Kitakawa) house and its garden well testify to Horiguchi's transition from expressionist to modernist, while nonetheless maintaining a certain regard for Japanese tradition.[14]

A bright watercolor rendering of the preliminary scheme for the house reveals a lingering interest in the Amsterdam School; like the Shien-sô, its juxtaposition of primary forms appears to some degree clumsy and unconvincing as a resolved composition [figure 3-21]. In the rendering, and like the Shien-sô, the roof of the Kikkawa house reads as a pyramid of tile set hesitatingly upon a white box. Like certain couples who have lived together for many years, the two elements live in proximity but do not truly converse.

The design phase for the Kikkawa house spanned more than three years marked by Horiguchi's continually increasing rationalization of the scheme. The resulting design was credibly modernist and a milestone in the development of modern Japanese architecture, and yet the house fits uncomfortably within the Western canon because it leaves so many of its architectural components undigested [figure 3-22].[15] Moreover, it eschews the calm resolution of Horiguchi's Wakasa house to follow at decade's end.

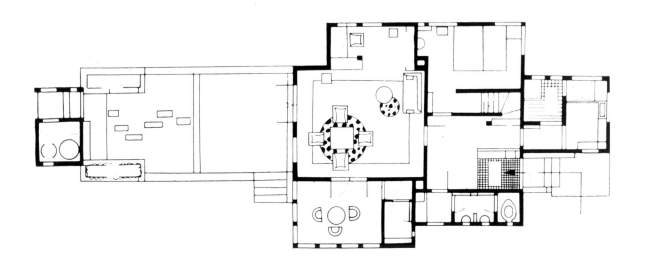

3-21
Sutemi Horiguchi.
Kikkawa house.
Meguro, Tokyo,
1930.
Preliminary study.
［HA, MU］

144 >

3-22
Kikkawa house.
Meguro, Tokyo.
Garden façade.
［Yoshio Watanabe,
HA, MU］

In planning the Kikkawa house, Horiguchi devoted considerable attention to the existing site vegetation, solar orientation, and a potential view of Mount Fuji to the west, gained principally from terraces on the upper floor. In an explanation of his thoughts, he noted that the house was sited to consider a *nara* (oak) tree near the guest room, an *enoki* (Japanese hackberry) on the east side of "madam's room," and a large Himalayan cedar.[16] The plan is difficult to characterize given the extensive floor area of the house (roughly 13,000 square feet) and the panoply of separate rooms—virtually nothing remains of the fluid spaces of the traditional Japanese house except in the private spousal domain, and in the zone assigned to domestic help [figure 3-23]. As always in the Japanese house, the living and formal dining areas and guest rooms were situated along the south of the main block, while offices occupied the southeastern rank— clearly the most public zone of the house.

Buried within the simple massing of the plan was a labyrinth of service spaces, such as those needed for food preparation and storage, and a small, intimate dining area. A narrow courtyard brought light and air into the middle of the house, as well as conjuring its most poetic moment [see figure 3-25]. The rooms are mostly Western in feeling, with public as well as some private spaces on the ground floor, and bedrooms and family rooms assigned to the upstairs. In contrast to the simplified delineation of the enclosed ground floor and more open upper level of the Wakasa house at decade's end, a nervous and somewhat still traditional energy marked the Kikkawa elevations, especially the south façade whose vertical planes joined two roof levels in striking zigzag fashion, stacking one set of eaves one upon another.

The Kikkawa house was designed to have been built of reinforced concrete, but when this proved impractical—probably due to governmental restrictions on key building materials like steel—Horiguchi returned to common wood-frame construction. Like Le Corbusier—whose nearly contemporary Villa Savoye is a concrete frame with brick infill, thereafter stuccoed to give the impression of concrete—Horiguchi too rendered his construction visually homogenous by coating the timber structure with hard plaster. Unfortunately, in Japan stucco suffers under high humidity and intense precipitation, although freeze-thaw cycles in most coastal areas are minimal. Interestingly, the Kikkawa foundations perpetuated centuries-old building practices, with large stones installed at the base of the principal wood posts, thereafter supported by smaller stones rather than backfilled with gravel as is common practice in the United States. Thus, only the outer walls benefited from cast-concrete foundations. As in its architectural style, the construction technique used to build the Kikkawa house was a fusion of native and imported practices.

The energetic composition of the Kikkawa façade extended to the complexity of its landscape in what, taken as a whole, was Horiguchi's closest approximation of the Western gardenesque style. A purely decorative narrow band of water poured southward from the living room; its flow terminated in a circular flower bed that might have well fit without notice in any nineteenth-century Parisian park [figure 3-24]. Horiguchi explained that this channel was designed to serve two functions: drainage and cooling through

3-23
Sutemi Horiguchi.
Kikkawa house.
Meguro, Tokyo,
1930.
Plan.
[HA, MU]

3-24
Kikkawa house.
Meguro, Tokyo.
View to the garden.
[Yoshio Watanabe,
HA, MU]

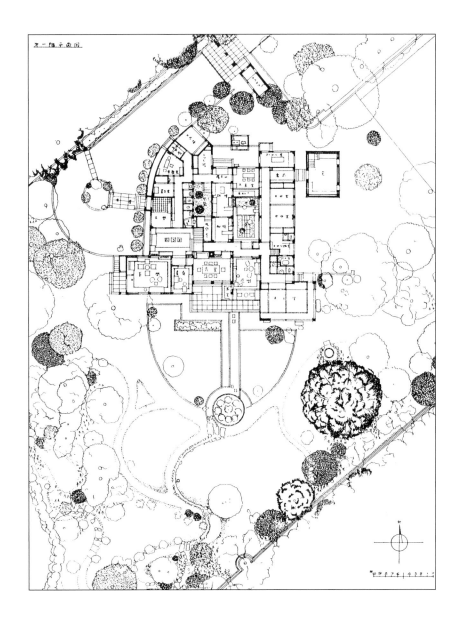

evaporation. Just precisely how this would be accomplished is left unexplained and to the imagination of the reader. A prow-shaped concrete curb in the form of a double great arc linked one slightly raised portion of lawn to the geometry of the house, distinguishing it from the more freely treated areas of garden beyond. As the footprint of this large house filled more than one-third of the site, shrubbery and trees were relegated to its periphery. Separate areas within this outer green band were enriched with meandering paths, seating, and other garden features. Like almost all of Horiguchi's work of the period, the Kikkawa garden adumbrated planning that would become the norm for Japanese houses on small lots in the postwar period: an approach that has been termed the "open center." That is to say, the house roughly occupies the center of an expanse of lawn, while dense plantations of shrubs anchor the limits of the site, creating visual interest and insuring privacy from neighbors.

Of all the diverse landscape features of the Kikkawa house, it was the tiny internal *tsuboniwa* (courtyard garden) that first caught the eye of architect Raymond McGrath and landscape architect Christopher Tunnard thereafter. It remains in the Western garden imagination as one of Horiguchi's signature works [figure 3-25].[17] This small space, a double square in proportion, brought light and air to the corridors and service areas surrounding it. Most landscape designers would recoil at the limits imposed by such a restricted space granted only periodic sunlight, but Horiguchi triumphed with a solution that was almost a diagrammatic overlay and conflation of Asian and Western approaches. A central walk shaped an axis through the middle of the courtyard, an axis that in fact led nowhere and terminated at the rear wall. Fed by an elevated fountain-head, a small pool halted the thrust of the walkway. To this point, the composition could be read as almost classical. But against this primary structure, Horiguchi poised three circular elements: two round stepping-stones and a third component enacted in clipped plants (*ibuki,* or Chinese juniper). This composition was set off by an asymmetrically placed evergreen white *tsubaki* (*Camellia japonica*) that complemented the horizontal movement of the pathway with a strong vertical, and diagonally joined the vegetal circle in the foreground with the corresponding features behind it. The wall surfaces were sheathed in light yellow ceramic tiles that enlivened the space with warm reflected light.

The composition occupied the courtyard while at the same time forming it. Its vegetation and built elements engaged the walls of the house, but the true dynamism of the composition derived from the deft counter-play of circular forms against the courtyard's structural order. The American landscape architect Fletcher Steele, writing somewhat earlier of modern garden design in France in the 1920s, referred to this relationship as an "occult balance": far from symmetry yet ordered, far from chaotic yet vibrant.[18] In its essence, the Kikkawa court seemed to cite the play of square stepping-stones and gravel at the Katsura Villa in Kyoto, not by rehearsing the imperial garden's shapes but in the superimposition of one system of order upon another [figure 3-26]. This suggests that Horiguchi kept one eye directed to the present, while the other maintained a view of and strong attachment to the past.

3-25
Sutemi Horiguchi.
Kikkawa house.
Meguro, Tokyo,
1930.
Internal court.
[*Architectural
Beauty
in Japan*]

3-26
Katsura Villa.
Kyoto, 1620s–1670s.
Overlay of
stepping-stones.
［Marc Treib］

With the completion of the Kikkawa house Horiguchi had demonstrated his design skill and proclaimed his generalized faith in a new architecture for Japan. Accompanying his growing professional reputation as an architect was his acclaim as an author. Two important articles from the early 1930s elucidated Horiguchi's concern for the Japanese adoption of modernism as a support for contemporary living. The first of these writings argued for a way of building securely reflecting its time; the second article, which we shall discuss first, displayed the author's support for a new, modern architecture. The second article, in turn, demonstrates his passion for formulating new ideas for making a modern Japanese garden.

> Japanese Spirit & Taste

"Japanese Taste Expressed in Modern Architecture" was prompted by the outcome of the 1931 architectural competition for the Tokyo Imperial Household Museum (today the Tokyo National Museum) in Ueno Park.[19] The building program, typical of museums of the time, called for major display spaces, administrative, work, and storage areas, and the other rooms required by an institution of this type and status. While theoretically the style of the building was left open, in the growing climate of nationalism that accompanied the rise of a militaristic regime, government buildings had begun to reject Western architectural styles in a newly instituted search for a way of building that would reflect Japanese tradition. Despite the seeming freedom in the objective list of required spaces, the competition brief informed competitors that the building should be designed "in an Eastern style that is based on Japanese taste, so that it will preserve harmony with the contents of the museum."[20] For example, the architect Chuta Itô—professor of architecture at the Tokyo Imperial University and a member of the competition jury—would shortly conceive his design for the 1934 Hongan-ji temple at Tsukuji in Tokyo as a neo-Indian pile whose Orientalizing manner was equally foreign to Japan in stylistic terms as was its weighty stone construction [figure 3-27]. Western classicism had impressed Itô, who reasoned that if Greece and Rome had provided the prototypes for neoclassicism in the West, Japan should seek its Buddhist roots in India. Based upon a related logic, Kenzô Tange later won the 1941 competition for a Japan–Thailand Cultural Center in Japanese-occupied Bangkok with a design whose roof forms borrowed in equal measure from the revered grand shrine complexes at Ise and the extinct *shinden* style that had once characterized the aristocratic mansions of Kyoto of the Heian era toward the end of the first millennium CE.

The architect Shin (or Jin) Watanabe won the Tokyo Imperial Household Museum competition with a building in what later came to be generally termed the Imperial Crown Style (*teikan yoshiki*) [figure 3-28]. These were fireproof buildings of masonry-faced reinforced concrete and steel, thus making full use of contemporary Western technologies—but capped by a form of roof—"the imperial crown"—and employing decorative and other auxiliary elements drawn from historical construction in wood, notably Buddhist temples. Horiguchi was troubled by the winning scheme.

One unpremiated competitor was Kunio Maekawa, a young architect recently returned from employment in the office of Le Corbusier

SUTEMI HORIGUCHI / AHEAD THROUGH THE PAST

in Paris.[21] The Maekawa proposal eschewed any tinge of historicism. It instead offered a building configured as an H in plan, with boxed masses that recalled, rather directly, Le Corbusier's rejected entry to the 1927 competition entry for the League of Nations in Geneva. Although the scheme received no recognition, Maekawa's design caught the eye of Horiguchi, who wrote a strident retort attacking the jury's selection. We live, he argued, in a modern world and our buildings—especially major cultural structures—should therefore make use of all newly available means in order to develop an architectural expression that accords with modern technology and life.[22]

In rejecting the jury's decision, together with what he perceived as the superficiality of the winning scheme, Horiguchi entered into a complex abstract philosophical discussion of beauty. In this essay, attempting to come to terms with his own predilection for Western modernism, he pragmatically divided the concept of beauty into two basic types. The first was beauty as understood by the mind; the second was emotional, felt rather than consciously pondered. Within the classification of intellectual beauty were two subcategories, one based on function and the other on organization, in which modernist architecture was assessed in terms of its aim and purpose (including layout). In turn, Horiguchi's beauty of emotion comprised three subcategories: beauty "naturally" induced as a product of function, beauty "intentionally" produced by functional concerns, and the overall resultant beauty of general architectural expression.

In the remainder of the essay, Horiguchi expanded upon these categories and toward the end of the article used them as an armature for his condemnation of the winning design. To start with, he argued, utilitarian beauty can only be ephemeral. We appreciate the form of the battleship because it represents the most direct expression of the functional demands placed upon it. As soon as a subsequent model surpasses the performance of its predecessor, the splendor of the earlier battleship will be immediately diminished and its form rendered passé. Organization is more apparent in a building than in a ship or in a machine; gravity is the defining factor for architecture, although new structural systems and materials have today provided the means for overcoming its forces. It should be noted that by the date of the museum competition, a comparison of buildings to machines, ships, and airplanes was well established, most famously in Le Corbusier's quip that the house was to be a "machine for living."

In discussing emotional beauty, Horiguchi admitted that the distinctions between these categories were not as clear as he would prefer and that our regard for functional beauty is to some degree also based on emotion. Horiguchi acknowledged sympathy with the architectural critic and philosopher Takao Itagaki, who held that functionalism alone was insufficient: there must also be a new architecture somehow expressive of the age.[23] Ultimately, it is morphological beauty that trumps all other categories. The problem with the Imperial Crown Style, Horiguchi asserts, is that it conflicts with the beauty of pragmatism. Nor is the stylistic approach in accord with the contents of the museum, as the objects on display are Chinese and Korean as well as Japanese. It is certainly out of accord with its times: the era of the train and the airplane. "No matter how graceful the oxcart was, we ride on trains and in airplanes."

Japan was no longer a feudal society and its architecture should express its modern condition. In summary, Horiguchi insisted that architecture should "express Japanese culture using the most advanced technology so that its purely elemental tastes emerge in the use of color, proportion, balance, and harmony." It is clear that Horiguchi had virtually accepted wholeheartedly the need for modernization and modernity, as had much of Japanese society by that time. However, within several years his stance would revert, so to speak, to one far more tolerant of history, in style sharing affinities to the mock-nationalist style he had condemned in this essay.

> Modernity & Its Discontents

During the Meiji era (1868–1912), in the course of several decades of intense industrialization accompanied by equally rapid urbanization and a net demographical shift, the Japanese had accepted whole hog what their newly expanded world offered. There were new ways of dress, new art forms, new communication technologies, new building types, new transportation systems. From the status of an essentially feudal culture for nearly three centuries, albeit one centered on a premodern infrastructure, Japan had emerged as a modern nation and naval power in her own right, capable of crushing Imperial Russia in a pivotal naval battle in the Straits of Tsushima in May 1905.[24] Many of Japan's writers supported the project for modernization, among them the members of the Meiji-era Shirokaba literary group and later the novelist and cultural critic Jun'ichiro Tanizaki.[25] In *Naomi*, first published in serial form in 1924—Tanizaki chronicled the changes in the life of this *moga*—a contraction derived from the Japanese pronunciation of "modern girl"—and her shift from a working-class traditional lifestyle to one marked by modern and excitingly foreign ways. Unlike her infatuated protector and lover, Naomi throws herself into the contemporary worlds of Western food and dress, ballroom dancing, and jazz. Through this transformation, she emerges as the queen bee in a circle of friends and admirers, but this popularity is accompanied by a noticeable decline in her character. Built in Western style, her home on the perimeter of Tokyo had, tellingly, first served as an artist's studio and residence. In Tanizaki's writing, architecture signals the life changes accompanying the modernization of the nation and its brash young capital. Although focusing on women, Tanizaki also characterizes the broader Japanese psyche, at least to some degree. "The greatest weakness of Japanese women is that they lack confidence," he writes.

> As a result, they look timorous compared to Western women. For the modern beauty, an intelligent, quick-witted expression and attitude are more important than lovely features. If she lacks true confidence, simple vanity is enough: to think "I'm smart," or "I'm beautiful," makes a woman beautiful.[26]

Yet even in Tanizaki's writings of the 1920s, the reader senses a hesitation in the wholesale adoption of things foreign to Japanese tradition—as represented in the figure of Naomi's beleaguered husband Jôji, who is much older than his young wife—and a lingering nostalgia for those things and values that have been lost. While accepting to some degree the changes brought by a flood of Western products, there remained a melancholy regret for those aspects of Japanese culture overlooked, denounced, and vanished. In the later post-World War II years, such losses were spiritual as well as material, a belief and experience Horiguchi himself shared with the novelist.

In their writings, other authors also reflected on that sense of loss. Yasunari Kawabata wove the plot of *Thousand Cranes* around the cult of tea and its accompanying wares.[27] He too reflected an uneasy regard for the transition to internationalism. "There had been a certain incongruity, as when someone living in a European house wears a kimono," he notes of one tea gathering.[28] Throughout the story of the entwined relations of two generations, Kawabata uses ceramics from the ancient Shino and Karatsu kilns to paint his characters, synecdochically examining their psyches through an examination of water jars and tea bowls. Perhaps Horiguchi shared such feelings. As a student of tea, the architect was continually reminded of the need for custom, for discipline, for a concern with the smallest detail, and for the time-honored ritual itself. His sensitivity to these concerns emerged in a key article not only as indicative of his own development—but also in the formulation of ideas for a modern Japanese garden.

It becomes clear that by the end of the 1930s, with the completion of the Kikkawa and Wakasa houses, Horiguchi had reached a more or less uncritical acceptance of modernism. Over time, however, his continued and increasingly engaged studies of the tea ceremony and its architecture would influence both his thinking and designs. For one, the *sukiya* teahouse sought a tranquil and natural simplicity, a simplicity differing from modernist architectural sentiment. In Europe, modern architects challenged the past and achieved simplicity primarily by discarding and removing the elements and ornaments of architectures past. This was an approach born as a reaction against the reiteration of historical architectural styles, moving away from neoclassicism toward a functionalism well captured by Le Corbusier in his celebrated assertion that the house is essentially a vehicle to support living.[29] Although most readers at that time, and since, have taken the statement far too literally, his notion framed the house as essentially a device to support the lives of its inhabitants. That belief might not be impugned, but it lacked a dimension beyond the merely functional. In time, like the authors cited above, Horiguchi turned from his essays in the International Style to a manner at once more inclusive of Japanese tradition and an architecture that offered psychological as well as physical well-being.

Horiguchi was not alone in his discontent with rationalist modernism. In several parts of the world, from the start of the 1930s architects turned away from heroic modernism to ways of building that acknowledged the conditions of the local environment, cultural and material traditions, and national history. Le Corbusier had substituted naked tree trunks for architectural columns in his unrealized 1930 design for a second house for the Errázuriz family in Zapallar, Chile—soon to be famously reinterpreted by Antonin Raymond and realized in Karuizawa, Japan, in 1933. After serving as chief architect for the high modernist Stockholm Exhibition in 1930, Gunnar Asplund began to incorporate more vernacular sources into his work, for example, at his own summer house at

154 >

Stennäs or in the celebrated Woodland Cemetery, designed in collaboration with Sigurd Lewerentz [figure 3-29]. In neighboring Finland, after the completion of the tuberculosis sanatorium in Paimio in 1933, Alvar Aalto likewise reconsidered the country's vernacular tradition and began to integrate selected elements drawn from common domestic and farm buildings, for example, at his Villa Mairea in Noormarkku, completed in 1939. Neither a wholesale rejection of modernism nor a nostalgic neo-vernacular manner, the evolving mode represented an amalgam in which one style or the other might prevail—but never in complete isolation.

There was also the matter of scale. Residences and their gardens required approaches more individual and detailed than those for larger buildings. In Horiguchi's work, this schism resulted in buildings of radically differing types. In his residential and restaurant designs after the Pacific War, Horiguchi modernized tradition with an architecture graced by exquisite detailing. In contrast, at Meiji University, where Horiguchi served as professor of architectural design, his buildings were so stripped of ornamentation that they bordered on mere engineering solutions. The care so extensively demonstrated in his house designs resides only in the interiors of the Meiji University buildings, for example, in their lecture halls. But such undertakings were still two or more decades in the future, following

in the wake of the horrific destruction brought by war. Before accepting this stripped modernist manner of his postwar university work, Horiguchi had sought more specifically to resolve the dichotomy he perceived in the opposition of East and West. Interestingly, he did not look to advanced contemporary art for inspiration and forms, as did Christopher Tunnard, but instead toward the past, namely to the works of the eighteenth-century Japanese Rimpa School of painting and decorative art.

> ## Ahead Through the Past

The *sukiya* style adopted for teahouse and villa designs had roots in the lowly farmhouses of the countryside.[30] Under the social strictures of the Tokugawa shogunate that governed the country for well over two and a half centuries, farmers and artisans ranked socially above merchants but below the nobility and samurai. If not precisely Jean-Jacques Rousseau's noble savage, the farmer of this quasi-feudal period lived an honest and worthy life, his house directly reflecting in its materials his agrarian activities and social status.[31] The rural farmhouse had developed variously throughout the archipelago in accord with local climatic conditions and an unwritten societal tenet holding that being cool in summer trumped being warm in winter. Solutions to architectural problems, evolving over centuries, responded to sumptuary restrictions placed on materials and building pretensions. When the tea masters looked to *minka-zukuri* (farmhouse style) as a source for tea architecture, however, they did not unreservedly elevate

the forms of the farmers' and artisans' houses to a higher aesthetic level. Instead, they appropriated and reconfigured elements of that architecture into a style appropriate to the practices of serving and drinking tea in different milieus, places, and eras. Yet despite this disconnect between architectural sources and their redirected applications, a line of conduct nonetheless developed. Simplicity, unlike in Western modernism, derived not from reduction, but from intensification and condensation. Architectural richness, in turn, emerged over time through compressed layers of consideration. Over time rain exposes the straw and aggregates of earthen walls and enriches its texture. As it weathers and erodes, thatch grants the teahouse a softer profile. Over time the teahouse, both inside and out, acquires *sabi*, a patina of venerability. These qualities are not achieved through a process of reduction, but instead by way of a compression of materials and emotions whose release occurs over an elapse of time.

3-30
Kôrin Ogata.
Red and White Plum Blossoms.
Early eighteenth century.
[Atami MOA, Wikimedia Commons]

> Autumn Grasses

The second of Horiguchi's key writings of the 1930s, "The Garden of Autumn Grasses" (*Akikusa no niwa*) treated the subject of garden design directly. In this article published in 1934, Horiguchi laid the theoretical foundation for a garden appropriate for modern Japan—retrieving the nation's past to avoid conflating the modern situation with internationalism. In his text, the architect focused not on the gardens of the Edo period or the dry gardens that had preceded them as sources for the new landscape, but instead on the gold- and silver-grounded paintings of the eighteenth-century Rimpa School. The best known of the Rimpa artists included Kôrin Ogata, his younger brother Kenzan Ogata, Hon'ami Kôetsu, and Tawaraya Sôtatsu, whose works displayed a lavish freedom, elegant and sophisticated, achieved by setting the intricately rendered subject against a simple background [figure 3-30].[32] Although the astute compositions and skill of the brush drive the paintings, the orthogonal field resulting from the application of gold leaf in small rectangular sheets created both the ground and counterpoint to the floral designs. Whether executed on ceramics or the surfaces of the *fusuma* (opaque sliding panels used to divide larger interior spaces into rooms), these works were characterized by a dazzling beauty that would qualify as *hade*, rather than the austere beauty of *shibui* that had been more characteristic of the *sukiya* style.[33]

From these Rimpa works, Horiguchi extracted a simple manner for modern garden design: by isolating the plant or rock, and setting it against an unadorned background he could create a three-dimensional, living tableau to be enjoyed from a veranda or the internal spaces of the house. His idea, he readily admitted, derived from the historical dry garden, especially Ryoan-ji. Like the display of flowers within the *tokonoma* (ceremonial alcove) of the teahouse, isolation heightens the form and presence of each element, a characteristic of the dry gardens that dates back at least as far back as the fifteenth century.[34] What was new, and to some degree modern, was the intention behind the use of this idea and the extended spaces with which Horiguchi surrounded them. An early nineteenth-century screen painted by Hoitsu Sakai, today in the Tokyo National Museum, depicts the theme of summer and autumn grasses [figure 3-31]. Here the ground is silver leaf rather than gold, but the delicate tracings of

3-31
Sakai Hoitsu.
*Flowering Plants of
Summer and Autumn.*
c. 1821.
［Tokyo National
Museum,
Wikimedia
Commons］

blades of drooping pampas grass and tints of fall color in the leaves of the ivy evoke the melancholy that accompanies the passage of a moribund autumn into winter.[35] The screen is remarkably close in figure and mood to Horiguchi's compressed and walled garden enclosing the Okada house, whose completion would parallel the publication of Horiguchi's article.

The hybrid style of the Okada house itself belies the period of its construction in 1933–1934 and the nature of the commission. Horiguchi did not begin the design of the house from the start but received the scheme for a building already designed by another architect; this was one of the factors contributing to its stylistically mongrel design [figure 3-32].[36] Built of wood in the traditional manner, with only one Western-style room of reinforced concrete, the Okada house in its relative simplicity looks earlier in date than the Kikkawa house, whose design actually preceded it by three years. Without knowing the exchanges between client and architect, it is impossible to determine if the historical manner was his patron's programmatic demand, or whether this part of the house was previously designed, or perhaps already existing. In any event, if the house is considered merely as a representative work of Horiguchi's mature Japanese modernist period, it appears to some degree disappointing.

In shape, the plan approximates the figure of a square doughnut enclosing a small courtyard, with circulation facilitated by a single corridor [figure 3-33]. Every major space opened outward to some part of the garden. Typically for its era, and its near-central Tokyo location, the house occupied the center of the lot and filled more than half of it. Also typically, a boundary wall marked the limits of the site and stymied intruding eyes; moreover, these smooth wall surfaces provided Horiguchi with the plain backgrounds he sought when designing the garden. Sliding outer panels of wood and inner panels of rice paper or glass infilled the post-and-beam structural frame of wood. If Horiguchi's earlier interest in Dutch architecture had drawn on the forms of the Amsterdam School, the Okada house suggested the play of planes characteristic of the Dutch De Stijl. Ceramic pantiles covered the roof, chosen for their durability and flame resistance. The solid walls of the Western room, only a part of which appears in any existing photograph, uncomfortably abutted the zone of traditional construction. In all, the room appears as an addition, like the relatively fireproof plastered storehouses (*kura*) externally linked to traditional residences.[37] Horiguchi considered the Okada house transitional, admitting that he had made no effort to harmonize the architectural styles of the two

To achieve congruence between interior and exterior, no naturally shaped stones were set in the garden beyond the Western-style room. Instead, Horiguchi deemed the geometry of ashlar blocks and clipped lawn more suitable, a combination that recalls the rectangular stepping-stones in the shallow pool of the Shien-sô. "Elements such as the *tsukubai* [a rock carved to hold water for drinking or washing hands] were set in the farthest location from the Western-style room."[39] Nor were there stone lanterns. Water would provide the harmonious transition between stones in their natural state and those already processed and squared. To Horiguchi's way of thinking, things natural were endemic to Japan and tradition, things geometric, to the West and modernity.

Horiguchi explained that in the ambient Okada landscape he had attempted to create a "garden of grasses."[40] "What would happen," he asked rhetorically, "if a plain gold screen was placed behind the autumn grasses? Would the new composition appear like a work by Sôtatsu or Kôrin? This idea motivated me to design a garden of autumn grasses."[41] Although the idea may not have existed in his thinking at an earlier date, Horiguchi now applied it to a garden in Ômori in southern Tokyo. He knew of no Western precedent for this landscape, although aspects of what he proposed bore an oblique relation to the historical English landscape garden and the way its plants were originally used. Although the painted subjects on *byobu* (folding screens) or *fusuma* were frequently those of autumn grasses, Horiguchi pursued a garden of plant materials indicative of spring and autumn. A generation later, the artist reflected on the ideas he had used in the Okada garden:

> The grasses used here [were] all closely related to the life of the Japanese and to their literary and artistic traditions, and have a direct, emotional appeal to them. To capture the beauty of nature by means of compositional treatment of such sparse materials in such a restricted space is one of the traditional techniques of Japanese gardening, as it is of Japanese painting.[42]

As his source Horiguchi cites Rimpa paintings, although in designing the garden he has transformed their painted forms into "lines and dots from *susuki* [Japanese pampas grass], *hagi* [bush clover] and *nadeshiko* [fringed pink]...clumps of Japanese pampas grass have individualized shapes, and moreover, the beauty as a whole is well composed" [figure 3-34].[43] Without question, grasses in nature are beautiful, but they achieve an even higher level of splendor in works by the likes of Sôtatsu and Kôrin, in whose paintings the dimly brilliant gold or silver leaf sets off the work's vegetal subjects. Meanwhile, in the new garden, the white plastered boundary wall assumed the role of the flat ground of the painting, against which the individual shapes of Horiguchi's grasses and shrubs literally and visually thrived.

Whatever care one may take in composing a garden, every plant nonetheless responds to the periodic cycles of birth, fruition, decline, and demise. As a garden may tend to appear sad or depleted during the winter months, visual interest turns to the stones, which in some ways serve as surrogates for the vegetation at rest. Although the wall surfaces are plain, the dense plantings of trees rising behind them add color and variation to the garden, even in winter when the grasses have been cut back. At that moment, the dogwood and the oak will visually prevail as pine needles fall and cover the moss. The wall becomes a neutral band set between the ground plane and the upper palisade of trees that showcases the individual plants, selected for their shape, texture, and color. By this time, Horiguchi either must have acquired an enviable knowledge of plants or collaborated with an experienced gardener or horticultural specialist. His plant selection produced a palette of rich effects, changing throughout the year, with each species carefully selected for its prime appearance in a certain month. For spring grasses he specified *tosamizuki* (spike winter hazel), a trio of Japanese pampas grasses, bush clover, and *nogiku* (wild chrysanthemum) all played off against the white surfaces of the perimeter wall. A sprinkling of pine needles amplified the visual texture of a ground plane carpeted by moss.

3-32
Sutemi Horiguchi.
Okada house.
Ômori, Tokyo, 1934.
House seen
from garden.
〔*Japanisches*
Wohnhaus der
Gegenwart〕

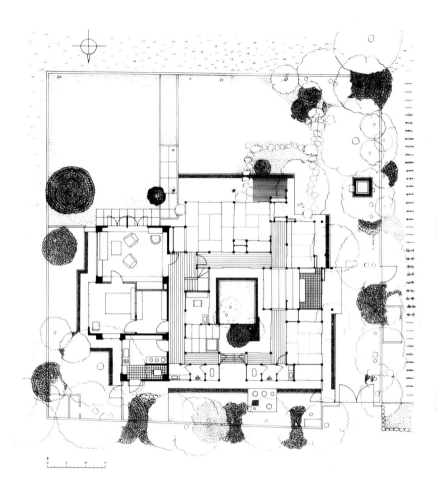

3-34
Sutemi Horiguchi.
Okada garden.
Ômori, Tokyo, 1934.
[*Architectural
Beauty in Japan*]

3-35
School of
Tawaraya Sôtatsu.
*Flowers and
Butterflies*
(central panels),
1730–1770.
[Indianapolis
Museum of Art;
Wikimedia
Commons]

As November ended, signaling the onset of winter, the severe pruning of the garden's vegetation granted prominence to the neighboring trees, species which included *arakashi* (Japanese blue oak, *Quercus glauca*) and *natsutsubaki* (pseudo- or summer camellia, Japanese *Stewartia*). Red flowers enlivened February's short days; in March the *tosamizuki* (spike winter hazel, *Corylopsis spicata*) bloomed with small yellow flowers, complementing the *kantsubaki* (midwinter camellia) which blossomed over an extended period.

Horiguchi explained that the *shojobakama* (Japanese hyacinth), *tatsunamiso* (Japanese skullcap), and other varieties were planted to invigorate the handsome green of the *Eizan-goke* moss. Another intended effect paired *shida* (fern) with *giboushi* (plantain lily) and *hototogisu* (toad lily). "Though smaller than the autumn plants and inferior to the beauty of the spring plants," the author admitted, "these are lovely flowers."[44] His listing continued: "in April the *hime torano-o* (*Veronica linariifolia* Pallas) stands with its long small purple ears; and in May the *tatsunamiso* blooms with white and purple flowers."[45] In his positioning and pairing of species, Horiguchi made no effort to replicate how they grew in the wild. By definition, a garden recomposed nature according to artistic principles and the designer's intentions. While the paintings of the Rimpa artists provided the inspiration for this garden, it was Horiguchi's knowledge of vegetal forms and color—and perhaps most of all his botanical knowledge of their blooming period—that insured the success of the design [figure 3-35]. As a total work of art Horiguchi's garden of autumn grasses resembled an *ikebana* composition writ large, sufficiently large to view, if not to truly inhabit.

The Okada landscape embodied more dimensions than the astute selection of plants alone. The ground was modeled in relief, a common feature in Horiguchi's designs. The lawn terrace outside the Western-style room rose two steps higher than the adjacent garden of grasses, which faced the house's principal living space, an eight-mat *tatami* room. A small wooden deck outside the tea room extended the ground plane of the *tatami* and drew the interior outward [figure 3-36]. A support post stood in a narrow pool to link the two levels; its sidewalls formed the transition between the house and the south perimeter wall. A translucent prism, a glass lantern, marked the intersection of water, grass, and stone. A gravel trough collected rainwater from the encircling eaves that extended almost completely around the house as a linear element that linked tradition and modernity. In all, the Okada design offered a living picture that provided mental provocation and visual delight throughout the year, with seasonal changes that reflected the passage of time and the flow of life.

The garden's conception and execution were nothing short of exquisite. Every rock, every plant, every blade of grass appears carefully considered and arranged, although each element allowed for natural processes to work their magic at the right time of year. Some few drawings in the archives and a handful of photographs by Yoshio Watanabe—as perfect in their compositions as the garden elements were in theirs—comprise the sole record of the Okada garden, the Garden of Autumn Grasses. Although the house plan was logical and the proportions of the room and walls refined and polished, here the garden outshone the architecture. As architecture, the Okada house marked a pause, if not

3-36
Sutemi Horiguchi.
Okada garden.
Ômori, Tokyo, 1934.
Bamboo terrace
and grasses.
[*Architectural
Beauty in Japan*]

a retreat, from Horiguchi's pursuit of modernism; for the garden, it represented a major step forward, but a step forward through the past.

> Mirei Shigemori

Sutemi Horiguchi was not alone in his quest for a modern garden for twentieth-century Japan. If Horiguchi looked to Rimpa painting as a source for making a modern garden, the younger Mirei Shigemori (1896–1975) sought other, more contemporary sources in modern art. First trained as a painter at the Tokyo University of the Arts, and then long involved with invigorating the practice of *ikebana*, Shigemori applied ideas drawn from painting to garden making.[46] Like Horiguchi, Shigemori was also interested in Japan's historical glories. During the 1930s, he and a team of students measured and recorded a significant number of historical gardens ultimately published in no fewer than twenty-four volumes as *An Illustrated History of the Japanese Garden*.[47] Horiguchi owned a complete set of the books and no doubt used them as a reference source for his individual garden elements, if not for the overall planning of the garden. Given Horiguchi's absorbing interest in the architecture and gardens of the tea ceremony, Shigemori's books were an essential source.

Shigemori's best-known work was also one of his earliest: the suite of gardens at the Hôjô (Abbot's Quarters) of Tôfuku-ji, in south-eastern Kyoto. Realized in 1939, at the height of Japanese military expansion in Asia and on the brink of war with the West, the gardens are remarkable not only for their erudition and abstraction but also for their departure from the rigid strictures of historical Japanese garden making. Unconventionally, one enters the temple from the south on a raised wooden walk. Its elevation offers the first glimpse of the south garden and a corresponding space constructed of gravel and bridge foundation stones reconfigured as the astronomical constellation of the Great Bear. The main Hôjô garden, executed in the dry garden (*kare-sansui*) style, literally turns tradition on edge. The rocks stand proudly vertical—as knife blades, thin and brittle—departing radically from the horizontal orientation and deeper setting more common for stones in historical gardens. The gravel area adjoins low mounds covered with moss set along a sweeping diagonal, in a manner recalling the motifs appearing on Edo-period kimonos, a dynamic Shigemori gesture that denounced the stasis traditionally sought by Japanese garden makers [figure 3-37]. The theme of the checkerboard first appears in the west garden, there executed in low shrubbery cut geometrically as low cubes. To the north, in the garden to the building's rear, this motif continues as a play of square paving stones arranged within a sea of moss [figure 3-38]. Both laterally and to the rear, the density of the squares dissipates and gradually merges with the masses of shrubbery that conceal the ravine behind them and the stream far below.

In their use of geometric motifs, the Tôfuku-ji gardens share few similarities with the Okada garden realized only several years before. The confined Okada garden was necessarily compressed in form and space, with vegetation and rocks freely arranged within its walls. Although inspired by Rimpa paintings, the garden could also be taken as a modern realization of the *kare-sansui* style, where grasses and plants stand as surrogates for rocks and

3-37
Mirei Shigemori.
Tôfuku-ji Hôjô.
Kyoto, 1939.
South garden.
[Marc Treib]

3-38
Tôfuku-ji Hôjô.
Kyoto, 1939.
North garden.
[Marc Treib]

shaped shrubs.[48] Shigemori, in contrast, applied an abstract geometric pattern to govern the Hōjō gardens, although the motifs were executed using traditional materials and gardening techniques. While both gardens drew from sources in painting or textiles, the thinking behind and the resulting forms of each of the landscapes significantly diverged.

In the postwar years Shigemori's position as one of a handful of signature garden designers became more secure, and he executed designs for both new temple gardens and the renovation of older ones. The term "restoration" is always problematic in Japan, as gardens predating the Meiji period were usually configured and constructed directly on-site with few or no drawings to guide their construction. This dearth of graphic material provides any garden designer charged with a process of restoration a wide berth within which to work. Shigemori's garden for the Reiun-in, a sub-temple of Tōfuku-ji, applied his signature swirls and patterns—executed in red-tinted concrete and infilled with colored gravel—hardly historical motifs. His design for the garden at Ryogin-an (1964), another sub-temple of Tōfuku-ji, departed even further from tradition [figure 3-39]. Low curbs of cement—a device Shigemori used in numerous of his patterned works—delineated swirling shapes invoking the image of a tiger. Here the garden was conceived as a subject for viewing, a painting turned horizontally, less affected by the seasons—except perhaps by snow in winter—rather than as an artwork unfurled before the eyes to be taken in and considered. Its role in religious practice continued the traditions of the Zen sect, yet its forms were strikingly original.

At Kōmyō-in, in contrast, Shigemori returned to stones as his primary medium. But these are stones of a mass and placement hardly characteristic of Japanese garden norms. The scale of both garden and stones has been inflated, with the spaces between them, rather than the greater space around them, emerging as more prominent [figure 3-40]. Furthermore, what are we to make of the 1971 gardens for the Matsuo Taisha Shrine in western Kyoto? In the central area of the shrine a winding rill descends the slope recalling the meandering stream (*yarimizu*) of the ancient Nara period. Surfaces of broken ceramic tiles confine the streambed, in a material and manner that speak more of the Japanese appreciation for the Catalan architect Antoni Gaudí than the natural environment of the Ise shrines. Shigemori knew garden history well, and such turns from its prescriptions were never total. In the Garden of Ancient Times, to the rear of the Matsuo Taisha, for example, large stones stand vertically in a field of uncut grasses [figure 3-41]. In the introduction to his voluminous *An Illustrated History of the Japanese Garden*, he offered, "The rock itself is the embodiment of time immemorial. The landscape, that folds together these rocks... celebrates 'the eternal abode of the immortals,' [and] symbolizes the gathering spot of the nation's culture as well as prosperity for all eternity."[49] The effect is primitive and speaks to origins long ago. In fact, the arrangement of the stones cites the ancient *iwakura*, a preliterate Japanese use of standing stones to demarcate a site of veneration.

Like Horiguchi, Shigemori used history and tradition as he saw fit, although the latter used it more willfully, shifting between historical

3-39
Mirei Shigemori.
Ryûgin-an, Tôfuku-ji.
Kyoto, 1964.
[Marc Treib]

3-40
Mirei Shigemori.
Kômyô-in, Tôfuku-ji.
Kyoto, 1971.
[Marc Treib]

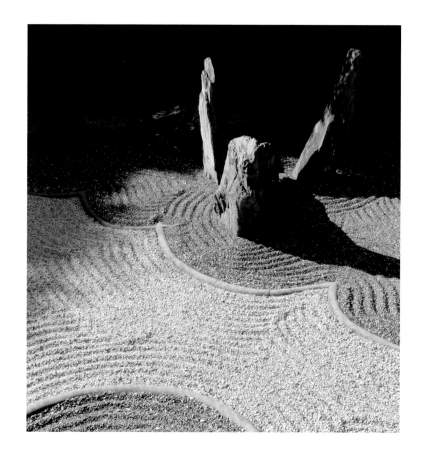

reference and invention as suited his purpose. Horiguchi never traversed the boundaries of propriety to an equal degree. Perhaps it was his training as an architect and his search for order and tranquility that led him to eschew the raucous and atavistic play of forms that seems to drive many Shigemori works. It seems a case of the classic Horiguchi versus the mannerist, or even the baroque, Shigemori. Or perhaps, as often occurs in Japan, Horiguchi, then settling into middle age, became less interested in mere innovation and more dedicated to achieving equilibrium and beauty. Whatever the reason, Horiguchi's landscapes tended to be more introspective than demonstrative, ever refined and ever elegant.

> A Last Prewar House

Somewhat unusual in relation to Horiguchi's earlier house plans was the figure of the pure rectangle sustained over the three floors of the 1939 Wakasa house [figure 3-42]. Its lowermost floor was semi-subterranean and devoted to services: a garage and storage room to one side and domestic quarters to the other, an open porch separating them. The main floor centered on a living room whose south façade was extensively glazed to visually enfold the garden [figure 3-43]. It was aligned with, but did not connect with, a lap pool that drew the eye to the far end of the site. An external walkway, elevated above ground level, extended the full length of the ground floor and encouraged each room to open outward. On the upper floor, bedrooms were conceived in a Western rather than Japanese style, and the sole *tatami*-floored room occupied the southwest corner for use as a children's playroom and nursery.

Construction began in reinforced concrete, but due to wartime building restrictions, the second floor was built of wood. Mosaic tiles uniformly covered all exterior surfaces. The Wakasa house may indeed have been Horiguchi's purest exercise in the modernist manner, with its façades inventively treating the second floor as a thin continuous plane whose irregular crenellation gave it the air of fingers reaching for the sky. These rhythmic verticals offered a counterpoint to the overall horizontal thrust of the elevations. As a totality, the composition of house and landscape represented an integrated play of lines and volumes set in orthogonal counterpoise.

In order to achieve a southern aspect for the garden and the principal internal spaces of the house, the structure was set at an angle of almost 45 degrees to its lot lines [figure 3-44]. An approach road entered at the southeast corner of the site, headed north, and terminated with a southwest bend that revealed the house's northern façade and the view it framed. To accommodate the turning radius of an automobile, at this point the drive expanded into an auto court.

The garden design relied heavily on expanses of lawn, in all probability chosen as the ground against which to pit the figure of the house, with the bulk of the trees and shrubs clustered along the site's perimeter. Local species were planted to form a privacy screen, as well as to offer sensual delight. The dominant garden element was not planted, however, but manmade, a narrow lap pool set perpendicular to the length of the house, a functional version of the ornamental rill at the Kikkawa house constructed almost a decade

3-41
Mirei Shigemori.
Garden of Ancient
Times.
Matsuo Taisha.
Kyoto, 1975.
[Marc Treib]

3-42
Sutemi Horiguchi.
Wakasa house.
Shibuya, Tokyo,
1939.
Elevation and
section.
〔HA, MU〕

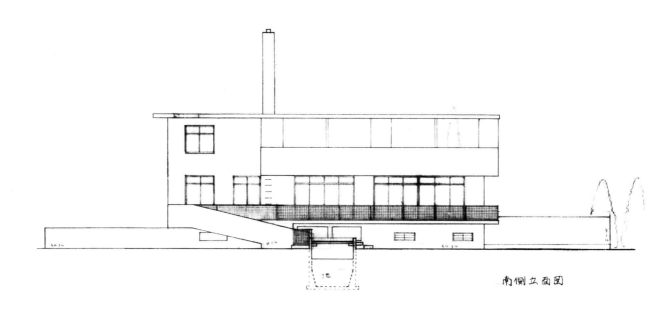

南側立面図

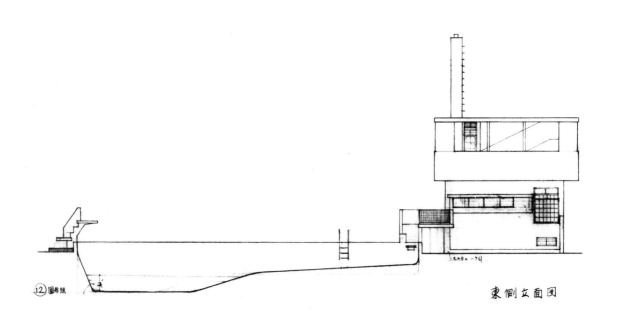

⑫圖番號

東側立面図

3-43
Wakasa house.
Shibuya, Tokyo.
Ground-floor plan.
［HA, MU］

3-44
Wakasa house.
Shibuya, Tokyo.
Site plan.
［HA, MU］

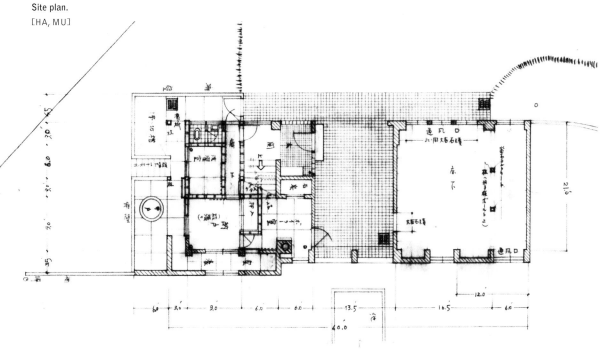

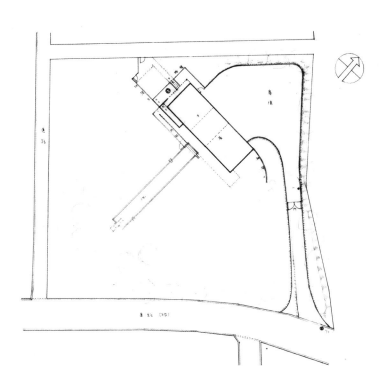

before [figures 3-45, 3-46]. The pool was raised and flanked by low white walls whose material and texture matched those of the residence. In form and configuration the pool became a compositional anchor, and in reflective terms a foil for the architecture—a fragment of the building set into the landscape. It was at once a functional, architectonic, and poetic gesture.

> Commemoration

War produces the dead; the dead deserve commemoration. In 1939, prior to the all-out war with the West, a competition was organized to design a Memorial Tower for Fallen Soldiers, the Chûreitô, dedicated to those who had sacrificed their lives in the long, undeclared Second Sino-Japanese War, during Japanese military operations elsewhere on the Asian mainland, and in other theaters of war. Bizarrely, the project was linked with the planning of the 1940 Tokyo Olympic Games, whose several proposed venues explain the diverse nature of the competition entries. The program for the memorial itself, on an as-then-unspecified site, called for a tower of suitably sober and uplifting mien honoring the sacrifice of all who had given their lives for the homeland. The competition received nearly 1,700 entries from both professionals and laypersons, including notable submissions from several up-and-coming younger architects.[50]

Many of the architect-designed submissions, such as those by Kunio Maekawa and Junzô Sakakura, sought to configure the required tower as a full or truncated pyramid.[51] Other competitors interpreted the competition brief more liberally and chose obelisks or block forms. Horiguchi proposed a columbarium as the memorial tower, itself to be only one element of those comprising a larger complex. Set on a site adjacent to the Yasukuni Shrine—the national military memorial cemetery—the Horiguchi scheme was truly monumental in its vision and dimensions.[52] In the scheme he proposed a national plaza, a museum, and several athletic stadiums, including one to accommodate 100,000 spectators; the plan of another stadium suggests that it would be dedicated to baseball [figure 3-47]. In a later text accompanying the publication of the premiated entries, Horiguchi explained that because Japan would become the center of the Greater East Asian Co-Prosperity Sphere, he had drawn upon the architectural traditions of several cultures. "Today, we cannot be satisfied with only the Japanese mind," Horiguchi declared." We must capture the minds of the entire world. We have to do this [in our role] as the center of Asia."[53] All this, he stressed, could not be embodied in mere functionalist architecture: "It should be a place where the spirits dwell. It can be a sculpture. It can be a forest-like garden."[54] He proclaimed that his design was to incorporate influences as wide-ranging as the ancient Imperial *kofun* (keyhole-shaped tumuli), porticoes characteristic of Shinto shrines such as the complex on Miyajima, Buddhist stupas, and the rose windows of Christian cathedrals.[55] His design was rigorously symmetrical and characterized by a precinct-within-precinct layout that recalled the sequencing of the increasingly sanctified zones of the Ise shrines.

Paving, hedges, and sheets of water defined the outer area of the memorial [figure 3-48]. A loggia surrounded the central tower as a boundary to the inner zone; its configuration suggested the *shinden* style of

3-45
Sutemi Horiguchi.
Wakasa house.
Shibuya, Tokyo,
1939.
[*Architectural
Beauty in Japan*]

3-46
Wakasa house.
Shibuya, Tokyo.
The garden from
the living room.
[HA, MU]

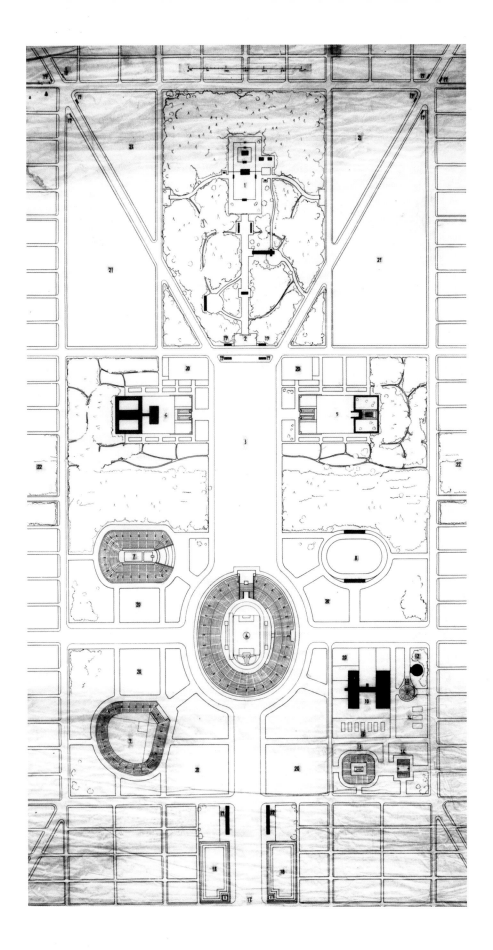

Heian-period palaces, with the tower replacing the central pavilion (*shinden*), or the earliest Japanese Buddhist temples like Tennô-ji in Osaka. "To possess greater meaning," Horiguchi believed the tower "should not only enshrine ashes from the ultimate battle but serve as a pantheon for all time."[56] Evidencing a strong Buddhist connection, the rings on the mast standing before the tower recalled the finials of the religion's pagodas, although principally intended to reinterpret the five-ringed symbol of the international Olympic Games [figure 3-49].[57] A wall of closely planted red cedar trees completed the definition of this precinct and was conceived to merge with the proposed greenbelt beyond the borders of the memorial.

It is difficult to imagine that any entry to the competition accorded equal attention to the elements of the commemorative landscape. In Horiguchi's site design the vast entry court featured white sand, red pines, camellias, the *sakaki* (*Cleyera japonica*) sacred to Shinto, and flowering plants selected for their seasonal bloom. Taken as a working whole the Chûreitô would become a part of a greater landscape enfolding the wooded areas of the Yasukuni Shrine occupying its nucleus. Cedar, with the evergreen *sakaki*, is the preferred species in this zone of the memorial: the overall impression created should be dark and subdued, Horiguchi reasoned. In contrast, the Chûreitô courtyard landscape was to be "bright" in its blending of newly planted zelkova trees with pines.[58]

Horiguchi's entry was among those selected for further elaboration in the competition's postponed second stage. But as wartime conditions in Tokyo worsened, and air raids became more frequent, the project duly faltered and was ultimately abandoned.

> War Years & Thereafter

During the war years, for reasons as yet undetermined, Horiguchi left Tokyo and his family and spent two years at the temple of Jikô-in outside Nara [figure 3-50]. The temple dates only to the seventeenth century but is well known for the relation among its garden, temple buildings, and outlying teahouses. Horiguchi saw in its garden a perfect landscape, a garden reflecting nature itself. Striking in its simplicity, the garden was less a subject as such than a foreground for the landscape beyond: "There, against nature spread out vast in the distance the garden functions as a frame; to be precise, the garden was created expressly to complement that scene."[59] Poets had long celebrated the temple's carefully positioned and artfully shaped shrubbery, together with the long views over the Yamato Plain gained from its veranda. In *Architectural Beauty in Japan*, Horiguchi echoed these sentiments: "The worth of the building lies in the combined beauty of the building and its well cared-for garden that commands to the east a distant view of the mountains of Nara.[60]

The Jikô-in garden appears as a simple unity that uses carefully positioned vegetation rather than stones as its primary features. It is less these elements in themselves, however, than their arrangement and interplay that distinguish the design. No doubt the two years Horiguchi spent at the Jikô-in, removed to some degree from the tumult and devastation of war,

3-47
Sutemi Horiguchi.
Chûreitô
(Memorial Tower
for Fallen Soldiers).
Tokyo, 1939.
Site plan.
[HA, MU]

3-48
Sutemi Horiguchi.
Chûreitô
(Memorial Tower
for Fallen Soldiers),
Tokyo, 1939.
Shrine courtyard
plan.
〔HA, MU〕

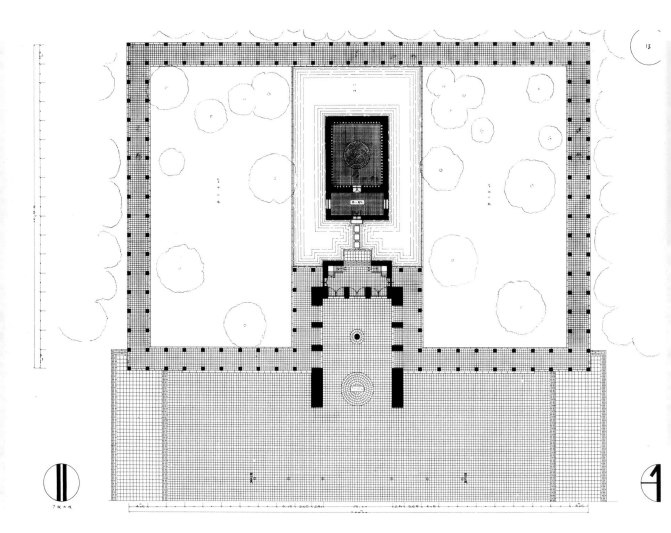

3-49
Chôreitô
(Memorial Tower
for Fallen Soldiers).
Tokyo.
Perspective.
〔HA, MU〕

3-51
Kenzô Tange.
Garden, Kagawa
Prefectural Offices.
Takamatsu, 1958.
〔Marc Treib〕

further inspired him to reexamine the place of tradition in modern Japan.[61] And from this point forward he sought, like the novelists discussed above, to align Japanese custom with contemporary life, avoiding wherever he could manage, the inevitable rupture imposed by the forms and apparatus that accompanied imported cultural forms.

Horiguchi was scarcely alone in his quest. The Pacific War proved to be a disaster for Japan, with the country left in ruins, its population seriously reduced and demoralized, and its economy in shambles. After the heady days of the 1930s, replete with early military successes and a broad swath of territory occupied in Asia and the Pacific, Japanese military and naval victories seriously declined after America's entry into the war following the attack on Pearl Harbor in December 1941. Half a year later, the Battle of Midway stemmed the tide of territorial gains and shifted the possession of naval dominance in the Pacific. Thereafter, American firebombing decimated sixty percent of Tokyo's buildings, and similar conditions characterized every major city; Hiroshima and Nagasaki had shuddered under the fatal jolt of the new and frightening atomic age, whose final consequences were largely unknown at the time. At war's end in August 1945, Japan accepted unconditional surrender and foreign occupation for the first time in its multimillennial history. The Allied occupation sought to dismantle the country's military-industrial alliance, the *zaibatsu* and their interlocking directorates—while attempting to impose a newly "democratic" constitution on the beleaguered nation.

Although this was a trying time, especially in terms of basic existence, hope began to emerge, with faith in the future renewed. For the majority of the population, the war's end brought sheer relief regardless of the associated military and political consequences. They would say *shoganai*— "it cannot be helped." In response, the country was, however tentatively, reborn, as survivors carried on in a determined fashion, creating new lives as best as they could. Recovery began, and within a decade a newly industrializing Japan was once more on its feet, aided in part by the termination of the occupation in April 1952. Beginning in June 1950, the United States and its allies restyled Japan as a supply base in their battle against Communist military incursions on the adjacent Korean peninsula: an early belligerent action of the Cold War.[62]

For Japanese architects and garden designers, the opportunities to rethink their ideas and practice were plentiful, if also challenging. So much of the country's built fabric had been destroyed that regaining any semblance of normalcy would require enormous efforts at repair, as well as a vast quantity of new construction. Most of the physical recovery, however, would be placed in the hands of the major construction companies with their enormous design departments and privileged position in the construction of government-sponsored infrastructure. The design of public architectural commissions, such as city halls, concert halls, and museums, would be directed to architects in the smaller offices, who would also design most private residences. But the question of what style in which to build faced the new generation of architects. The single greatest influence of the time was Le Corbusier, especially on the three younger Japanese architects who had worked in his office during the prewar years:

3-50 (*opposite*)
Sadamasa Katagiri.
Jikô-in.
Nara, c. 1664.
[Marc Treib]

successively, Junzô Sakakura (1901–1969), Kunio Maekawa (1905–1986), and Takamasa Yoshizaka (1917–1980). While Maekawa basically opted for reliance on the Swiss-French architect's in-situ concrete work in Marseille and at Chandigarh and elsewhere in India, Sakakura—whose training had been primarily in structural design—favored construction using dry systems such as steel or precast concrete once wartime building restrictions had been lifted and such materials were more available.[63]

It was Kenzô Tange (1913–2005), however, whose voice would remain the most identifiable and influential during the decades after the establishment of peace; Tange was also the first Japanese architect to achieve a truly international reputation in the postwar period.[64] Like contemporaries such as Kiyoshi Seike and Junzô Yoshimura, Tange looked to a renewed Japanese tradition, as we have already seen in the case of Horiguchi. With other architects in their coterie, they developed a manner termed *Japonica*, which sought to fuse the architecture of the Japanese past with postwar international currents. Tange's own house, built in 1953, was located in the southern suburbs of Tokyo. It could only have been Japanese, given its insistent horizontal lines and dignity of proportions. Yet its plan nonetheless revealed the influence of Mies van der Rohe, particularly his steel-and-glass Farnsworth house in rural Illinois built two years before. Tange, however, built in wood as the steel needed for a structural frame of reinforced concrete was still not easily procured in Japan. The fluidity of the spaces of the Tange house owes to historical Japanese architecture, although it is also not far from what Mies had achieved in the singular "universal spaces" of buildings such as his house in glass and steel.

In multistory construction, Tange transposed the forms of wooden post-and-beam architecture into those of reinforced concrete. Protruding beam-ends marked works such as the 1958 Kagawa Prefectural Office in Takamatsu and the 1960 Kurashiki City Hall, although their overall massing and dense concrete walls speak equally of the influence of Le Corbusier. In the garden for the prefectural offices, Tange channeled Shigemori more than Horiguchi [figure 3-51]. Rocks stood on end around and within a small pond, the entirety a mannerist version of the Japanese garden—a design conceived, perhaps, with a nod to his friend Isamu Noguchi, the Japanese-American sculptor who had lived in Japan in the early 1950s.[65]

Clearly, Horiguchi was evolving in a different direction, partly in order to secure relevant commissions: a return to tradition was deemed appropriate, an approach less internationally oriented and more related to Japan's timber-framed architecture of prior centuries. In Nagoya, he designed two premises for the Hasshôkan restaurant that demonstrated what depth his knowledge of Japanese building art had achieved. The site for the downtown Nakamise branch of the restaurant was small and extremely constricted. The challenge facing Horiguchi was to design interior dining spaces and the restful outdoor settings to complement them—at least visually [figures 3-52, 3-53]. The garden expanded the dimensions of each room and supported a visual flow from inside to out. Views outward were partially deflected by adroitly positioned wooden fences; these paired with floor-to-ceiling sliding *shôji* faced the veranda

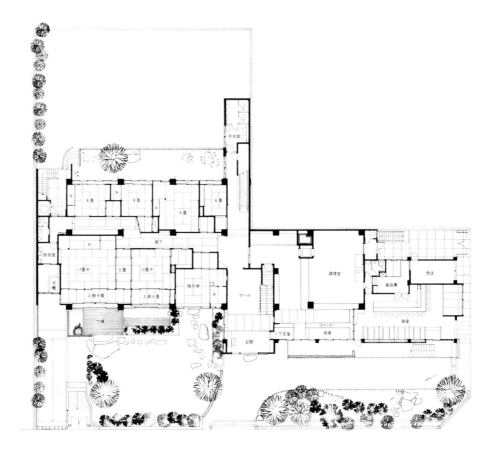

and multiplied the number of possible views and spatial configurations across the glazed window wall [figure 3-54].

As the presence of traffic and passersby disturbed the tranquility of the downtown site, Horiguchi devised an ingenious solution for the rank of rooms that faced a park on the opposite side of the street. In accord with tradition, he proposed a white stuccoed wall along the boundary of the site; like a traditional Buddhist temple hall, the building comprised an island within these confines. But to avoid having the wall limit the view, he banked earth almost to its full height and planted shrubs linearly along its crest. These shrubs, which concealed the *kawara* (tiles) that capped the wall, were carefully trimmed and varied in their heights and shapes. The net effect of this maneuver merged garden and shrubbery within the walls into the tree canopies "borrowed" from the park across the street, a skillful application of traditional *shakkei* ("borrowed scenery") techniques, here used to resolve a problematic modern situation. The presence of vegetation continued on the upper floors as well, where *kaizuka ibuki* (*Juniperus sinensis*) and red-pink *sazanka* (*Camellia sasanqua*) were planted. From the street below, this line of vegetation softened the edge of the building, naturalizing the architecture, at least to a certain degree.[66]

The design of the Hasshōkan's main premises presented Horiguchi with a far more challenging task, namely a complex program and larger set of completely new structures to be located outside central Nagoya [figure 3-55]. With more land available than at the restaurant's later downtown branch, the dining rooms and services were configured more traditionally as a series of pavilions within a garden. That the emperor was to visit the restaurant would justify an especially sophisticated design for one pavilion, to be named the Miyuki-den. Every detail of this room and its surrounding verandas was consummately studied, composed, and executed. In contrast to the Nakamise branch of the Hasshōkan, the main room followed centuries-old rules for proportions, although its ceiling appears to have been set higher than normal for rooms of the given floor area. The colors throughout the space were muted and harmonious, the sole visual accent being a mural of Horiguchi's design executed in imperial purple and related soft hues. Rather than the intimate spaces of the teahouse, the Hasshōkan recalled the grander dimensions of Kyoto villas such as Katsura or those that today comprise the temple of Manshu-in in the same city—that is to say, "imperial" in their scale and dimensions. The finest *hinoki* cypress was the primary building material and the *tatami* were likewise of regal quality. The flooring mutated from *tatami* to planed wooden surfaces on the veranda, to flooring of bamboo spaced at intervals to allow rainwater to drain any surface directly exposed to weather. Today we might regard the fluorescent lamps that run the length of the ceiling as garish and cold in their light quality. At the time of construction in 1956, however, this lighting medium represented the height of modernity and a source of illumination suitable for an imperial visit.

Today, the garden is blanketed by masses of azaleas and other species of shrubs to such a degree that it is difficult to discern Horiguchi's intention for the landscapes other than to encase each pavilion in a

3-54
Sutemi Horiguchi.
Hasshōkan, Nakamise.
Nagoya, 1967.
Looking to the
garden.
[Marc Treib]

sea of greenery.[67] Even in early photos, no clear idea behind the garden design is evident. In brief, the Hasshōkan might be read as an imperial retreat far removed from the hubbub of the city that demonstrated Horiguchi's ability to work within traditional modes while reinvigorating them with an air of contemporaneity [figure 3-56]. At first glance, it all appears stylistically traditional, with nothing changed, nothing new added; seen over time, however, it becomes more obvious that properties such as scale and detail qualify these works as modern interpretations of centuries-old rules and patterns.

In the immediate postwar period, it was not at all unheard of for architects to extend their design interests out of doors. During the 1960s, for example, Isoya Yoshida (1894–1974) designed two handsome gardens for buildings related to the arts. With a building sympathetic to *Japonica* values, Yoshida's 1960 Gotoh Museum at the southern edge of Tokyo expresses its trabeated concrete structure through contrasts of color. An astringent landscape, more grassed courtyard than a garden in any normal sense, complemented the building on its south façade.[68]

To a large degree, the same description applies to Yoshida's premises for the 1958 Japanese Academy of Art center situated in Ueno Park, even though its central zone is surfaced with coarse gravel rather than lawn [figure 3-57]. This space, confined between two wings of the building, opens to a grassed terrace overlooking the city—whose effect today, like that of the Gotoh Museum, has been completely destroyed by the subsequent urban construction it faces. Other architects, such as Kiyoshi Seike, typically positioned a residence within a lawn bounded by shrubbery. Kenzō Tange, as noted above, was more adventurous in his search for newer landscape forms for the Kagawa Prefectural Office and other public works. But no other architect attempted to formulate a detailed theory of the new Japanese garden as early or with the same depth of consideration as Sutemi Horiguchi.

> Postwar Garden Design

The landscape designer most closely allied with the ideas and principles of Horiguchi at this time in the 1950s would have been Kinsaku Nakane (1917–1995). Hailing from Kansai, the Kyoto-based Nakane worked as a garden maker as much as a garden designer; that is to say, he was responsible for the construction of his landscapes as well as their conception. Although his realized works in the prewar period had been limited, by the 1950s Nakane had assumed a preeminent position in the Kyoto garden world.[69] In design approach, Nakane departed to some degree from age-old practices, by virtue of his first producing design studies on paper or in models prior to actual layout and construction. Work on a given garden scheme would commence with a conceptual sketch, thereafter developed, adjusted, and perfected during realization. The principal stones served as the armature for a more detailed fulfillment using secondary rocks and vegetation. In addition to his design practice, Nakane also wrote about gardens and appreciated their history. Engaged in garden restoration in the postwar years, he was induced to establish a relation to the past. In Japan, as already noted, documents to guide the restoration of historical gardens are rare. Therefore, in gardens like those

3-55
Sutemi Horiguchi.
Hasshōkan.
Nagoya, 1956.
View of pavilion.
[HA, MU]

3-56
Hasshōkan.
Nagoya.
Veranda.
[Marc Treib]

adjacent to the main hall at Nanzen-ji, the so-called Leaping Tiger Garden, Nakane reinterpreted what had once existed rather than trying to recreate its original form [figure 3-58]. Inspiration, and perhaps early photographs, guided the work.[70]

In later years, Nakane, like Horiguchi, would occupy a prestigious position in academia. After years of teaching, he became president of the Osaka University of Fine Arts in 1987 and held that office until his death in 1995. Given that landscape architecture was his principal vocation, his production of garden designs was considerably greater than that of Horiguchi, and one of his later works, the garden for the Adachi Museum of Art, ranks as a modern masterpiece executed in a more traditional, if still modern, manner [figure 3-59].[71] Like Horiguchi at the Hasshōkan, Nakane used banked earth to cleverly screen an undesired visual element, in this case, a major highway adjacent to the site. Yet despite the considerable invention that characterized the design, in its isolation of dwarf pines in the White Gravel and Pine Garden, one sees soft echoes of the grasses featured within the white walls of Horiguchi's Okada house some four decades earlier.[72]

Horiguchi similarly pursued an academic career, no surprise considering his extensive knowledge of tea, Japanese architecture and history, his interest in German and Dutch architecture, and his continually growing volume of published writings. From 1946 to 1949, he served as an instructor in architecture at the University of Tokyo, his alma mater. As a professorship was not forthcoming, however, when offered a position subject to tenure at Meiji University—at the time based solely in the convenient central Ochanomizu district of Tokyo—he accepted. There he remained until his retirement in 1970, even though like many academics he was severely unsettled by the radical student movement of the late 1960s, which seemed to undermine his credibility and to some degree his confidence.

> Books in English

In 1956 Horiguchi published his first book in English, *Architectural Beauty in Japan*, followed by *Tradition of* [the] *Japanese Garden* in 1962.[73] Until that time, literature on Japanese architecture and gardens in foreign languages had been limited, and much of what had been published first appeared in German. As noted earlier, Josiah Conder had published *Landscape Gardening in Japan* as early as 1893, a book heavily based on native Japanese gardening manuals in its characterization of garden elements and types. Conder's book spoke only of the past—a virtual summary of Edo-period garden making—with nothing of contemporary Meiji-period gardening practice or achievements. Ironically, Conder showed considerable sensitivity for things Japanese. He became a close friend of the artist Kawanabe Kyōsai and authored a book about him; he also became accomplished in monochrome painting. Above all, he sought to soften, if not completely resolve, the distinctions between English and Japanese landscape practices—despite his limited competence as a practicing architect.[74] When he proposed landscapes in the Japanese manner, however, he was politely rebuffed by clients and told, in effect, that Japan already had gardeners for landscapes in that manner; "we want modern, that is to say, a European garden." Conder's sensitivity as a garden

3-57
Isoya Yoshida.
Courtyard of the
Japan Academy of
Arts center.
Tokyo, 1958.
［Marc Treib］

3-58
Kinsaku Nakane.
Leaping Tiger
Garden.
Nanzen-ji Hôjô.
Kyoto, 1960s.
［Marc Treib］

designer, it should be recalled, was evident in the amply landscaped grounds of the Furukawa residence discussed earlier.

Jirô Harada's *Japanese Gardens* appeared in English in 1936 and was long the sole work on the subject in that language. A German-language edition of Tetsuro Yoshida's *The Japanese House* was issued in 1935 with an English-language edition (including Yoshida's writings on gardens) appearing only some twenty years after. He followed this study with another text solely devoted to the Japanese garden in 1957.[75] The pair of Yoshida's books endured as the standard references on the subject until the 1950s. At that time the Japan Travel Bureau (JTB) republished a series of small handbooks on Japanese culture—first issued in the 1930s—both as cultural propaganda and to support tourism. The series was broadened in the postwar recovery years to include sundry volumes on architecture, gardens, theater, flower arrangement, and *sakura* (Japanese flowering cherry trees).

In 1953, Arthur Drexler organized the exhibition *The Architecture of Japan* at the Museum of Modern Art in New York and wrote the accompanying publication. The project included the erection of a Japanese "house" in the museum's garden, whereas in fact the design was based on a temple building in the *shoin* style.[76] Drexler's exhibition and book revealed a changed attitude toward Japan, one that encouraged visitors to look beyond the recent war years, as well as to Japan's premilitaristic past, to reveal a culture sensitive to a refined sense of beauty from which America had much to learn. Japan's position as a newly democratic ally during the Korean War was no doubt also a consideration, but in general, apart perhaps from those who had suffered in the war, a new American attitude toward Japan was emerging. That the popular lifestyle magazine *House Beautiful* published two issues devoted to the aesthetic of *shibui*, the astringent category of beauty the Japanese hold in the highest regard, suggests how widespread the interest in Japan had become.[77] While there may not yet have been a specific reader demand for books on the subjects of the art, architecture, and gardens of Japan at this time, without question, the need existed.

More serious, if narrowly focused, scholarship was evident in two books by Kenzô Tange that appeared in the early 1960s.[78] Tange's study of Katsura—with a glowing foreword by Walter Gropius—presented the building and its garden through extensive drawings and elegant black-and-white photographs by Yasuhiro Ishimoto. In turn, *Ise: Prototype of Japanese Architecture*, which followed five years later, examined the religious ritual of rebuilding and the architectural ideas that produced Shinto's pair of imperially related Grand Shrines at Ise. The book, for the first time, offered an international readership extensive documentation of the landscape and its numerous religious and secular structures. Tange contended that the architecture of the shrines embodied the merger of prehistoric Jômon and later Yayoi cultural values and as such provided a basis for Japanese culture. Like Horiguchi, perhaps with less scholarship and greater self-interest in the promotion of his own work, Tange sought the roots for the present in a far more remote past, anxious meanwhile to transcend the recent decades and promote a state of tradition-related modernity.

3-59
Kinsaku Nakane. Garden of the Adachi Art Museum. Yasugi, 1970+.
[Marc Treib]

Horiguchi's *Architectural Beauty in Japan*, which features an essay by Yôichirô Kôjiro, is more an album of projects than an in-depth study of Japanese buildings and gardens. In the essay that forms the opening section of the book, Horiguchi first examines times before the present. The story he tells is today familiar, beginning with prehistoric settlements during the long Jômon era, followed by the briefer Yayoi period with its *kofun* (tumuli). For Horiguchi, this transformation of the landscape was the country's first true architectural act. His narrative also provided a tentative description of the emergence of Shintô—and the formal shrine complexes that reached a climax with the construction of the Grand Shrines at Ise that accompanied the elevation of Shintô to the state religion. Horiguchi then jumps to the arrival of Buddhism in the sixth century and the impact of Chinese-style temple and palace architecture from the eighth century onward. The first truly monumental idiom was the *shinden* style imported from mainland Asia, thereafter modified and adapted by the Japanese relatively soon following its arrival.[79] With the mature *shoin* style—Horiguchi was soon to become the prime expert on the subject—the author's first discussion of the garden appears. In it, he notes both the *kare-sansui* (dry garden) that precedes the *shoin-zukuri* as well as the *roji* (so-called dewy path) of the tea ceremony that was a nearly contemporary development.

With a huge leap, the discussion then lands in the Meiji period where "Roman style buildings of stone and brick" were qualified as imports from Europe. "But nearly all of these were destroyed in earthquakes," Horiguchi notes, with seeming satisfaction. Then follows modern architecture: "before the Pacific War there had been a tendency to reproduce Japanese-style buildings, using iron frames and ferro-concrete." Happily, these practices died with the cities that fell to the bombings. Of current architectural practice, he writes, "[Their] construction is European but the proportions and coloring reveal Japanese taste."[80] This would be a fair assessment of Horiguchi's own late institutional work, especially the buildings on the three campuses of his own Meiji University.

Yôichirô Kôjiro's essay "Modern Art and Japanese Architecture" then follows, first tracing the influence of the Japanese print on such European movements as Art Nouveau and, thereafter, on the architecture of Frank Lloyd Wright. He quickly passes through De Stijl, Bauhaus, and Purism, and arrives at Horiguchi's own designs, noting how he, like anyone else interested in the *sukiya* style, must be struck by the work of Piet Mondrian. "The ceiling and sliding doors of the second floor room in the Hotel Hasshôkan," Kôjiro writes, "show interesting color patterns composed of vermillion, yellow, viridian and blue colored papers."[81] Their effect is to "give the room an unusual color rhythm, making the room a complete world of art, a Mondrian world in three dimensions." Thus, a "striking modernity" has been achieved, albeit "according to the traditional principles of wooden construction."[82]

Kôjiro then introduces two of the main figures in Japanese architecture during the early 1950s, citing Antonin Raymond's striking 1951 Reader's Digest Building in Tokyo, with its garden by Isamu Noguchi, and the works of Kenzô Tange, particularly his landmark 1952 Peace Park and memorial at Hiroshima. Here, according to the writer, the formula employed by Horiguchi has been inverted, with Western architecture now graced by a Japanese sensibility: "As Japanese we cannot help feeling a certain affinity between these buildings with unconcealed steel frames and Japanese houses with their bare wooden framework." Modular construction also entered into the picture, another tie linking tradition and modern architecture. While certain architects such as Frank Lloyd Wright in his design of the 1939 Kaufmann house, Fallingwater, in Mill Run, Pennsylvania, and Richard Neutra in his 1947 Tremaine house in Montecito, California, have achieved a strong connection to nature, they have never quite attained the historic integration achieved in Japan. In other words, "There was still the glass separating them; only visual continuity was achieved, and that this lukewarm compromise with Nature could not satisfy people became evident as life in the cities became more and more mechanized."[83] The tone of the writing is chauvinistic.

At this point Kôjiro unabashedly again refers the reader to the work of his master: "A profound feeling for Nature is expressed in the series of gardens designed by Sutemi Horiguchi, the autumn-plants-garden of the Okada House, the court of the Kikkawa House, and the gardens of the Hotel Hasshôkan, all of which are small confined spaces." Of the latter, he stresses the impact of a dry stream comprised of black and white pebbles.[84] "The secret of modern garden design," he concludes, "must lie in the choice of natural objects and their composition."[85] This is a philosophical and aesthetic stance found in other Japanese arts, such as flower arranging, calligraphy, and the tea ceremony, and returns the discussion to tradition.

Craft is essential for any creation of beauty, Kôjiro believes. Among the works he praises are Pietro Belluschi's 1951 First Presbyterian Church in Cottage Grove, Oregon, and exports such as the house by Junzô Yoshimura constructed in the garden of the Museum of Modern Art the year of the book's publication [figure 3-60]. Yet he again returns to Horiguchi, in this case the Japanese pavilion for the São Paulo Bienal. "The proportions seem to embody the logical beauty of *shinden-zukuri* and the refinement of *sukiya-zukuri* construction, although these are not apparent as styles" [figures 3-61, 3-62, 3-63]. How is this achieved? "Its modern beauty can move us without a knowledge of Japanese architecture," Kôjiro contends. "Here the garden itself is an object."[86] Today, however, we read Belluschi's church as a far more contemporary essay than Horiguchi's pavilion. While both employed wood construction expressed inside and out, the pavilion clings to traditional imagery, models, and materials, and there is something in the proportions that appears too tall for the interval between the structural posts. The pavilion's garden featured a shallow pond upon which some of the pavilion's posts stood, each supported on a single stone; a lawn abutting the water in a graceful curve; and rockwork used as stepping-stones to cross the pond [figure 3-64].[87]

Horiguchi's *Tradition of* [the] *Japanese Garden*, like *Architectural Beauty in Japan* published by the Kokusai Bunka Shinkôkai, followed in 1962.[88] As with the earlier book, the sole authorship of its companion volume is credited to Horiguchi, although Yôichirô Kôjiro wrote the book's extensive summary history of the Japanese garden. For his part, Horiguchi took a

3-60
Pietro Belluschi.
First Presbyterian
Church.
Cottage Grove,
Oregon, 1951.
［Marc Treib］

3-61 *(opposite below)*
Sutemi Horiguchi.
Japanese Pavilion.
Ibirapuera Park.
São Paulo, Brazil,
1954.
［Marc Treib］

3-62
Japanese Pavilion.
Ibirapuera Park.
São Paulo, Brazil.
Perspective study.
［HA, UM］

3-63
Japanese Pavilion.
Ibirapuera Park.
São Paulo, Brazil.
Plan.
［Pavilion brochure］

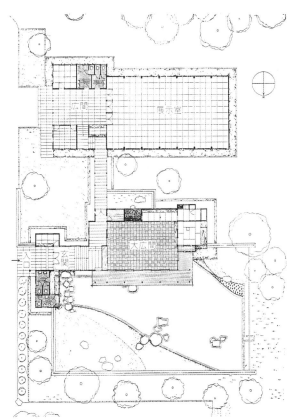

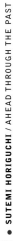

3-64
Sutemi Horiguchi.
Japanese Pavilion.
Ibirapuera Park.
São Paulo, Brazil,
1954.
View over the pool
and garden.
[Marc Treib]

3-65
Itsukushima shrine.
Miyajima,
founded 811.
Torii (Gate).
[Marc Treib]

more philosophical turn when explaining the history of garden making in Japan, now returning to the subject after more than a decade. First, like Tunnard, he positioned the garden within the greater landscape, which is to say within "scenery," as he termed it.[89] Also like Tunnard, Horiguchi asserted that in Japan no division of labor or thought separates architecture, garden, and landscape. "One finds it hard to draw a line between the garden and its surrounding landscape, because every segment of the landscape is in itself a garden and every branch of a tree is as graceful as a flower in a flower arrangement."[90] But he also took pains to specify that the first Buddhist temples constructed in Japan (in the Nara period, 710–794 CE) were imports from the Asian mainland and in those early centuries those buildings must certainly have stood at odds with the Japanese landscape. Over time, however, native builders achieved a greater harmony between architecture and landscape, as represented by the Shintô shrines on Itsukushima (on Miyajima in today's Hiroshima Prefecture) [figure 3-65]. Despite these various architectural adaptations, true Japanese placemaking, Horiguchi contends, actually began with the sacred designation of a great tree, the four vertical posts of the *himorogi* used to sanctify a building site or other locale, and the rocks of the *iwakura* which invite a *kami* (deity) to descend. However common such basic acts of demarcation may have been to many early societies, they assumed a form particular to Japan.

In the Japanese garden, or in site planning at the greater scale, nature and artificiality blend their identities into a composite in which neither is easily distinguished nor extracted. "Architecture and gardens are melted together by their common denominator which is nature."[91] He identifies the Tokugawas' shogunal mausoleums at Nikkô as the foremost example of give-and-take between the artifice of architectural ideals and the matrix furnished by the site's dense cryptomeria forest and irregular topography [figure 3-66]. One does not destroy nature to achieve an abstract ideal, Horiguchi argues, but instead the maker must use nature to create architecture as a phenomenon positioned between abstraction and reality. One needs the forest to shape buildings, which are unable to achieve form or identity on their own. This interweaving of nature

3-66
Tôshôgû Shrine.
Nikkô,
c. 1615+.
[Marc Treib]

and design is also evident in the practice of borrowed scenery, referred to earlier in discussing the Hasshôkan Nakamise. Here, nature, surrounding or distant, is drawn into the garden as a feature equal to, or surpassing in prominence and power, the rocks, shrubs, or trees that may constitute the foreground of the design.

Horiguchi then turns to gardens created explicitly for contemplation, where artifice seems to take the upper hand: "It is neither architecture nor nature, only a garden. Its construction is nothing but an outline to frame nature. The stones and trees are a substitute for black ink."[92] In his discussion of the tea garden, he stresses that its form as a human construct should not be apparent, that any indication of artifice should be withheld: it should not emulate nature but "be" nature—so as not to distract from the ceremony held within the teahouse. The essay closes with "gardens that are not [called] gardens," referring to a group that includes the primeval *iwakura* described earlier, but also the ancient burial mounds dating from the fourth and fifth centuries also cited above.

As in *Architectural Beauty in Japan*, the authorship of the extended captions that accompany photographs is divided between Horiguchi and Kôjiro, with Horiguchi's entries centering on gardens from the earliest times. He explains how elements from the burial mounds would become common in later Japanese gardens, for example the "hill garden" type of later centuries.[93] In a like manner, the presence of *iwakura* testifies to the regard, even sanctity, accorded stones that provides the basis for the dry gardens of the Muromachi period—and Shigemori's Garden of Ancient Times at the Matsuo Taisha. One understands from his descriptions that Horiguchi envisions history as recurrent and relevant to the making of the garden, from primeval to modern times; we cannot escape the past and should, therefore, use the lessons of history and precedent to profit from them. As the author had embraced Rimpa paintings and screens as sources for a modern garden in the 1930s, he now commits to the even deeper presence of history within the Japanese present—and calls attention to its usefulness as a fecund guide for the future of garden making.

Horiguchi authored over three-quarters of the caption entries, each displaying a depth of historical knowledge accompanied by acute observations about the significance of each respective site. He reviewed three projects by Jihei Ogawa, noting his disappointment with the garden of the Heian Shrine: "The main building and garden fail to create an artistic atmosphere of unity"—certainly a fair assessment.[94] He is more positive about the 1950s Jônan-gû gardens by Kinsaku Nakane, particularly the rockwork positioned on its south lawn, and Mirei Shigemori's 1939 Kômyô-in: "The glittering white sand and green moss seen through a bamboo screen are a delight to the eye of a camera" [figure 3-67; see also figure 3-40].[95]

For works with greater modern ambitions, the baton was handed to Kôjiro. About Meiji University's recent Izumi campus, Kôjiro writes, "Horiguchi succeeded in creating a natural garden by following the contours of nature, making use of naturally growing trees, placing stepping stones and surrounding them with grass and shrubbery...a garden design technique which follows the natural order."[96] In a like judgment, he regarded the 1957 Iwanami garden in Tokyo, also by Horiguchi, as "the perfect example of the spirit and technique of *tsuboniwa* [courtyard garden], a traditional garden, applied to a modern home."[97]

3-67
Kinsaku Nakane. Muromachi-Momoyama garden, Jônan-gû shrine. Kyoto, 1960s. [Marc Treib]

200 >

From these writings we can discern that Horiguchi had passed from a stage in the 1930s when modernity entered his purview with greater force, through a more tradition-bound postwar phase, and finally to a garden that at its most successful should merge with nature and become virtually indistinguishable from it. Despite this conceptual position, in writings Horiguchi often claimed that a garden is always a product of artifice that embodies the interplay between what exists and what may transform it. Naturalism may have constituted Horiguchi's highest aspiration, but in actuality, its realization eluded him and proved unattainable.

> The Academic Campus

Meiji University provided Horiguchi with a secure academic position; it also brought him a series of architectural and landscape commissions. The university, which had gained increased academic respectability during the 1950s, was rapidly expanding at the time of his appointment as professor in 1952. By the end of the decade, the university required additional land to augment the acreage of its original Ochanomizu campus in central Tokyo. Early in the 1960s, the university began to develop the Izumi campus on the periphery of the city and five years later expanded the offerings of its Ikuta campus west of Shinjuku, where it already maintained an agricultural program. On these three sites Horiguchi designed a library and several multistory classroom and lecture-hall buildings, many of which were realized through collaboration with the office of Masao Hayakawa, a former student with whom Horiguchi had maintained a close personal and professional bond. Given his teaching responsibilities and writing, from the early 1950s on Horiguchi relied on Hayakawa for technical support and to see his designs through construction. Credit nonetheless rested with Horiguchi, so that the precise arrangement between the two architects, and their individual design contributions, remains undetermined.

The buildings at Meiji University will not be those for which Sutemi Horiguchi will be best remembered. For the most part their architecture displays little of the feeling or details characteristic of his more personal efforts in the domain of house or garden. Instead, they look to structures more directly expressive of their engineering and construction, a manner pioneered during the late 1930s by Tetsurô Yoshida in his central post offices for Osaka and Tokyo. The classrooms, lecture halls, and laboratories for Meiji University proudly announced their construction in concrete by their exposure of structure, but only in the buildings' proportions, monochrome white set off by railings and trim of royal blue, and certain interior details do they exhibit any real distinction. Within the Izumi campus main building, for example, the large rooms are cleverly inserted into a trabeated concrete slab and frame structure in a manner that completely belies their volume and shape [figures 3-68, 3-69]. To encourage cross ventilation, the building's circulation was set outside the main block and treated as a play of ramps that smoothed the open-air movement of students between classes. Horiguchi explained his intentions with notable care:

> Students attending two-hour-long lectures in a building planned for 900 students usually have to move from one classroom to another. During the short intermission he has to relax and refresh his mind; thus, fresh air and sunshine are a great necessity. Japanese schools are generally located in congested city areas, where the only place to enjoy sunshine and fresh air is on the roof. This campus is fortunate in being located in a comparatively open suburban area, and offered a possibility for arranging something unusual for a Tokyo school.[98]

While an acceptable vehicle for circulation in fine weather, the open ramps have created problems on inclement days by exposing students to the forces of nature, for example in the driving rains of May and June—although a secondary circulation system of internal stairs does offer alternate routes. A single spiral stair on the exterior of one Ikuta campus building stands out as a rare moment of bravado and showmanship, as well as a departure from the orthogonal form of the building [figure 3-70]. For the most part, however, the design of buildings produced by Horiguchi on all three campuses was underplayed, essentially neutral in aspect, and undistinguished.

The configuration of paths linking the academic buildings was carefully considered: in places walkways were angled to adjust the perception of the surrounding space; in other areas they meandered beneath existing tree cover and were paved only with loose gravel. Paths marking the shortest distance between building entrances also traversed the central lawn in a style that has returned to recent Japanese campus planning. "The irregularity of the network of paths was purposely arranged with the intention of keeping students off the flower beds and lawn," Horiguchi explained rather dryly, no doubt to deflect any criticism of his scheme.[99]

While the buildings themselves today display little architectural interest and seem to repeat academic building patterns seen throughout Japan both then and now, certain areas of the landscape nevertheless confirm Horiguchi's abiding interest in the garden. These are for the most part low-key and dependent on lawn, using simple outlines of shrubbery and the placement of benches as graphic lines set against the grassed ground. The construction of newer buildings and the destruction of several of Horiguchi's own earlier designs have radically changed and eroded the built nature of the three campuses with their shared idyllic vision of education in multistory blocks set amid swashes of greenery. In places, however, Horiguchi's original vision persists, although an effort may be required today to identify and decipher his intentions.

> Culmination: Uraku-en

Late in life, in his seventh decade, Horiguchi completed a large garden that in many ways represents the culmination of his long career in landscape design. The site was far from Tokyo, part of an ambitious plan to develop the town of Inuyama, just sixteen miles (22 kilometers) from Nagoya. The client was the owner of the Meitetsu Railway, who had preserved buildings from the Meiji and Taishô periods and assembled them in an open-air museum planned by the modernist architect Yoshirô Taniguchi. Meiji Mura, as the "village" is called, has served as an experiment in both preservation and development, a cultural park intended also as a tourist destination for this region served by the Meitetsu Railway. The original plan also included the construction of the Meitetsu Hotel in Inuyama. On its grounds—as an additional act of preservation—the celebrated Jo-an teahouse would be re-erected in a garden envisioned as a setting suitable for this national treasure. Horiguchi was chosen to design and lay out this garden, a project that began around 1970.

The history of the Jo-an traces back to 1618, when Urakusai Oda, a brother of Nobunaga Oda, the noted warlord who nearly succeeded in unifying Japan, sponsored a teahouse to be built within the grounds of the Kennin-ji temple in Kyoto. Over the intervening centuries, the building had fallen into disrepair, and in 1908 it was sold to the Mitsui family who moved the building to the grounds of their residence in Tokyo. Some thirty years later, the diminutive structure continued its peregrinations, this time to Oiso-machi in Kanagawa Prefecture, where the Mitsui family possessed a seaside villa. Finally, around 1970, it became the property of Meitetsu, was moved to Inuyama, and became the central feature of Horiguchi's design, paired with the larger *shoin*-style pavilion of which it was now considered to be part.

One can read the garden design either centrifugally— that is, by starting with the Jo-an and moving outward—or centripetally, by first looking at the greater site with the teahouse as its conceptual center [figure 3-71]. In either case, the garden for the Jo-an and its *shoin* are of a different character than the landscape that surrounds it: first, in the use of elements of the dry garden style for the formal approach and, secondly, the tea garden as an immediate

3-68
Sutemi Horiguchi.
Meiji University
Izumi campus.
Tokyo, c. 1960.
[Marc Treib]

3-69
Sutemi Horiguchi.
Meiji University,
Sokoku-sha.
Tokyo, 1960s.
[Marc Treib]

3-70
Meiji University,
Sokoku-sha.
Tokyo.
Spiral stairs.
[Marc Treib]

3-71 *(overleaf)*
Sutemi Horiguchi.
Uraku-en.
Inuyama, 1972.
General view.
[Marc Treib]

setting to the south. In fact, Horiguchi changed the orientation of the teahouse—which had originally faced east—to bring it into accord with the Japanese norm of positioning a garden to the south of the house or temple. On the northern side, a straight path of natural stones traverses the broad sea of gravel surrounding the entrance [figure 3-72].

Following the entrance into the courtyard through a roofed gate, the path takes two right-angled bends, indicating we have entered the *gyo*, or semiformal zone of the garden. Late-Edo-period aesthetics relied in large measure on the play of *shin-gyo-so*—that is, the interweaving of formal, semiformal, and informal elements—not merely juxtaposing these, as was more common in the West, but embedding one order within another. Historically, such formal orderings were applied at both macro- and microscales, from the overall planning of temples to the selection and arrangement of stepping-stones within the garden, and even in the shearing of shrubs [figures 3-73, 3-74, 3-75]. In the courtyard, for example, Horiguchi balanced fields of gravel with round planes of moss. These defined zones planted with bamboo and a single *Uraku-tsubaki* (the uraku camellia associated with the original maker of the teahouse).[100] The court does not lead to the tea room, however, but to the entry of the *shoin*. Invited to tea, one entered instead from the opposite side of the garden, that is, through a separate approach from the south.

To the east lies a tea garden that follows historical patterns more directly. By contrast, an area to the west shows how Horiguchi often interpreted history more freely, reconfiguring it to accord with modern taste. Although schooled in tea and a master of theories of Japanese aesthetics, Horiguchi remained at heart an architect who sought some degree of freedom from the strictures of tradition. Unlike a master gardener in Kyoto, who as a scion of generations of garden makers would be bound to continue age-old patterns and techniques, Horiguchi could reinterpret and even deny convention.[101] Plantings of azaleas and other low shrubs enclose a central lawn that meanders and changes its configuration as it moves away from the path.

The Jo-an and *shoin* gardens fit comfortably within the larger landscape whose feeling of a public park displaces the intimacy of the tea ceremony. A large lawn dominates the western portion of the Uraku-en, interrupted in one area by a freely shaped field of gravel, in another by an elevated seating area, rectangular in plan, and in yet another by a raised mound with a structure that recalls a Western gazebo. The paths are discontinuous, beginning in some areas with stepping-stones set in gravel, and ending, bafflingly, in grass or moss. Are we meant to tread on these plants, or should we merely stop and carefully regard each one of them? As if in response, a seat farther on bids us to continue. Other details are equally anomalous if viewed in relation to historical precedents. Certain rocks stand on end as vertical counterpoints to the flow of the contours; others have edges that hover above the ground, a practice prohibited in older practices. While a number of features engage the eye and body of visitors, certain discontinuities mystify them. The Uraku-en is a complex work, especially at the scale of the intimate element, whether plant or stone.

3-72
Sutemi Horiguchi.
Uraku-en.
Inuyama, 1972.
Entrance court.
[Marc Treib]

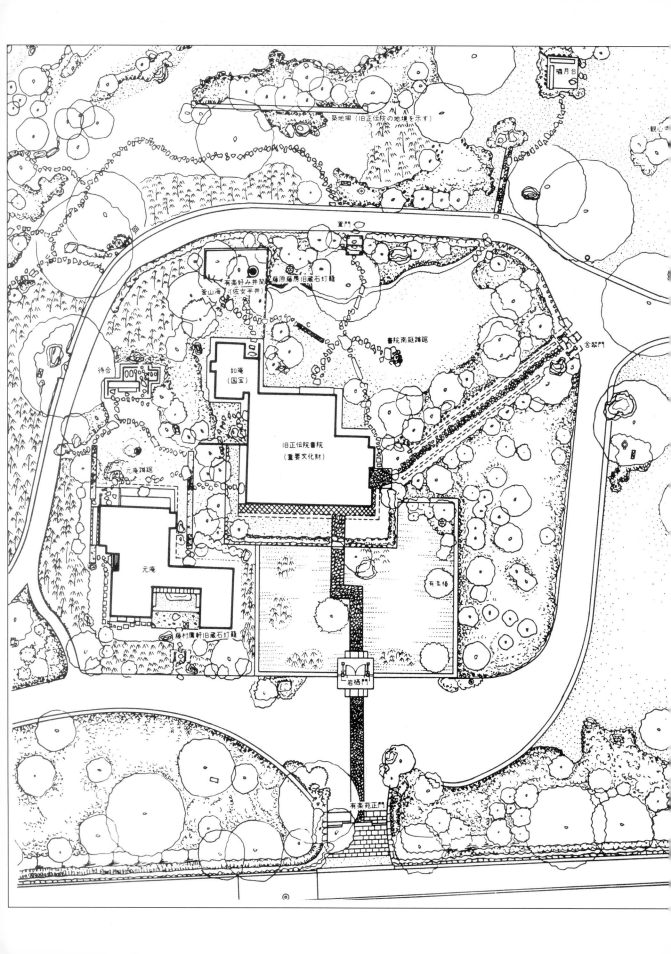

3-73 [opposite]
Sutemi Horiguchi.
Uraku-en.
Inuyama, 1972.
Site plan.
[HA, MU]

3-74
Uraku-en.
Inuyama.
Rock and azaleas.
[Marc Treib]

3-75
Uraku-en.
Inuyama.
Clipped shrubs.
[Marc Treib]

Despite the skill and care in the planting of the hedges and the manipulations of views, the eastern section of the garden appears to be less developed, even if meant to establish the setting for a second teahouse by Urakusai Oda—albeit only a replica. Perhaps the garden has changed over time with the addition of visitor facilities and the planting of specimen camellias over a mound that feeds a small falling rivulet and a tiny pond, the latter traversed by a natural bridge with a lozenge-shaped stone as its key element [figures 3-76, 3-77].

How should one read the garden of Uraku-en? Is it modern or traditional?[102] Certainly, it is far easier to evaluate architectural modernism—that is if we accept either French or German buildings of the 1920s as its foremost exemplars. In 1932 Henry-Russell Hitchcock and Philip Johnson defined what for a long time would be called the International Style, although over time we have learned that there were in fact numerous species of modern architecture—Japanese modernism, in which Horiguchi was a key player, among them.[103] But how do we evaluate a landscape in which vegetation takes the spotlight and hard elements play only minor roles: the more so in Japan, when the principal structures of a garden may be some four hundred years old?

Perhaps modernism in the garden is best defined in the negative. The Uraku-en is neither a stroll garden nor a tea garden nor a dry garden—instead, it duly incorporated selected aspects of each type and reconfigured them. This condition in itself is hardly unique, as even the very greatest Japanese seventeenth-century estates are known to have comprised multiple zones: some for walking and viewing, others for tea and rest or contemplation. But at Uraku-en we are able to follow the relationships among these zones and their constituent elements, especially in the semiformal courtyard, which is hardly characteristic of Edo-period villa gardens. The placement of the elevated stone seating area in the midst of a lawn is a strong, almost perverse, departure from tradition and is in many ways inexplicable. It is composed of various shapes of stones that embody *shin-gyo-so* principles, but in plan its figure is a pure square. The plan suggests that four paths lead to it as a culminating feature and yet these paths are discontinuous and difficult to discern, at least in their present state. Then comes the extensive use of hedges as walls to define subzones of the garden, and the novel character and siting and varied orientation of stones. In places, the rockwork even recalls Mirei Shigemori's quite unconventional vertical settings of stones, at times thin and bladelike. Interesting, too, is the shift from large stones to small gravel in the dry "sea" at the site's western edge. But perhaps of all these readings, it is the discontinuities in the pathways that appear new and challenging. A path may end in a lawn; a path through grass and moss may erupt into a composition of stones that suggests continuation but does not support it. These various disjunctures are visually intriguing but intellectually troubling. Was all this intentional on the designer's part, or something that occurred during construction despite extended periods of on-site supervision, or merely the product of the forty-five years that have elapsed since the opening of the Uraku-en? Difficult to say. Over the years, elements of the garden have no doubt changed. On a visit some twenty years ago, for example,

3-76
Sutemi Horiguchi.
Uraku-en.
Inuyama, Japan.
1972.
Stone benches.
［Marc Treib］

the edges of the gravel "sea" were carefully defined along a crisp line; today the gravel is dissipated into the lawn and the effect has been lessened. In the opposite corner of the site, the multiplication of camellia specimens has undermined what was originally a purer design. Landscapes by nature are ever in flux, even those under the care of a Japanese master gardener. Yet despite these departures from the original design—or the changes that have accompanied growth and replacement—one nonetheless reads Horiguchi's intentions; more importantly, one can also still experience the spaces and forms that resulted from them.

> In Closing

The design of the Uraku-en, in some places puzzling, was Horiguchi's last major landscape work. In some ways, that design represents a zenith, derived from years of acquired knowledge and work at the desk, in the studio, and in the field. In its design, Horiguchi had returned to a resolutely Japanese manner; to identify his inventions and reinterpretations of traditional practice demands a sophisticated eye. Perhaps the key problem that faced Japanese garden designers in search of a modern manner was the inherent modernity that characterized so many historical gardens, which in their reduction and elegant play of forms and space suggested to the casual visitor properties seemingly shared with the work of modernist designers. Despite the beauty of the Uraku-en, the now-vanished garden of grasses for the Okada house remains Horiguchi's signature work. As the Shien-sô had represented his fusion of an expressionist vision with *minka*-based traditions, the Wakasa house, if not its garden, represented Horiguchi's utmost facility with Western modernism. The Okada house—due to its domestic program and Horiguchi's adaptation of a design by another architect—yielded a hybrid architecture that lucidly, if perhaps somewhat accidentally, reflected cosmopolitan Japanese society in the period of the prewar 1930s: rooted in the East, but avidly searching for—and acquiring—technology, products, and not least of all, art forms from the West. Yet Horiguchi's own assimilation of the past and his choice of Rimpa paintings as conceptual models for his work assured that no matter the particular forms and their modernity, the ensemble would nonetheless be Japanese in spirit. In the end, the resulting garden was quite Japanese in form as well. In the design of the areas around the Western wing of the Okada house, Horiguchi succeeded in producing the foremost example of a truly Japanese garden for the modern period.

3-77
Sutemi Horiguchi.
Uraku-en.
Inuyama, Japan,
1972.
A sophisticated
play of formalities
enacted in stone.
[Marc Treib]

4. >   Afterword

Little remains today of any landscape by either Christopher Tunnard or Sutemi Horiguchi,the subjects of this book. The total number of their design works was quite limited to begin with, and the passage of time, changes in ownership, and subsequent development have all taken their toll on the few projects that were ever realized. Landscapes are fragile things, subject to the whims of their proprietors and the environmental forces that bear upon them. Though deed restrictions may control the management of the landscape before and after construction, it is more difficult to stem the effects of a drought or to tame the destruction brought by typhoon winds. Gardens are far more tenuous than the houses they complement and, being more vulnerable, far more susceptible to the modifications that accompany the transfer of ownership, whether within or external to the families of their original sponsors. This story of the ephemerality of landscape architecture is, of course, a familiar one and it applies equally to the works by the two landscape designers presented in this book.

       Of Christopher Tunnard's projects, we can cite three that endure, at least in part. While the Chermayeff house at Bentley Wood has survived to large measure intact, an addition to one side of the original block mars its purity. Happily, the current owner has begun to restore the building and its terraces and is committed to returning the property to as near its designed state as possible. The landscape designed by Chermayeff and Tunnard, on the other hand, appears irrevocably altered. True, the long view over the Downs remains, but residential and commercial construction encroaches on the once open vista, and more consequentially, the topography has been modified by a fishpond regraded from the original contours after the Chermayeffs departed for the United States. Perhaps this basic aspect of the landscape will also be restored in time. The house and garden at St. Ann's Hill have fared far better. The house stands in almost pristine condition, renovated more than once by owners subsequent to the Mr. Schlesinger who constructed the house—although the interiors today reflect the new century more than the time of their making, given the additions and modifications that have been made over the years. Like Bentley Wood, however, the landscape is less original in its condition, in this case due largely to the growth of its shrubs and trees. The curving pool still exists, and when house and pool are viewed from the landscape, one garners a rather convincing picture of the ensemble at the time of its completion in 1938 [see figure 2-45]. Due to a complete and sympathetic restoration, the Warren garden in Newport is today the purest example of Tunnard's garden art. This was also Tunnard's last realized design and as such is different in form and nature from the projects in England that preceded it. The garden is curious in its design, biomorphic in the shaping of its shrubbery, and almost baroque in the configuring of its central space and use of shallow basins with water jets at their centers. Although these basins are today inactive, as a complete work the Warren garden nonetheless fares as the best existing representative of Tunnard's landscape designs. It should be noted, however, that while the basic structure of the design remains, the forms of the individual hedges vary considerably from those at the time of the garden's origin. These differences will be evident when comparing the plan for the garden with recent photographs.

Of Horiguchi's prewar landscapes nothing survives, and even most of his key buildings—such as the 1930s weather station on Oshima—have been demolished. The Okada and Kikkawa houses are long gone, although his minuscule Koide house has been moved to the Edo-Tokyo Outdoor Museum west of Shinjuku and restored. The little garden that now surrounds the house illustrates none of Horiguchi's ideas for the modern Japanese garden so brilliantly represented at the Okada house, which followed some few years after the Koide project. The pairing of the inexorable forces of war and urbanization have destroyed all prewar Horiguchi landscapes, and even the majority of his postwar works have been modified to a significant degree. Of those that remain, the landscape setting for the exclusive Hasshôkan restaurant in Nagoya is the best example, perhaps more for its architecture than the landscape, which by the early 1990s when I visited the site had matured to a state that concealed the designer's original intentions (perhaps it has been restored since then, however). Today, the most complete Horiguchi landscape is the garden of Uraku-en in Inuyama, constructed in 1972; like the Warren garden for Tunnard, it was Horiguchi's last major landscape.

With most of their landscapes gone, we must regard the writings of both protagonists as their principal contributions to the formulation of a modern landscape architecture and the broader history of landscape design. Without question, Tunnard's *Gardens in the Modern Landscape* was the right manifesto at the right time, and its influence was widespread both in the English-speaking world and abroad. In many ways, the book was far ahead of Tunnard's own landscape designs at the time, or any that followed. Unlike the transience of natural environments, books tend to endure. Garrett Eckbo's 1950 *Landscape for Living*, the first book to surpass in scope and depth Tunnard's call for the modern garden, has enjoyed two new printings in recent years, and Thomas Church's *Gardens Are for People*, first published in 1955, has remained in print ever since.[1] A paperback facsimile of *Gardens in the Modern Landscape*'s 1948 edition appeared in 2014, bringing to a new generation of landscape students Tunnard's provocative call for a modern landscape enacted with a broad vision.[2] Yet, as discussed in the Tunnard half of the book, despite his theoretical provocations and exotic Japanese references, Tunnard remained rooted in the thinking of the English landscape garden and the picturesque—in all, what he proposed was more advanced than what he designed. These landscapes were all in his past as from 1950 on Tunnard's contributions were to be found in historical preservation and city planning, and not in landscape architecture.

Sutemi Horiguchi outlived Tunnard by almost two decades and operated in a broader field of design, primarily in architecture, but also as a cultural figure. As an author, historian, professor, and poet, he exerted a direct impact on several generations of architecture students—although given his position within a school of engineering, he was no doubt more influential in architecture than in landscape architecture. Yet as late as the 1970s Horiguchi designed landscapes of note, albeit tending to be more traditional in aspect than the landmark garden for the Okada house designed some four decades prior. That particular garden remains iconic, primarily as witnessed in the handful of stunningly revealing photographs by Yoshio Watanabe that beautifully captured the moment as well as the idea: the transformation of the two dimensions of Rimpa screen paintings into the three dimensions of a modern garden [see figure 3-34].

It could be said that conceiving a modern landscape was far easier than producing an actual one. Tunnard and Horiguchi both attempted to formulate and to realize a modern landscape and they did succeed, at least to some degree. Their works remain today primarily in prints, drawings, and photographs, although—as noted above—some gardens also survive in reality. Witnessed historically, in almost all instances the word preceded the deed, or as the novelist J. M. Coetzee phrased it, "It is a world of words that creates a world of things."[3] Executed landscapes by Tunnard and Horiguchi were certainly not without their limits as embodiments of their ideas. And while the validity of their thinking may be questioned, it cannot be completely dismissed; nor can we dismiss their contributions to conceiving a modern landscape architecture—which were, without question, significant.

Notes

1. > Thinking a Modern Landscape Architecture

1 Le Corbusier, *Towards a New Architecture*, 1923, reprint, New York: Dover, 1986; and Henry-Russell Hitchcock and Philip Johnson, *The International Style*, 1932, reprint, New York: W. W. Norton, 1966.

2 The use of the term "axiom" was borrowed from Peirce Lewis' "Axioms for Reading the Landscape: Some Guides to the American Scene," in *The Interpretation of Ordinary Landscapes: Geographical Essays*, ed. D. W. Meinig, Oxford: Oxford University Press, 1979, pp. 11–32.

3 Marc Treib, "Transitional, Modern, Modernistic, Modernist," *Journal of Landscape Architecture*, Spring 2014, pp. 6–15.

4 Dorothée Imbert, *The Modernist Garden in France*, New Haven, CT: Yale University Press, 1993.

5 From this group I exclude Pierre-Émile Legrain's 1924 Tachard garden in La Celle-Saint-Cloud, which appears to have made a more radical break with the past in terms of its structure and the positioning of its elements. See Imbert, *Modernist Garden*, pp. 112–123.

6 Stephen Kern, *The Culture of Time and Space: 1880–1918*, Cambridge, MA: Harvard University Press, 2003.

7 Garrett Eckbo, conversation with Marc Treib, Berkeley, CA, June 1988.

2. > Christopher Tunnard

1 Christopher Tunnard, "Landscape Architecture in the U.S.A.," typescript, no date, 1940s, p. 1. Christopher Tunnard Papers, Yale University Library, New Haven, CT, Later published as "Landscape Architecture in America," *Architects' Yearbook*, 1945, pp. 34–35.

2 Christopher Tunnard, *Gardens in the Modern Landscape*, London: Architectural Press, 1938. References to this edition will appear in the notes and captions without a date. References to the 1948 edition will be so noted.

3 Raymond McGrath, *Twentieth-century Houses*, London: Faber & Faber, 1934.

4 Emily Carr, *The Book of Small*, 1942, reprint, Vancouver: Douglas & McIntyre, 2004, p. 19.

5 Ibid., p. 98.

6 Some estimates suggest as many as 65,000 Canadians gave their lives in the war.

7 Butchart Gardens, http://www.butchart gardens.com/the-gardens/our-history/our-history.html, accessed 1 February 2012.

8 Lawren Harris (1885–1970) moved to British Columbia in 1940 and lived there the rest of his life.

9 According to Jacques and Woudstra, Christopher Coney Tunnard "was from landed gentry, being the second son of Charles Thomas Tunnard of Frampton House, near Boston, Lincolnshire." Sir Bernard Burke, *A Genealogical and Heraldic History of the Landed Gentry of Great Britain*, ed. A. Winthrop Thorpe, 13th ed. (London: Burke's Peerage, 1921), cited in David Jacques and Jan Woudstra, *Landscape Modernism Renounced: The Career of Christopher Tunnard (1910–1979)*, London: Routledge, 2009, p. 15.

10 Christopher had a younger brother, Peter Kingscote Tunnard (1919–1940), http://www.thepeerage.com/p21743.htm, accessed 20 January 2018; "Interview with Peter Humphrey Tunnard," interview by David Jacques, 9 January 1990. I thank Rusty Tunnard for providing me with a copy of this interview. For some additional biographical background, see also Jane Brown, *Eminent Gardeners: Some People of Influence and Their Gardens, 1880–1980*, London: Viking Penguin, 1990, although the reader should be warned the the Tunnard chapter is riddled with factual errors.

11 Alan Peat and Brian A. Whitton, *John Tunnard: His Life and World*, Aldershot, Hampshire, UK: Scolar Press, 1997, p. 16.

12 Although he moved to Cornwall in 1933, he does not seem to have been an active participant in the artist group there.

13 Peat and Whitton, *John Tunnard*, p. 79.

14 "Although John and Christopher had some contact with each other, it seems unlikely that Christopher's work had any direct influence on John's art." Peat and Whitton, Ibid., p. 19.

15 Christopher Tunnard, Curriculum Vitae, 1 November 1954. Tunnard Papers, Yale. About that same time his family left Canada for Ireland. "Interview with Peter Humphrey Tunnard," interview by David Jacques, 9 January 1990.

16 Letter from F. G. Ogilvie, "Report of H.M. Inspector for the Year 1907–08," *Journal of the Royal Horticultural Society* 34, 1908, p. 303.

17 Ibid., p. 304.

18 *School of Horticulture Prospectus, Journal of the Royal Horticultural Society* 33, 1908, p. 341.

19 *RHS Gardens Club Journal*, 1929, p. 28. Tunnard was ranked sixth of 13 matriculants. The *RHS Gardens Club Journal* lists him as receiving a certificate, although in his own CV Tunnard refers to the degree as Diploma in "Horticulture and Landscape Design."

20 *RHS Gardens Club Journal*, 1930, p, 26.

21 Percy S. Cane, *The Earth Is My Canvas*, London: Methuen, 1956; Percy S. Cane, *The Creative Art of Garden Design*, London: Country Life, 1966.

22 Percy S. Cane, *Garden Design of To-day*, New York: Charles Scribner's Sons, 1936, p. 12.

23 Christopher Tunnard, "Application to Join the Institute of Landscape Architects," 29 December 1934. He was granted associate status, but within three years became a full member. Landscape Institute Archives.

24 As a gross generalization I have found that most of the "modern" landscape architects I have studied utilized a reduced and consistent palette of plants or have relied on selections drawn from ecological analysis. The late Richard Haag, who practiced in Seattle, was a notable exception. For those who work primarily as garden designers the story is quite different, and employing a panoply of plants is basic to what they do. Of Tunnard's generation Francisco Caldeira Cabral's training in agronomy, art, and landscape design certainly rivaled, if not surpassed, the Canadian's knowledge, albeit in different areas. See Teresa Andresen, *Francisco Caldeira Cabral*, Reigate, Surrey, UK: Landscape Design Trust, 2001; and Teresa Andresen, ed., *From the National Stadium to the Gulbenkian Garden: Francisco Caldeira Cabral and the First Generation of Portuguese Landscape Architects*, Lisbon: Calouste Gulbenkian Foundation, 2003.

25 J. L. Martin, Ben Nicholson, Naum Gabo, eds., *Circle: International Survey of Constructive Art*, London: Faber & Faber, 1937.

26 Interestingly, Le Corbusier provided a text, "The Quarrel with Realism," arguing for the transformation of the "real world" through painting rather than through its replication as an image. Of course, his architecture was also included in that section of the book.

27 Gabo explained their ideas in this way: "It has revealed an [sic] universal law that the elements of a visual art such as lines, colours, shapes, possess their own forces of expression independent of any association with the external aspects of the world; that their life and their action are self-conditioned psychological phenomena rooted in human nature; that those elements are not chosen by convention for any utilitarian or other reason as words and figures are, they are not merely abstract signs, but they are immediately and organically bound up with human emotions." Naum Gabo, "The Constructive Idea in Art," in Martin, Nicholson, and Gabo, *Circle*, p. 7.

28 Henry-Russell Hitchcock, "Gardens in Relation to Modern Architecture," in *Contemporary Landscape Architecture and Its Sources*, San Francisco: San Francisco Museum of Art, 1937, p. 15.

29 Victoria and Albert Museum, "Daily Mail Ideal Home Exhibition: Records, 1910–1990," Victoria and Albert Museum: Archive of Art and Design, http://www.vam.ac.uk/_data/assets/pdf-file/0013/250114/dealhome-aad-1990-9_20140709.pdf, accessed 9 January 2018.

30 John Summerson, "The MARS Group and the Thirties," in *English Architecture, Public and Private: Essays for Kerry Downes*, ed. John Bold and Edward Chaney, London: Hambleden Press, 1993, p. 305; and Modern Architecture Research Group (MARS), exhibition catalog, 1938, p. 23.

31 As quoted in Louise Campbell, "The MARS Group, 1933–1939," *Transactions (Royal Institute of British Architects)* 8, 1985, p. 70.

32 George Bernard Shaw, Introduction, *New Architecture*, London: MARS (Modern Architecture Research Group), 1938, p. 3.

33 This trinity characterizing "well building," derives, of course, from the Roman Vitruvius, and was given its English words by Henry Wotton in the sixteenth century.

34 Louise Campbell cites the MARS plan for London prepared between 1938 and 1942, and credits the contribution of Elizabeth Denby as well as Tunnard. Given Tunnard's departure for the United States less than a year after the exhibition, one wonders in exactly what way he participated.

35 MARS, exhibition catalog, p. 20.

36 "Mars versus Jupiter," *Landscape and Garden*, Spring 1938, p. 53.

37 Ibid.

38 A Member of the MARS Group, "Modern Architectural Research and Landscape Planning," *Landscape and Garden*, Summer 1938, p. 101.

39 John Summerson to Ben Nicholson, 31 December 1940, Nicholson Papers, Tate Archives, quoted in Alan Powers, "John Summerson and Modernism," in *Twentieth Century Architecture and Its Histories*, ed. Louise Campbell, London: Society of Architectural Historians of Great Britain, 2000, pp. 166 and 167 respectively.

40 Ibid., p. 167.

41 Tunnard's projects included the gardens for the "All-Europe House, St. Ann's Hill," "Informal Water at Aldbury," "Entrance Planting at Highpoint II," and the "Garden for Restaurant, Lawn Road Flats, Hampstead." Christopher Tunnard, *Garden and Landscape: An Exhibition Organised by the Institute of Landscape Architects*, London: Institute of Landscape Architects, 1938, p. 4.

42 Ibid, p. 5.

43 Ibid., p. 7.

44 "Work of the Landscape Architect," *Landscape and Garden*, Summer 1939, p. 104.

45 In June 1936, when he applied for membership to the Institute of Landscape Architects, Tunnard's address was given as Salcott, Fair Park Road, Cobham, Surrey.

46 "Television of Garden Planning," *Landscape and Garden*, Summer 1938, p. 118.

47 This is a hypothetical interpretation; it could be that the photo was taken only partway through the program and that there would be more planting to come by the end of the presentation. Fletcher Steele, *Design in the Small Garden*, Boston: Atlantic Monthly Press, 1924.

48 "Television of Garden Planning," p. 118.

49 J. M. Richards, *Memoirs of an Unjust Fella: An Autobiography*, London: Weidenfeld & Nicolson, 1980, no pagination (photo insert).

50 Christopher Tunnard, "Garden and Landscape: The Sectional Layout of a Small Garden Plot," *Architectural Review*, March 1939, p. 199.

51 Arthur C. Tunnard, "The Influence of Japan on the English Garden," *Landscape and Garden*, Summer 1935, p. 51.

52 Ibid. However, the influence of Japanese art on Western modern art, particularly by the woodblock print, has been well established. See Christopher Benfey, *The Great Wave: Gilded Age Misfits, Japanese Eccentrics, and the Opening of Old Japan*, New York: Random House, 2003. And, yes, the French still refer to what we know as the English garden as the *jardin anglo-chinois*.

53 Jacques and Woudstra note that Tunnard borrowed books on the subject from the Royal Horticultural Society's Lindley Library, including Arthur Lindsay Sadler, *The Art of Flower Arrangement in Japan: A Sketch of its History and Development* (London: Country Life, 1933). Jacques and Woudstra, *Tunnard*, p. 96.

54 *Gardens in the Modern Landscape*, p. 6.

55 This and the information to follow is from Bernard Leach, *Beyond East and West: Memoirs, Portraits and Essays*, London: Faber & Faber, 1978.

56 Sôetsu Yanagi, *The Unknown Craftsman: A Japanese Insight into Beauty*, adapted by Bernard Leach, Tokyo: Kodansha International, 1972.

57 Arthur C. Tunnard, "Interplanting," *Landscape and Garden*, Autumn 1935, pp. 110–112.

58 Christopher Tunnard, "Garden-Making on the Riviera," *Landscape and Garden*, Spring 1936, p. 32.

59 Tunnard, "Garden-Making on the Riviera," p. 33.

60 Christopher Tunnard, "Garden Design at Chelsea Show, 1936," *Landscape and Garden*, Summer 1936, p. 90.

61 Ibid. Eighty years later, people still ask this question.

62 Christopher Tunnard, "Garden Work," *Landscape and Garden*, Spring 1937, p. 39. Additional images of the project appeared in the autumn 1938 (p. 163) and spring 1939 (p. 39) issues of the same journal.

63 Christopher Tunnard, "Planning the Town Garden," *Decoration*, Summer 1939, p. 31.

64 Ibid., p. 34.

65 In 1939 the Architectural Press would also publish *The Modern Flat*, co-authored by Yorke and Frederick Gibberd, followed in the postwar years by Peter Shepheard's *Modern Gardens*, in 1954.

66 *Gardens in the Modern Landscape*, p. 6.

67 Ibid., p. 7.

68 Ibid., p. 9.

69 Ibid., pp. 11–12.

70 Ibid., p. 21.

71 Ibid., p. 23.

72 For example, see Lester Collins, in his review of the second edition, in *Landscape Architecture*, April 1949, p. 147.

73 Reginald Blomfield, *Modernismus*, London: Macmillan, 1934, p. 59.

74 *Gardens in the Modern Landscape*, p. 62.

75 Ibid., p. 74. Compare with Nikolaus Pevsner's pronouncement that "a bicycle shed is a building; Lincoln Cathedral is a piece of architecture." *An Outline of European Architecture*, 1942, reprint, Harmondsworth, UK: Penguin, 1957, p. 23.

76 *Gardens in the Modern Landscape*, p. 69.

77 Ibid., p. 80.

78 *Gardens in the Modern Landscape*, 1948, p. 94.

79 Ibid.

80 Ibid.

81 Ibid., p. 87.

82 Ibid., p. 82. The term "occult balance" probably derives from Fletcher Steele's "New Pioneering in the Garden," *Landscape Architecture*, October 1930. Reprinted in *Modern Landscape Architecture: A Critical Review*, ed. Marc Treib, Cambridge, MA: MIT Press, 1993, pp. 108–113.

83 *Gardens in the Modern Landscape*, 1948, p. 84.

84 Ibid., p. 90.

85 One of the original editions made it to the University of Tokyo architecture school library; in Israel, in 1941, Tunnard was not only cited but also paraphrased in instructions to those creating landscapes under conditions quite different from those of England. Jakob Schwarzmane (Jakob Shur), "Towards a New Technique in the Garden—an Adaptation of Tunnard's Gardens in the Modern Landscape," *Alon L'Ganan* (Gardener's Newsletter) 13–14, 1944, pp. 4–5 (p. 5 in Hebrew). I thank Elissa Rosenberg for bringing this reference to my attention.

86 Mary McLeod, "Domestic Reform and European Modern Architecture: Charlotte Perriand, Grete Lihotzky, and Elizabeth Denby," in *Modern Women: Women Artists at the Museum of Modern Art*, ed. Cornelia Butler and Alexandra Schwartz, 2010, p. 185.

87 Elizabeth Denby, *Europe Re-housed*, London: George Allen & Unwin, 1938.

88 "The All-Europe House," *Journal of the Royal Institute of British Architects*, June 1939, p. 26.

89 The caption reads, "Terrace-houses ingeniously sited for the maximum privacy." Denby, *Europe Re-housed*, p. 71.

90 *Gardens in the Modern Landscape*, 1948, p. 145.

91 H. F. Clark, *The English Landscape Garden*, London: Pleiades Books, 1948.

92 Probably a corrupted version of "1934."

93 Reginald Blomfield, *The Formal Garden in England*, London: Waterstone, 1892; William Robinson, *The Wild Garden*, London: John Murray, 1870.

94 Although the Keene landscape project is not identified, it seems obvious that Tunnard used it as the basis of his case study. Christopher Tunnard, "Garden and Landscape: The Country Acre; A Typical Garden Problem." *Architectural Review*, February 1939, p. 96.

95 *Gardens in the Modern Landscape*, p. 93.

96 See Laura Cohn, ed., *Wells Coates: Architect and Designer, 1895–1958*, Oxford: Oxford Polytechnic Press, 1979. Interesting in a different way from the radical modernism of the building's architecture were its occupants, who over time included émigré architects, artists, and even spies. See Jill Pearlman, "The Spies Who Came into the Modernist Fold: The Covert Life in Hampstead's Lawn Road Flats," *Journal of the Society of Architectural Historians*, September 2013, pp. 358–381.

97 Alan Powers, *Serge Chermayeff: Designer, Architect, Teacher*, London: RIBA, 2001, p. 120.

98 Both paintings are in the collection of Tate Britain.

99 Powers, *Serge Chermayeff*, p. 129.

100 As it happens, Chermayeff would not enjoy the sculpture for long. By 1939, about a year after occupancy, he was considering immigration to the United States due to the onset of war. His financial condition was also precarious and final payment for the work was never made. Realizing the importance of the sculpture, the Contemporary Art Society gathered support for its purchase and donation to the Tate Gallery—today Tate Britain—where it still resides. Moore, however, seems to have preferred its being displayed outdoors. See Henry Moore, "*Recumbent Figure*, 1938," and "Sculpture in the Open Air, 1955," reprinted in *Henry Moore: Writings and Conversations*, ed. Alan Wilkinson, Berkeley: University of California Press, 2002, p. 258.

101 Moore, "*Recumbent Figure*, 1938," p. 259; and Powers, *Serge Chermayeff*, pp. 128–129.

102 Moore, "*Recumbent Figure*, 1938," p. 259.

103 Barbara Tilson, "The Battle for Bentley Wood," *Thirties Society Journal*, 5, 1985, pp. 24–31.

104 Christopher Tunnard, "Planning a Modern Garden: An Experience in Collaboration," *Landscape and Garden*, Spring 1939, p. 23.

105 Ibid., p. 23.

106 Ibid., pp. 25–26.

107 Ibid., p. 25.

108 Ibid.

109 Ibid.

110 "Bentley, Notes on the Work to be Carried Out in the Autumn, 1938," typescript, no date. H. F. Clark Papers, Royal Commission on the Ancient and Historical Monuments of Scotland (now Historic Environment Scotland, hereafter HES).

111 Tunnard to Serge Chermayeff, 19 February 1928. H. F. Clark Papers, HES.

112 Lance Neckar, telephone conversation with Serge Chermayeff, October 1989. See his "Christopher Tunnard: The Garden in the Modern Landscape," in *Modern Landscape Architecture*, ed. Treib, pp. 144–158.

113 Ibid., p. 27.

114 Ibid., p. 26.

115 Dorothée Imbert, *The Modernist Garden in France*, New Haven, CT: Yale University Press, 1993.

116 The architect was Oliver Hill; construction was completed in 1938. See Alan Powers, *Oliver Hill: Architect and Lover of Life, 1887–1968*, London: Mouton, 1989, pp. 30, 75; and Tunnard, "Planning the Town Garden," *Decoration*, p. 31. Percy Cane had designed a garden for Schlesinger, which is where Tunnard may have met him. Jacques and Woudstra, *Tunnard*, p. 20.

117 Charlotte Talbot, "The £9m Chertsey home with secret split bedroom honoured for role in UK's LGBTQ+ heritage," 16 Oct 2016, "SurreyLive," http//www.getsurrey.co.uk/new/surrey-news/9m-chartsey-home-secret-split-12033664.

118 Reginald Blomfield would no doubt have sneered at the design: "One does not want to live either in a conservatory, or in rooms which appear to be suggested by the operating rooms of a hospital." *Modernismus*, p. 57.

119 Serge Chermayeff and Wells Coates also had worked for McGrath.

120 Lance Sieveking, *The Eye of the Beholder*, London: Hulton Press, 1957, p. 71. I thank Alan Powers for bringing this source to my attention. Tunnard seems to have also designed a garden for Nash at his home in Hampstead, or at least provided a list of plants to be used in an existing garden. Plant list addressed to Paul Nash, no date, H. F. Clark Papers, HES.

121 Sieveking, *Eye of the Beholder*, p. 71.

122 Ibid., p. 72.

123 Ibid., pp. 72–73.

124 Henry Hubbard and Theodora Kimball, *An Introduction to the Study of Landscape Design*, New York: Macmillan, 1917; Madeline Agar, *Garden Design in Theory and Practice*, London: Sidgwick & Jackson, 1911; and G. C. Taylor, *The Modern Garden*, London: Country Life, 1936.

125 Soukop's *Donkey* (1935) is one of the favorite pieces of visitors. On the landscape of Dartington Hall, and the contributions of Beatrix Farrand and Percy Cane to its shaping, see Reginald Snell, *From the Bare Stem: Making Dorothy Elmhirst's Garden at Dartington Hall*, Exeter, Devon, UK: Devon Books, 1989.

126 At the time of my first visit to St. Ann's Hill in 1989, the sculpture lay behind the house in the woods, probably unceremoniously disposed of by a subsequent owner.

127 *Gardens in the Modern Landscape*, pp. 11–12.

128 Ibid., p. 74.

129 Christopher Tunnard, "Landscape Design at the Paris International Congress: What Other Countries Are Doing," *Landscape and Garden*, 1937, pp. 78–83.

130 Ibid., p. 78.

131 *Gardens in the Modern Landscape*, pp. 81–82. Steele was commenting on the Tachard garden in La Celle-Saint-Cloud by Pierre-Émile Legrain. Steele, "New Pioneering in Garden Design," p. 192.

132 Christopher Tunnard, "Landscape Design at the Paris International Congress," p. 80.

133 Ibid., p. 81.

134 Ibid., p. 83.

135 Ibid.

136 Ibid., p. 80.

137 The definitive study of the life and work of this Belgian landscape architect is Dorothée Imbert, *Between Garden and City: Jean Canneel-Claes and Landscape Modernism*, Pittsburgh: University of Pittsburgh Press, 2009.

138 *Gardens in the Modern Landscape*, p. 65.

139 Ibid., p. 80.

140 Imbert, *Between Garden and City*, pp. 119–120.

141 Tunnard seems to have spoken at least passable French.

142 Tunnard, "Landscape Architecture in the U.S.A.," p. 8, Tunnard Papers, Yale.

143 Christopher Tunnard and Jean Canneel-Claes. Manifesto. Brussels: Association Internationale des Architectes de Jardins Modernistes (International Association of Modernist Garden Architects), no date (c. 1938), p. 3.

144 Letter from Tunnard to Loftus Hare, 7 May 1938, reproduced in Dorothée Imbert, "Landscape Architects of the World, Unite! Professional Organizations, Practice, and Politics, 1935–1948," *Journal of Landscape Architecture*, Spring 2007, p. 12. In the letter Tunnard explains that due to the political climate in Germany, he cannot support any event sponsored by the National Socialist regime. The following year England would be drawn into the conflict and Tunnard would return to Canada, entering service in the Royal Canadian Engineers.

145 Ibid., p. 16.

146 Tunnard, "Landscape Architecture in the U.S.A." Tunnard Papers, Yale.

147 This was not Hudnut's judgment alone. In writing to Tunnard about another matter, cultural landscape historian and *Landscape* magazine founder and editor John Brinckerhoff Jackson mentioned that "I have just been reading Gropius' sad little opus, 'Scope of Total Architecture[.]' I feel he is a very earnest and modest man, but what commonplace thoughts he expresses." 6 May 1955. Tunnard Papers, Yale.

148 Jill Pearlman, *Inventing American Modernism: Joseph Hudnut, Walter Gropius and the Bauhaus Legacy at Harvard*, Charlottesville: University of Virginia Press, 2007.

149 Dorothée Imbert has noted the irony that Tunnard's departure on 1 September 1939

coincided with Germany's invasion of Poland and the opening of the Second World War. "The AIAJM: A Manifesto for Landscape Modernity," *Landscape Journal*, Spring 2007, p. 8.

150 Eckbo did take one studio with Gropius, however, collaborating with four architecture students on a park design. Garrett Eckbo, *Landscape Architecture: The Profession in California, 1935–1940, and Telesis; Oral History Transcript*. Interviews conducted by Suzanne Riess, 1991. Berkeley: Regional Oral History Office, Bancroft Library, University of California, Berkeley, 1993, p. 16.

151 *Official Register of Harvard University, Department of Architectural Sciences, Containing an Announcement for 1940–41*, Cambridge, MA, 5 March 1940, p. 9. Tunnard also taught "occasional seminars" in this course. *Official Register of Harvard University, Department of Architectural Sciences, Containing an Announcement for 1940–41*, Cambridge, MA, 30 April 1941, p. 6.

152 *Official Register of Harvard University, The Graduate School of Design, with Courses of Instruction, 1940–41*, Cambridge, MA, 23 April 1940, p. 46.

153 Announcement of the joint Harvard and Smith College Summer School, 10 August 1940, unpaginated.

154 Christopher Tunnard, "Site Planning Course," syllabus. The letterhead upon which the syllabus is written bears the address 115 Mount Street, London. Tunnard Papers, Yale.

155 An article in the summer 1941 issue of *Task* magazine was based on a lecture he had given to his design studio—possibly for the "Site Planning" course—suggests that Tunnard also ran independent studios.

156 Final examination, Architecture 1c, Harvard University, 29 January 1942. Tunnard Papers, Yale. B9/F 15.

157 *Bulletin of the Summer Term, Graduate School of Design*, Harvard University, Cambridge, MA, 1942, p. 18.

158 Norton Newton, Memorandum to Mr. [Bremer] Pond, Architecture 1c, Harvard University, 25 April 1942. Tunnard Papers, Yale. B9/F 15.

159 Tunnard, Architecture 37b, no date. Tunnard Papers, Yale. B9-F15.

160 Hubbard and Kimball, *An Introduction to the Study of Landscape Design*. See note 124.

161 "Some of his [Tunnard's] decisions appear to us, a decade later, somewhat romantic, somewhat eclectic. 'Modern' has become a

style, no longer a method of approach. This book is no longer in the vanguard." Lester Collins, review of *Gardens in the Modern Landscape*, revised second edition, *Landscape Architecture*, April 1949, pp. 147–148. At that time, Tunnard had accepted an appointment in planning at Yale and was involved in his last landscape design projects.

162 Garrett Eckbo, *Landscape for Living*, New York: Duell, Sloan & Pearce, 1950.

163 "reads Christopher Tunnard's book Gardens in the Modern Landscape...and becomes aware of the significance of design in the environment. Decides on the spot to study design in architecture, with an emphasis on landscape design." *Lawrence Halprin: Changing Places*, ed. Lynne Creighton Neall, San Francisco: San Francisco Museum of Art, 1986, p. 115.

164 No date is provided on the short syllabus noting the lectures to be given, but the last bibliographic reference was 1948. Tunnard Papers, Yale. B37/F600.

165 Joseph Hudnut to Tunnard, 22 December 1942, Tunnard Papers, Yale. B8/F129.

166 Tunnard to Geoffrey Jellicoe, 11 May 1943. Landscape Institute Archives [hereafter LIA]

167 Jellicoe to Tunnard, 23 June 1943. LIA.

168 Christopher Tunnard, "Modern Gardens for Modern Houses: Reflections on Current Trends in Landscape Design," *Landscape Architecture*, January 1942, reprinted in *Modern Landscape Architecture: A Critical Review*, ed. Treib, p. 161.

169 Ibid., p. 164.

170 Ibid., p. 165.

171 Ibid., p. 162.

172 In 1945, at the time of his move to New Haven, he also married Lydia Evans.

173 Jellicoe to Tunnard 27 September 1946. LIA.

174 Tunnard to Jellicoe, 26 February 1947. LIA.

175 Mrs. Gordon Browne (Secretary, Institute of Landscape Architects), to Tunnard, 2 June 1947. LIA.

176 Tunnard, "Town and Country Landscape, U.S.A.," lecture prospectus, dated only 1947. Tunnard Papers, Yale.

177 Tunnard to Mrs. Gordon Browne, 2 December 1949. LIA.

178 Tunnard to Secretary of Institute of Landscape Architects (Mrs. Gordon Browne), 30 July 1945. LIA.

179 In a letter, Ian McHarg, professor of landscape architecture at the University of Pennsylvania, asks Tunnard what "writings, past and present" he would recommend for a research project, noting, "Your own work 'Gardens in the Modern Landscape' still remains the best thought on the subject." Ian McHarg to Tunnard, 26 January 1958. Tunnard Papers, Yale.

180 Christopher Tunnard, "Architecture and Art," *Task*, no. 7–8, 1948, p. 84.

181 Christopher Tunnard, "Art and Landscape Design," presented at Ann Arbor Conference on Esthetic Evaluation, University of Michigan, 2–3 April 1948. Text published in *Landscape Architecture*, April 1949, p. 107.

182 Ibid.

183 Ibid., p. 108.

184 Lewis Mumford, in "What Is Happening to Modern Architecture?" *Museum of Modern Art Bulletin*, Spring 1948, p. 3.

185 Ibid., pp. 3 and 7 respectively.

186 Christopher Tunnard, in "What Is Happening to Modern Architecture?" *Museum of Modern Art Bulletin*, Spring 1948, p. 14.

187 Christopher Tunnard, "Landscape Design and City Planning," in *Landscape Design*, San Francisco: San Francisco Museum of Art, 1948, p. 11.

188 The book remained in print until 1962.

189 *Gardens in the Modern Landscape*, 1948, p. 6.

190 Ibid., p. 7.

191 Tunnard, "Modern Gardens for Modern Houses," p. 162.

192 Cullen (1914–1994) had begun contributing articles and visual essays to *The Architectural Review* in the 1940s. These were collected and organized as *Townscape*, London: Architectural Press, 1961.

193 See Mathew Aitchison, ed., *Nikolaus Pevsner and the Picturesque*, Los Angeles: Getty Research Institute, 2010.

194 Royal Barry Wills popularized the style through his active architectural practice and through his pattern books such as *Houses for Good Living*, New York: Architectural Book Publishing, 1940; and *Better Houses for Budgeteers: Sketches and Plans*, New York: Architectural Book Publishing, 1941.

195 While staking out the territory for modern residential design in brief introductions, these books are compilations of work being done around the United States, no doubt to establish the ubiquity of the new manner. James Ford and Katherine Morrow Ford, *The Modern House in America*, New York: Architectural Book Publishing, 1940; and James Ford and Katherine Morrow Ford, *Design of Modern Interiors*, Architectural Book Publishing, 1942.

196 G. Holmes Perkins, interview with author, University of Pennsylvania, Philadelphia, 17 May 1994. Perkins moved to the University of Pennsylvania as the dean of the School of Fine Arts in 1951 and held that position for two decades.

197 G. Holmes Perkins to Marc Treib, 23 November 1993.

198 Ibid.

199 G. Holmes Perkins, interview with author, University of Pennsylvania, Philadelphia, 17 May 1994.

200 *Gardens in the Modern Landscape*, p. 63.

201 Tunnard also consulted with Perkins on the project for the Forbes house in Sudbury, Massachusetts, 1939–1940, mostly in terms of siting and the managing of views over the adjacent field. G. Holmes Perkins, interview with author, University of Pennsylvania, 17 May 1994.

202 When I visited the house in 1994 and interviewed Koch, he was living there as owner and tenant—and somewhat unfortunately had compromised the house's modernist expression with a mansard roof that all but buried the elegance of the original structure. Carl Koch, interview with author, 15 May 1994.

203 The site plan published in James Ford and Katherine Morrow Ford, *The Modern House in America*, p. 110, shows no traces of the Tunnard design.

204 *Gardens in the Modern Landscape*, 1948, p. 168.

205 Christopher Tunnard, *A World with a View: An Inquiry into the Nature of Scenic Values*, New Haven, CT: Yale University Press, 1978, p. 52.

206 Paul Nash to Clare Nelson, 6 August 1934, in introduction to Nash's Redfern Exhibition catalog, 1937, quoted in James King, *Interior Landscapes: A Life of Paul Nash*, London: Weidenfeld & Nicolson, 1987, p. 179.

207 Tunnard, *World with a View*, p. 52.

208 *Gardens in the Modern Landscape*, 1948, p. 169.

209 James Thrall Soby, "Love Song to a House," unpublished typescript, no date, c. 1975, p. 6-1. I thank Kevin Shushtari, the current owner of the property, for providing me with information on Soby's years in the house and its subsequent history, photographs, and permission to visit.

210 Ibid., p. 6-3.

211 *Gardens in the Modern Landscape*, 1948, p. 174.

212 In his memoir Soby credits the terrace design to Hitchcock. But this may have been in an earlier form later expanded or redesigned by Tunnard a decade later. Soby, "Love Song to a House," p. 6-3. In subsequent years the landscape has been substantially modified. The site was divided in two with much of the original garden no longer a part of the original property. The swimming pool—or a new one—is substantially larger and steps have been added to breach the retaining wall and provide access to the pool.

213 "[Luther Ely] Smith's granddaughter [sic]," quoted in "Luther Ely Smith: Founder of a Memorial," *Museum Gazette* (National Park Service, U. S. Department of the Interior), March 2001, no pagination.

214 Ibid.

215 William M. Blair, "St. Louis Chooses Arch as Memorial, *New York Times*, 19 February 1948, p. 30.

216 Tunnard team proposal, entry no. 64, February 1948.

217 The Saarinen–Kiley scheme featured two lakes, most welcome features within the highly wooded park that brackets the Arch.

218 Alyssa Lozupone, *A Passion for Preservation: Katherine Warren and the Shaping of Modern Newport*, Carlisle, MA: Commonwealth Editions, 2015, p. 51.

219 Alyssa Lozupone, "Modernism Meets Preservation: Katherine Warren in Newport," 2 September 2016, "InCollect", https://www.incollect.com/articles/modernism-meets-preservation-katherine-warren-in-newport.

220 Tunnard's consulting firm, Tunnard and Harris, was commissioned to undertake a study of historic Newport in 1959, completing their report the following year. Lozupone, *Passion for Preservation*," p. 132, and note 243.

221 Peter Shepheard, *Modern Gardens*, London: Architectural Press, 1954, p. 81.

222 Ibid.

223 All quotations are from "Garden for

U.N. Headquarters," *Architectural Review*, November 1949, p. 335–336. There is a second, unidentified clipping featuring the same perspective view among the Tunnard Papers in the Yale University Archives. That the texts to both short articles are so similar suggests they were merely paraphrases of a press release issued by Tunnard.

224 For a comprehensive telling of the history of the Museum of Modern Art sculpture garden see Mirka Beneš, "A Modern Classic: The Abby Aldrich Rockefeller Sculpture Garden," in *Philip Johnson and the Museum of Modern Art*, ed. John Elderfield, *Studies in Modern Art 6*, New York: Museum of Modern Art, 1998, pp. 104–151.

225 Elizabeth Mock to Monroe Wheeler, 16 September 1943. MoMA Archives.

226 At that time Howard Myers was the publisher of *Architectural Forum*.

227 On the so-called cubist gardens from the 1920s, see Imbert, *Modernist Garden in France*.

228 These large pieces tend to be displayed in parks of far greater scale than the urban garden, for example, at the Storm King Art Center in New Windsor, New York—although the Nasher Sculpture Center in Dallas does feature *Eviva Amore* by di Suvero (2001).

229 The 2004 renovation and addition by Yoshio Taniguchi maintained the sculpture garden in form, if not without serious modifications. Among these are the principal entrance laterally, from its western end, rather than from the original entrance from the south.

230 On Joanna Diman, see Nicholas Adams, "Joanna Diman (1901–91): A 'Cantankerous' Landscape Architect at Skidmore, Owings & Merrill," *Journal of the Society of Landscape Historians*, September 2018, pp. 339–348.

231 Tunnard to Frazar B. Wilde, President, Connecticut General Life Insurance, 12 February 1957. Tunnard Papers, Yale.

232 In a letter dated 1 October 1960 to Takashi Asada, written following his participation in the World Design Conference in Tokyo, Tunnard wrote, "I would be grateful if you would list me as 'City Planner' since I have been teaching and practising this subject for the last years." He was appointed professor and chair of the department in 1962. Tunnard Papers, Yale.

233 Jacques and Woudstra even titled their book *Landscape Modernism Renounced*. I feel we would need to qualify the claim, distinguishing between Tunnard's thinking over time and the designs he realized.

234 Henry Hope Reed, *The Golden City*, Garden City NY: Doubleday, 1959; "Ars in Urbe," *Bulletin of the Associates of Fine Arts at Yale University*, April 1953. Tunnard loaned an etching of the Piazza San Marco in Venice to the exhibition.

235 Christopher Tunnard, "The Architecture of the Regional Landscape," Gulf States Regional Conference of the American Institute of Architects, Biloxi, MS, September 1953, typescript.

236 Christopher Tunnard and Boris Pushkarev, *Man-Made America: Chaos or Control?* New Haven, CT: Yale University Press, 1964, p. x. Pushkarev was an influential member of the Regional Plan Association who worked on the book with Tunnard at Yale. Among his contributions was the section on highway planning.

237 Ibid., p. 9.

238 Tunnard to Takashi Asada, Secretary, World Design Conference, 12 September 1959. Tunnard Papers, Yale.

239 Tunnard to Junzō Sakakura, Chair, World Design Conference, 4 April 1960. Tunnard Papers, Yale.

240 Tunnard, "Too Fast, Too Far...or, Around the World in Thirty Days," c. June 1960. Tunnard Papers, Yale. He began his travels with a visit to the San Francisco Bay Area and ended in New York, and ultimately New Haven.

241 Tunnard mentions the intended publication in a letter to Takashi Asada, 1 October 1960. Tunnard Papers, Yale.

242 Christopher Tunnard, "The Garden of the Silver Pavilion," typescript, p. 2. Tunnard Papers, Yale. One wonders if Tunnard's title is a play on the title of the 1956 novel by Yukio Mishima, translated as *The Temple of the Golden Pavilion*.

243 Ibid., p. 3.

244 Tunnard, *World with a View*.

245 Ibid., p. 3.

246 Tunnard, Letter to the Editor, *Architects' Journal*, 8 March 1946. Tunnard Papers, Yale.

247 Ibid., p. 185.

248 Ibid., p. 109.

249 Ibid., p. 41

3. > Sutemi Horiguchi

Most of the writings by Sutemi Horiguchi were first collected in a seven-volume series released by Kajima Shuppan-kai in 1978: *Horiguchi Sutemi sakhuin: Ie to niwa no kūkan kōsei* [Works of Sutemi Horiguchi: Spatial Composition of House and Garden]. Of particular interest are the volumes *Spatial Composition of House and Garden* and *Architectural Dialogues*.

1 Today, Gifu Prefecture remains a significant tea-producing region.

2 This subdivision and compression of historic estates into smaller plots recalls similar practices in England, where the grand eighteenth-century parks and gardens of the landed gentry were condensed into the modest estates of nouveau riche businessmen in the century that followed.

3 Only relatively recently have a major studies of Jihei Ogawa (Ueji) appeared in English, although his works—most often the Murin-an and Heian Shrine in Kyoto—are cited in most books on the Japanese garden. Hiromasa Amasaki, *Ueji no niwa: Ogawa Jihei no sekai*, Kyoto: Tankōsha, 1990; Hiroyuki Suzuki, *The Life and Times of Gardener Jihei Ogawa*, Tokyo: University of Tokyo Press, 2013; Yōzabôro Shirahata, ed., *Ueji, The Genius of Water and Stone*, Kyoto: Kyoto Tsushinsha Press, 2008; Tsuyoshi Tamura, *Art of the Landscape Garden in Japan*, Tokyo: Kokusai Bunka Shinkokai, 1936, pp. 186–190; Loraine Kuck, *The World of the Japanese Garden: From Chinese Origins to Modern Landscape Art*, New York: Weatherhill, 1968, pp. 250–252.

4 Hiroyuki Suzuki, Terunobu Fujimori, and Tokuzu Hara, *Josiah Conder: A Victorian Architect in Japan*, Tokyo: East Japan Railway Culture Foundation, 1997.

5 Josiah Conder, *Landscape Gardening in Japan*, 1893, reprint, New York: Dover, 1964.

6 David B. Stewart, *The Making of a Modern Japanese Architecture, 1868 to the Present*, Tokyo: Kodansha International, 1987, pp. 90–94.

7 Bunriha, *Bunriha Kenchiku-Kai no Sakuhin*, Tokyo: Iwanami Shôten, 1924.

8 Ken Tadashi Oshima, *International Architecture in Interwar Japan: Constructing* Kokusai Kenchiku, Seattle: University of Washington Press, 2010, pp. 39–50. Oshima cites Horiguchi as the group's intellectual leader.

9 Founded in 1897 as the Union of Austrian Architects, members included such now well-known architects as Josef Hoffmann, Koloman Moser, and Josef Maria Olbrich; the painter Gustav Klimt served as its first president.

10 Olbrich had died in 1908.

11 For a comprehensive study of the earthquake and public response to it, see Gennifer Weisenfeld, *Imaging Disaster: Tokyo and the Visual Culture of Japan's Great Earthquake of 1923*, Berkeley: University of California Press, 2012.

12 The house has been conserved at the Edo-Tokyo Open Air Architectural Museum outside Shinjuku in Tokyo.

13 Oshima, *International Architecture*, p. 118.

14 The client, "Motoaki Kikkawa (1894–1953), a member of the international elite of Japan, contacted Horiguchi, his high-school classmate, after an earlier dwelling was damaged in the Tokyo earthquake." Oshima, *International Architecture*, p. 99.

15 David B. Stewart notes that "it is altogether more conventionally Constructivist-minded in its welding together of mutually opposite planes and would scarcely have been out of place, say, on the outskirts of Brussels." He also notes that the house "lacked the value of a manifesto or icon," as had the Okada house and garden. *Modern Japanese Architecture*, pp. 144–45.

16 Sutemi Horiguchi, *Ichi Konkuriito Jūtaku Zuchū* [Illustrations of a Concrete House], c. 1932.

17 Tunnard notes the use of only three plants in the courtyard design. Christopher Tunnard, *Gardens in the Modern Landscape*, London: Architectural Press, 1938, p. 89. Raymond McGrath observes that "In place of the normal Japanese garden there is one more in harmony with such a new house as this and pleasingly designed with waterways and stretches of grass." *Twentieth-century Houses*, London: Faber & Faber, 1934, p. 190.

18 Analyzing the composition of Pierre-Émile Legrain's Tachard garden, Fletcher Steele wrote that "The semi-circular front lawn is no new thing. Nothing in the rear lawn—nothing save the relation of the parts and the use of what we formerly called formal elements arranged in occult unsymmetrical balance. In fact, the most arresting feature is the manner in which the main axis of the composition has been shattered and the cross axes diminished." From "New Pioneering in Landscape Design," "Landscape Architecture," October 1930; reprinted in *Modern Landscape Architecture: A Critical Review*, ed. Marc Treib, Cambridge, MA: MIT Press, 1993, pp. 113.

19 Sutemi Horiguchi, "Japanese Taste Expressed in Modern Architecture," *Shiso* 116, 1932. [Melanie Hong, trans.]

20 *Kenchiku zasshi*, December 1930, cited in Jonathan M. Reynolds, *Maekawa Kunio and the Emergence of Modernist Japanese Architecture*, Berkeley: University of California Press, 2001, p. 92.

21 In English, the most complete study of Maekawa's work is Reynolds, *Maekawa Kunio*.

22 Horiguchi, "Japanese Taste Expressed in Modern Architecture."

23 Hiroyaso Fujioka and Kentaro Mimura, "The Architectural View of the Architectural Critic Takao Itagaki," *UDC* 3, 1972, pp. 60–70.

24 With President Theodore Roosevelt's intervention on Russia's behalf, the Treaty of Portsmouth (1905) ended the hostilities. Japanese pride in their nation soared; Russia was abashed and weakened; and Roosevelt received the Nobel Prize for Peace, 1906.

25 The Shirakaba-ha (White Birch Society) was a literary group founded in 1910 that included the authors Naoya Shiga and Ton Satomi among others. Unlike the so-called three friends: pine, bamboo, and plum, the birch did not command literary significance in Japan. Here the reference was Leo Tolstoy, whose social exhortations were appreciated and adopted by the group, and to Russia itself. Like the Bunriha, the Shirakaba-ha stressed individualism, evident in its continued support of fiction written typically in the first person, as in the older "I-novel." Sôetsu Yanagi, who would later found the Nihon Mingeikan (Japan Folk Crafts Museum) and preserve native crafts, was also a member. The Great Kantô Earthquake ended the group's eponymous publication in 1923.

26 Jun'ichirô Tanizaki, *Naomi*, 1924, trans. Anthony Chambers, Rutland, VT: Tuttle, 1986, p. 51.

27 Yasunari Kawabata, *Thousand Cranes*, trans. Edward G. Seidensticker, New York: Berkley, 1958.

28 Ibid., p. 55.

29 Le Corbusier, *Towards a New Architecture*, 1923, trans. Frederick Etchells, 1931, reprint, New York: Dover, 1986, p. 4.

30 The *sukiya* style (*sukiya-zukuri*) evolved in the sixteenth century and matured in the early Edo period of the seventeenth century. As the style of "personal taste," its semi-conventions furnished the principal design mode for pavilions

for the tea ceremony, famously for the unique Katsura Imperial Villa outside Kyoto toward mid-century. It may be described as a vehicle of sophisticated rusticity, in its selection of elements adopted from the rural farmhouse style (*minka-zukuri*) and their transformation into "humble" structures for the elite. The noted sixteenth-century tea master Sen no Rikyu is often credited with its earliest manifestations.

31 Consider that the principal crop was rice and that rice also became a unit of currency measured in *koku*, approximately five bushels, or 6.37 cubic feet, deemed sufficient to feed one individual for a year.

32 Among the English-language studies on these artists are Felice Fischer, ed., *The Arts of Hon'ami Kôetsu: Japanese Renaissance Master*, Philadelphia: Philadelphia Museum of Art, 2000; Miyeko Murase and Takeshi Noguchi, *Irises and Eight Bridges: Masterpieces by Kôrin from the Nezu Museum and the Metropolitan Museum of Art*, Tokyo: Nezu Art Museum, 2012; and Hiroshi Mizuo, *Edo Painting: Sôtatsu and Kôrin*, Tokyo: Weatherhill / Heibonsha, 1972.

33 Among the several traditional classifications of beauty in Japan, three stake out the main range of possibilities: *jimi* is harmonious beauty (the term is now usually reserved for an unintentional exposure of poverty), for example, a mix of brown, ivory, and oatmeal tones; *hade* is brilliant beauty, like juxtaposing gold, red, and silver (with the usual connotation today of being vulgar or over-the-top); and *shibui* (its literal translation is "astringent"), which is usually regarded as the highest form, the product of harmony and dissonance (however, the term is sometimes today applied ironically).

34 The *tokonoma* is the ceremonial alcove in a teahouse or tea room, as well as in *shoin-zukuri* reception rooms, where the host displayed a painting, or example of calligraphy, and a restrained flower arrangement.

35 Matthew P. McKelway, *Silver Wind: The Arts of Sakai Hôitsu (1761–1828)*, New York: Japan Society, 2012.

36 The client for the Okada and later the Wakasa houses was a certain Kiyoshi Shibui, an art professor at Keio University in Tokyo. The two houses were each designed for one of his mistresses, a Miss Okada and a Miss Wakasa. Both residences were provided with only a single bedroom, but each also possessed a separate room for dressing and applying makeup. I cite this only as lore as no factual source for this information has been found.

37 Marc Treib, "The Japanese Storehouse," *Journal of the Society of Architectural Historians*, May 1976, pp. 124–137; Teiji Itoh, *Kura: Design and Tradition of the Japanese Storehouse*, Tokyo: Kodansha International, 1973.

38 Both house and garden were destroyed sometime prior to 1954.

39 Sutemi Horiguchi, "Akikusa no niwa" [Garden of Autumn Grasses], *Shisô*, 1934. [Melanie Hong, trans.] A second translator, Koichi Miura, in a personal note wrote that Horiguchi stressed that the word for grass, usually pronounced *kusa*, here should be pronounced with its alternate reading *sô*—thereby relating it to the three formal orders, of which *sô* constitutes the informal.

40 Ibid.

41 Ibid.

42 Sutemi Horiguchi, *Architectural Beauty in Japan*, New York: Studio Publications; Tokyo: Kokusai Bunka Shinkokai, 1956, p. 161.

43 Horiguchi, "Akikusa no niwa" [Garden of Autumn Grasses.]

44 Ibid.

45 Ibid.

46 The most substantial study of this garden designer is Christian Tschumi, *Mirei Shigemori: Modernizing the Japanese Garden*, Basel: Birkhäuser, 2007.

47 Mirei Shigemori, *Nihon teien shi zukan* [Illustrated History of the Japanese Garden], Tokyo: Yukosha, 1936–1939.

48 Even this practice has historical precedents, for example, in the garden at Shôden-ji, where clipped azaleas serve as surrogates for the more common rocks.

49 Shigemori, Nihon teien shi zukan [*Illustrated History*].

50 Reynolds, *Maekawa Kunio*, p. 124.

51 Ibid., pp. 122–124.

52 Sutemi Horiguchi, "Chûreitô no hyôgen to sonoichishian" [Soldiers' Memorial, Expression and Proposals], *Gendai Kenchiku*, April 1940, pp. 5–15.

53 Sutemi Horiguchi, "About the Expression of the Chûreitô and My Project," *Gendai Kenchiku*, April 1940. [Koichi Miura, trans.]

54 Ibid.

55 Ibid.

56 Ibid.

57 Oshima, *International Architecture*, pp. 240–241.

58 Ibid.

59 Sutemi Horiguchi, "The Lecture Hall at Jikô-in," in Sutemi Horiguchi, *Kusaniwa: Tatemono to chanoyu kenkyu* [Garden of Grasses: Research in Buildings and Tea], Tokyo: Hakujitsu shoin, 1948, reprint, Tokyo: Chikuma shobô, 1968, p. 211. [Melanie Hong, trans.]

60 Horiguchi, *Architectural Beauty in Japan*, p. 153.

61 See Jonathan M. Reynolds, *Allegories of Time and Space: Japanese Identity in Photography and Architecture*, Honolulu: University of Hawai'i Press, 2015.

62 W. G. Beardsley, *The Modern History of Japan*, New York: Praeger, 1974; Kazuo Kawai, *Japan's American Interlude*, Chicago: University of Chicago Press, 1979; and Gary D. Allison, *Japan's Postwar History*, Ithaca, NY: Cornell University Press, 1997.

63 Alfred Altherr, *Three Japanese Architects/ Drei japanische Architekten: Mayekawa, Tange, Sakakura*, New York: Architectural Book Publishing, 1968.

64 Among the earliest books on the architect to be published in English were Udo Kultermann, ed., *Kenzô Tange, 1946–1969*, New York: Frederick A. Praeger, 1970; and Robin Boyd, *Kenzô Tange*, New York: George Braziller, 1962.

65 See Marc Treib, *Noguchi in Paris: Isamu Noguchi and the UNESCO Garden*, San Francisco: William Stout, 2003.

66 Sutemi Horiguchi, "Nakamise Hasshôkan," no source, n.d. (probably c. 1962).

67 My visit was in 1994.

68 The sense of this relationship is now stifled by a recent high-rise development along the Tama River below the bluff on which the museum is situated—perhaps ironically—sponsored by the Tôkyu Group of which Gotoh was the founder. I thank David B. Stewart for bringing this to my attention.

69 Publications in Japanese: "A Man and His Work: Kinsaku Nakane," *Niwa / The Garden* 77, January 1991; *Kinsaku Nakane, Landscape Artist, Japanese Garden Exhibition*, Yokohama: Yokohama City Art Museum, 1998; *Tankô*, Special Issue, November 1994.

70 Of course, if the rockwork survived, it usually provided the structure for the restoration—but not always.

71 Takanori Adachi, *The Gardens of the Adachi Museum of Art*, Yasugi: Adachi Museum of Art, 2002.

72 As an additional dimension, Nakane was one of the few Japanese garden designers offering classes and apprenticeships open to foreigners. In that sense he may be regarded as an influential source for spreading the word about Japanese garden making in Europe, the United States, and elsewhere abroad.

73 Horiguchi, *Architectural Beauty in Japan*; Sutemi Horiguchi, *Tradition of* [the] *Japanese Garden*, Tokyo: Kokusai Bunka Shinkôkai, 1962.

74 Josiah Conder, *Paintings and Studies by Kawanabe Kyôsai*, Tokyo: Maruzen, 1911.

75 Jirô Harada, *Japanese Gardens*, 1936, reprint, London: The Studio, 1956; Tetsuro Yoshida, *The Japanese House and Garden*, New York: Frederick A. Praeger, 1955; Tetsuro Yoshida, *The Gardens of Japan*, New York: Frederick A. Praeger, 1957.

76 The *shoin* style, which superseded the *shinden* style, was named for the writing-desk alcove that was one of its distinctive architectural features—together with still moderately heavy square posts, ornamentally painted sliding wall panels, and areas of raised *tatami* denoting differences in status. The building, the Shofusô, was designed by Junzô Yoshimura and today resides within a Japanese-style garden designed by Tansai Sanô in Fairmount Park, in Philadelphia. Arthur Drexler, *The Architecture of Japan*, New York: Museum of Modern Art, 1955.

77 *House Beautiful*, August 1960 and September 1960.

78 Kenzô Tange, *Katsura: Tradition and Creation in Japanese Architecture*, New Haven, CT: Yale University Press, 1960; and Kenzô Tange, *Ise: Prototype of Japanese Architecture*, Cambridge, MA: MIT Press, 1965.

79 The *shinden* style takes its name from the palace's main pavilion, which was symmetrically flanked by pavilions linked to the *shinden* by raised, open loggia-like corridors. Fully developed by the tenth century CE, buildings in the style were characterized by heavy square posts, floors primarily of bare wood, and top-hinged, lattice wall panels that lifted upward and outward, rather than set in sliding groves.

80 Horiguchi, *Architectural Beauty in Japan*, p. 6. The book also presents Horiguchi's own fully designed Okada, Wasaka, and Kikkawa houses, in addition to the Hasshôkan interior.

81 Yôichirô Kôjiro, "Modern Art and Japanese Architecture," in *Architectural Beauty in Japan*, pp. 7–15.

82 Ibid., p. 9.

83 Ibid., p. 13.

84 Ibid., p. 14.

85 Ibid.

86 Ibid., p. 15.

87 The pavilion was renovated in 2013.

88 Horiguchi, *Tradition of* [the] *Japanese Garden.*

89 Or to be more specific, as the translator terms it.

90 Horiguchi, *Tradition of* [the] *Japanese Garden*, p. 9.

91 Ibid., p. 10.

92 Ibid., pp. 10–11.

93 Ibid., pp. 162–163.

94 Ibid., p. 176.

95 Ibid., p. 177.

96 Ibid., p. 179.

97 Ibid.

98 Ibid.

99 Ibid.

100 Horiguchi's explanation of his use of the Uraku bamboo and camellia in his contemporary article "Uraku-en Arekore" [Various Thoughts on Uraku-en], *SD* [*Space Design*], March 1973, pp. 38–39, testified yet again to the seriousness with which he always selected the plants for his gardens. [Melanie Hong, trans.]

101 This conflict between a modern and traditional approach is illustrated by the difficulties experienced by the sculptor Isamu Noguchi while working with Tōemon Sanō, from a multigenerational family of Kyoto gardeners, in the making of the landscape at the UNESCO House in Paris. See Dore Ashton, *Noguchi East and West*, New York: Alfred A. Knopf, 1992, pp. 146–147.

102 Marc Treib, "Landscapes Transitional, Modern, Modernistic, Modernist," *Journal of Landscape Architecture*, Spring 2014, pp. 6–15.

103 Henry-Russell Hitchcock and Philip Johnson, *The International Style*, New York: W. W. Norton, 1932. The authors cited three specific characteristics by which to identify the International Style: an emphasis on space over mass, pursuit of asymmetry, and a rejection of all applied ornament.

4. > Afterword

1 Garrett Eckbo, *Landscape for Living*, New York: Duell, Sloan & Pearce, 1950; Los Angeles: Hennessey + Ingalls, 2002; Amherst: University of Massachusetts Press, 2009; Thomas Church, *Gardens Are for People*, New York: Reinhold, 1955; most recently, third edition, ed. Michael Laurie and Grace Hall, Berkeley: University of California Press, 1993.

2 Christopher Tunnard, *Gardens in the Modern Landscape*, 1948, reprint, Philadelphia: University of Pennsylvania Press, 2014.

3 J. M. Coetzee, *In the Heart of the Country*, London: Vintage, 2004, p. 146.

Bibliography

——. *A World with a View: An Inquiry into the Nature of Scenic Values.* New Haven, CT: Yale University Press, 1978.

Tunnard, Christopher, and Jean Canneel-Claes. Manifesto. Brussels: Association Internationale des Architectes de Jardins Modernistes (International Association of Modernist Garden Architects), no date, c. 1938.

Tunnard, Christopher, and Boris Pushkarev. *Man-Made America: Chaos or Control?* New Haven, CT: Yale University Press, 1964.

Tunnard, Christopher, and Henry Hope Reed. *American Skyline: The Growth and Form of Our Cities and Towns.* New York: New American Library, 1955.

Articles

Tunnard, Arthur C. "The Influence of Japan on the English Garden." *Landscape and Garden,* Summer 1935.

——. "Interplanting." *Landscape and Garden,* Autumn 1935.

Tunnard, Christopher. "Architecture and Art." *Task,* 7–8, 1948.

——. "Art and Landscape Design." *Landscape Architecture,* April 1949. Paper presented at Ann Arbor Conference on Esthetic Evaluation, University of Michigan, 2–3 April 1948.

——. "An Artist in the Streets." *Magazine of Art,* February 1953.

——"The City and Its Interpreters." Review essay. *Journal of the American Institute of Planners,* November 1961.

——. "A City Called Beautiful." *Journal of the Society of Architectural Historians,* March 1950.

——. "Creative Urbanism." *Town Planning Review,* October 1951.

——. "Fire on the Prairie." *Landscape,* Spring 1952.

——. "The Future of Frank Lloyd Wright." *Landscape,* Spring 1954.

——. "Garden and Landscape." *Architectural Review,* April 1939.

——. *Garden and Landscape: An Exhibition Organised by the Institute of Landscape Architects.* London: Institute of Landscape Architects, 1938.

——. "Garden and Landscape: The Country Acre; A Typical Garden Problem." *Architectural Review,* February 1939.

——. "Garden and Landscape: The Sectional Layout of a Small Garden Plot." *Architectural Review,* March 1939.

Christopher Tunnard

Archives

Christopher Tunnard Papers, Yale University Library, New Haven, CT.

H. F. Clark Papers, Royal Commission on the Ancient and Historical Monuments of Scotland (now Historic Environment Scotland), Edinburgh.

Landscape Institute Archives, formerly in London, now at The Museum of English Rural Life, University of Reading. Royal Horticultural Society, London.

Royal Institute of British Architects, London.

Publications

by Christopher Tunnard

Books

Tunnard, Christopher. *The City of Man.* New York: Charles Scribner's Sons, 1953.

——. *Gardens in the Modern Landscape.* London: Architectural Press, 1938. Revised second edition, 1948.

———. "Garden and Landscape: Shrubs for a Roof Garden." *Architectural Review*, June 1939.

———. "Garden and Landscape: The Suburban Plot; A Standard Garden Problem." *Architectural Review*, January 1939.

———. "Garden Design at Chelsea Show, 1936." *Landscape and Garden*, Summer 1936.

———. "Garden-Making on the Riviera." *Landscape and Garden*, Spring 1936.

———. "Garden Work." *Landscape and Garden*, Spring 1937.

———. "Landscape Design and City Planning." In *Landscape Design*. San Francisco: San Francisco Museum of Art, 1948.

———. "Landscape Design at the Paris International Congress: What Other Countries Are Doing." *Landscape and Garden*, Summer 1937.

———. "The Leaf and the Stone: Neo-Romantic Aspects of Nature in the City Plan." *Magazine of Art*, February 1951.

———. "Modern Gardens for Modern Houses: Reflections on Current Trends in Landscape Design." *Landscape Architecture*, January 1942.

———. "Planning a Modern Garden: An Experience in Collaboration." *Landscape and Garden*, Spring 1939.

———. "Planning the Town Garden." *Decoration*, Summer 1939.

———. Response. In "What Is Happening to Modern Architecture?" *Museum of Modern Art Bulletin*, Spring 1948.

Unpublished Texts

Tunnard, Christopher. "The Architecture of the Regional Landscape." Gulf States Regional Conference of the American Institute of Architects, Biloxi, MS, September 1953. Typescript.

———. "Design & Environment." World Design Conference, Tokyo, 13 May 1960. Typescript.

———. "The Garden of the Silver Pavilion." Typescript, no date, c. 1961.

———. "How to Expand the Natural Environment." Harvard Urban Design Conference, 1 May 1965. Typescript.

———. "Impressions of Tokyo." Typescript, no date, c. 1961.

———. "Landscape Architecture in the U.S.A." Typescript, no date, 1940s.

———. "The Natural City." Typescript, no date, post-1971.

———. "Sharawadji Reconsidered." Talk for the Club, New Haven, CT, 16 April 1975. Typescript.

———. "Too Fast, Too Far...or, Around the World in Thirty Days." No date, c. June 1960. Typescript.

———. "Walter Gropius at Harvard." Annual Meeting of the Society of Architectural Historians, Boston, 1962. Typescript.

Publications by Others

Adams, Nicholas. "Joanna C. Diman (1901–91): A 'Cantankerous' Landscape Architect at Skidmore, Owings & Merrill." *Journal of the Society of Landscape Historians*, September 2018.

Aitchison, Matthew, ed. *Nikolaus Pevsner and the Picturesque*. Los Angeles: Getty Research Institute, 2010.

"The All-Europe House." *Journal of the Royal Institute of British Architects*, June 1939.

Andresen, Teresa. *Francisco Caldeira Cabral*. Reigate, Surrey, UK: Landscape Design Trust, 2001.

———, ed. *From the National Stadium to the Gulbenkian Garden: Francisco Caldeira Cabral and the First Generation of Portuguese Landscape Architects, 1940–1970*. Lisbon: Calouste Gulbenkian Foundation, 2003.

"Ars in Urbe." *Bulletin of the Associates in Fine Arts at Yale University*, April 1953.

Beneš, Mirka. "A Modern Classic: The Abby Aldrich Rockefeller Sculpture Garden." In *Philip Johnson and the Museum of Modern Art*, edited by John Elderfield. Studies in Modern Art 6. New York: Museum of Modern Art, 1998.

Benfey, Christopher. *The Great Wave: Gilded Age Misfits, Japanese Eccentrics and the Opening of Japan*. New York: Random House, 2003.

Blair, William M. "St. Louis Chooses Arch as Memorial. *New York Times*, 19 February 1948.

Blomfield, Reginald. *The Formal Garden in England*. London: Waterstone, 1892

———. *Modernismus*. London: Macmillan, 1934.

Brown, Jane. *Eminent Gardeners: Some People of Influence and Their Gardens, 1880–1980*. London: Viking Penguin, 1990.

Butler, Cornelia H., and Alexandra Schwartz, eds. *Modern Women: Women Artists at the Museum of Modern Art*. New York: Museum of Modern Art, 2010.

Campbell, Louise. "The MARS Group, 1933–1939." *Transactions* (Royal Institute of British Architects) 8, 1985.

———. ed. *Twentieth Century Architecture and Its Histories*. London: Society of Architectural Historians of Great Britain, 2000.

Cane, Percy S. *The Creative Art of Garden Design*. London: Country Life, 1966.

———. *The Earth Is My Canvas*. London: Methuen, 1956.

———. *Garden Design of To-day*. New York: Charles Scribner's Sons, 1936.

Carr, Emily. *The Book of Small*. 1942. Reprint, Vancouver: Douglas & McIntyre, 2004.

Church, Thomas. *Gardens Are for People*. New York: Reinhold, 1955.

Clark, H. F. *The English Landscape Garden*. London: Pleiades Books, 1948.

Cohn, Laura, ed. *Wells Coates: Architect and Designer, 1895–1958*. Oxford: Oxford Polytechnic Press, 1979.

Collins, Lester. Review of *Gardens in the Modern Landscape*, second edition. *Landscape Architecture*, April 1949.

Contemporary Landscape Architecture and Its Sources. San Francisco: San Francisco Museum of Art, 1937.

Cullen, Gordon. *Townscape*. London: Architectural Press, 1961.

Denby, Elizabeth. *Europe Re-housed*. London: Allen & Unwin, 1938.

De Waal, Edmund. *Bernard Leach*. British Artist Series. London: Tate Publishing, 2003.

Eckbo, Garrett. *Landscape Architecture: The Profession in California, 1935–1940, and Telesis; Oral History Transcript*. Interviews conducted by Suzanne B. Riess, 1991. Berkeley: Regional Oral History Office, Bancroft Library, University of California, Berkeley, 1993.

———. *Landscape for Living*. New York: Duell, Sloan & Pearce, 1950.

Engler, Mira. *Cut and Paste Urban Landscape: The Work of Gordon Cullen*. London: Routledge, 2016.

Ford, James, and Katherine Morrow Ford. *Design of Modern Interiors*. New York: Architectural Book Publishing, 1942.

———. *The Modern House in America*. New York: Architectural Book Publishing, 1940.

Gabo, Naum. "The Constructive Idea in Art." In *Circle: International Survey of Constructive Art*, edited by J. L. Martin, Ben Nicholson, and Naum Gabo. London: Faber & Faber, 1937.

"Garden for U.N. Headquarters." *Architectural Review*, November 1949.

Hitchcock, Henry-Russell. "Gardens in Relation to Modern Architecture." In *Contemporary Landscape Architecture and Its Sources*. San Francisco: San Francisco Museum of Art, 1937.

Hitchcock, Henry-Russell, and Philip Johnson. *The International Style*. 1932. Reprint, New York: W. W. Norton, 1966.

"House at Galby, Leicestershire." *Architectural Review*, November 1941.

Hubbard, Henry, and Theodora Kimball. *An Introduction to the Study of Landscape Design*. New York: Macmillan, 1917.

Hunt, John Dixon. "The Dialogue of Modern Landscape Architecture with its Past." In Treib, *Modern Landscape Architecture*.

Imbert, Dorothée. "The AIAJM: A Manifesto for Landscape Modernity." *Landscape Journal*, Spring 2007.

———. *Between Garden and City: Jean Canneel-Claes and Landscape Modernism*. Pittsburgh: University of Pittsburgh Press, 2009.

———. "Landscape Architects of the World, Unite! Professional Organizations, Practice, and Politics, 1935–1948." *Journal of Landscape Architecture*, Spring 2007.

———. *The Modernist Garden in France*. New Haven, CT: Yale University Press, 1993.

Jacques, David, and Jan Woudstra. *Landscape Modernism Renounced: The Career of Christopher Tunnard (1910–1979)*. London: Routledge, 2009.

Jellicoe, Susan. "The First Exhibition." *Landscape and Garden*, Autumn 1938.

Kern, Stephen. *The Culture of Time and Space, 1880–1918*. Cambridge, MA: Harvard University Press, 2003.

King, James. *Interior Landscapes: A Life of Paul Nash*. London: Weidenfeld & Nicolson, 1987.

Landscape Design. San Francisco: San Francisco Museum of Art and Association of Landscape Architects, San Francisco Region, 1948.

Leach, Bernard. *Beyond East and West: Memoirs, Portraits and Essays*. London: Faber & Faber, 1978.

Le Corbusier. *Towards a New Architecture*. 1923. Translated by Frederick Etchells, 1931. Reprint, New York: Dover, 1986.

Lewis, Peirce. "Axioms for Reading the Landscape: Some Guides to the American Scene." In *The Interpretation of Ordinary Landscapes: Geographical Essays*, edited by D. W. Meinig. Oxford: Oxford University Press, 1979.

Lippit, Yukio, and James T. Ulak. *Sōtatsu*. Washington, DC: Arthur M. Sackler Gallery, Smithsonian Institution, 2015.

Lozupone, Alyssa. *A Passion for Preservation: Katherine Warren and the Shaping of Modern Newport*. Carlisle, MA: Commonwealth Editions, 2015.

"Mars versus Jupiter." *Landscape and Garden*, Spring 1938.

Martin, J. L., Ben Nicholson, Naum Gabo, eds. *Circle: International Survey of Constructive Art*. London: Faber & Faber, 1937.

McGrath, Raymond. *Twentieth-century Houses*. London: Faber & Faber, 1934.

McLeod, Mary. "Domestic Reform and European Modern Architecture: Charlotte Perriand, Grete Lihotzky, and Elizabeth Denby." In *Modern Women: Women Artists at the Museum of Modern Art*, edited by Cornelia Butler and Alexandra Schwartz. New York: Museum of Modern Art, 2010.

Meinig, D. W., ed. *The Interpretation of Ordinary Landscapes: Geographical Essays*. Oxford: Oxford University Press, 1979.

A Member of the MARS Group. "Modern Architectural Research and Landscape Planning." *Landscape and Garden*, Summer 1938.

Modern Architecture Research Group (MARS). Exhibition catalog, 1938.

Moore, Henry. "*Recumbent Figure*, 1938," and "Sculpture in the Open Air, 1955." Reprinted in *Henry Moore: Writings and Conversations*, edited by Alan Wilkinson. Berkeley: University of California Press, 2002.

Mumford, Lewis. In "What Is Happening to Modern Architecture?" *Museum of Modern Art Bulletin*, Spring 1948.

Neall, Lynne Creighton, ed. *Lawrence Halprin: Changing Places*. San Francisco: San Francisco Museum of Modern Art, 1986.

Neckar, Lance M. "Christopher Tunnard: The Garden in the Modern Landscape." In Treib, *Modern Landscape Architecture*.

Pearlman, Jill. *Inventing American Modernism: Joseph Hudnut, Walter Gropius, and the Bauhaus Legacy at Harvard*. Charlottesville: University of Virginia Press, 2007.

———. "The Spies Who Came into the Modernist Fold: The Covert Life in Hampstead's Lawn Road Flats." *Journal of the Society of Architectural Historians*, September 2013.

Peat, Alan, and Brian A. Whitton. *John Tunnard: His Life and Work*. Aldershot, Hants, UK: Scolar Press, 1997.

Pevsner, Nikolaus. *An Outline of European Architecture*. 1942. Reprint, Harmondsworth, UK: Penguin, 1957.

Powers, Alan. *Oliver Hill: Architect and Lover of Life, 1887–1968*. London: Mouton, 1989.

———. *Serge Chermayeff: Designer, Architect, Teacher*. London: RIBA, 2001.

Reed, Henry Hope. *The Golden City*. Garden City, NY: Doubleday, 1959.

Richards, J. M. *Memoirs of an Unjust Fella: An Autobiography*. London: Weidenfeld & Nicolson, 1980.

Robinson, William. *The Wild Garden*. London: John Murray, 1870.

Shaw, George Bernard. Introduction. *New Architecture*. London: MARS (Modern Architecture Research Group), 1938.

Shepheard, Peter. *Modern Gardens*. London: Architectural Press, 1954.

Sieveking, Lance. *The Eye of the Beholder*. London: Hulton Press, 1957.

Snell, Reginald. *From the Bare Stem: Making Dorothy Elmhirst's Garden at Dartington Hall*. Exeter, Devon, UK: Devon Books, 1989.

Soby, James Thrall. "Love Song to a House." Unpublished typescript, no date, c. 1975.

Steele, Fletcher. *Design in the Small Garden*. Boston: Atlantic Monthly Press, 1924.

———. "New Pioneering in the Garden." *Landscape Architecture*, October 1930. Reprinted in Treib, *Modern Landscape Architecture*.

Summerson, John. "The MARS Group and the Thirties." In *English Architecture Public and Private: Essays for Kerry Downes*, edited by John Bold and Edward Chaney. London: Hambledon Press, 1993.

"Television of Garden Planning." *Landscape and Garden*, Summer 1938.

Tilson, Barbara. "The Battle for Bentley Wood." *Thirties Society Journal*, no. 5, 1985.

Treib, Marc, ed. *Modern Landscape Architecture: A Critical Review*. Cambridge, MA: MIT Press, 1993.

———. "Transitional, Modern, Modernistic, Modernist." *Journal of Landscape Architecture*, Spring 2014.

"What Is Happening to Modern Architecture?" *Museum of Modern Art Bulletin*, Spring 1948.

Wills, Royal Barry. *Better Houses for Budgeteers: Sketches and Plans*. New York: Architectural Book Publishing, 1941.

"Work of the Landscape Architect." *Landscape and Garden*, Summer 1939.

Yanagi, Sōetsu. *The Unknown Craftsman: A Japanese Insight into Beauty*. Adapted by Bernard Leach. Tokyo: Kodansha International, 1972.

Royal Horticultural Society Publications

Ogilvie, F. G. "Report of H.M. Inspector for the Year 1907–08." *Journal of the Royal Horticultural Society* 34, 1908.

RHS Gardens Club Journal, 1929 and 1930.

"School of Horticulture Prospectus." *Journal of the Royal Horticultural Society* 33, 1908.

Harvard University Publications

Bulletin of the Summer Term, Graduate School of Design, Harvard University, Cambridge, MA, 1942.

Official Register of Harvard University, Department of Architectural Sciences, Containing an Announcement for 1940–41. Cambridge, MA, 5 March 1940.

Official Register of Harvard University, Department of Architectural Sciences, Containing an Announcement for 1940–41. Cambridge, MA, 30 April 1941.

Official Register of Harvard University, The Graduate School of Design, with Courses of Instruction, 1940–41. Cambridge, MA, 23 April 1940.

Online Sources

The Butchart Gardens. ButchartGardens.com. http://www.butchartgardens.com/the-gardens/our-history/our-history.html. Accessed 1 February 2012.

Lozupone, Alyssa. "Modernism Meets Preservation: Katherine Warren in Newport." "InCollect," 2 September 2016. https://www.incollect.com/articles/modernism-meets-preservation-katherine-warren-in-newport.

"Luther Ely Smith: Founder of a Memorial." "Museum Gazette" (National Park Service, U.S. Department of the Interior), March 2001, no pagination. https://www.nps.gov/jeff/learn/historyculture/upload/luther_ely_smith.pdf.

Talbot, Charlotte. "The £9m Chertsey home with secret split bedroom honoured for role in UK's LGBTQ heritage." "SurreyLive," 16 October 2016. http://www.getsurrey.co.uk/news/surrey-news/9m-chertsey-home-secret-split-12033664.

Victoria and Albert Museum. "Daily Mail Ideal Home Exhibition: Records, 1910–1990." Victoria and Albert Museum: Archive of Art and Design. http://www.vam.ac.uk/__data/assets/pdf_file/0013/250114/idealhome_aad-1990-9_20140709.pdf. Accessed 9 January 2018.

———. *Kusaniwa: Tatemono to chanoyu kenkyu* [Garden of Grasses: Research in Buildings and Tea]. Tokyo: Hakujitsu Shoin, 1948. Reprint, Tokyo: Chikuma Shobô, 1968.

———. "The Lecture Hall at Jikô-in." In Horiguchi, *Kusaniwa* [Garden of Grasses].

———. *Tradition of* [the] *Japanese Garden*. Tokyo: Kokusai Bunka Shinkôkai, 1963.

Articles

"About the Expression of the Chureitô and My Project." *Gendai Kenchiku*, April 1940.

"Akikusa no niwa" [Garden of Autumn Grasses]. *Shisô*, 1934.

"Chureitô no hyôgen to sonoichishian" [Soldiers' Memorial, Expression and Proposals]. *Gendai Kenchiku*, April 1940.

"Japanese Taste Expressed in Modern Architecture." *Shisô* 116, 1932.

"Nakamise Hasshôkan." No source, no date, probably c. 1962.

"Uraku-en Arekore" [Various Thoughts on Uraku-en]. *SD* [*Space Design*], March 1973.

Publications by Others

Adachi, Takanori. *The Gardens of the Adachi Museum of Art*. Yasugi: Adachi Museum of Art, 2002.

Allinson, Gary D. *Japan's Postwar History*. Ithaca, NY: Cornell University Press, 1997.

Altherr, Alfred. *Three Japanese Architects / Drei japanische Architekten: Mayekawa, Tange, Sakakura*. New York: Architectural Book Publishing, 1968.

Amasaki, Hiromasa, ed. *Ueji no niwa: Ogawa Jihei no sekai*. Kyoto: Tankôsha, 1990.

Ashton, Dore. *Noguchi East and West*. New York: Alfred A. Knopf, 1992.

Asquith, Pamela J., ed. *A Japanese View of Nature: The World of Living Things by Kinji Imanishi*. London: Routledge Curzon, 2002.

Beasley, W. G. *The Modern History of Japan*. New York: Frederick A. Praeger, 1974.

Boyd, Robin. *Kenzô Tange*. New York: George Braziller, 1962.

Bunriha. *Bunriha Kenchiku-Kai no Sakuhin*. Tokyo: Iwanami Shôten, 1924.

Conder, Josiah. *Landscape Gardening in Japan*. 1893. Reprint, New York: Dover, 1964.

Sutemi Horiguchi

Archives

Sutemi Horiguchi Archives, Meiji University, Tokyo

Publications

by Sutemi Horiguchi

Books

Horiguchi, Sutemi. *Architectural Beauty in Japan*. New York: Studio Publications; Tokyo: Kokusai Bunka Shinkôkai, 1956.

———. *Horiguchi Sutemi sakhuin: Ie to niwa no kûkan kôssei* [Works of Sutemi Horiguchi: Spatial Composition of House and Garden]. Tokyo: Kajima Shuppan-kai, 1978.

———. *Ichi Konkuriito Jûtaku Zuschû* [Illustrations of a Concrete House]. Tokyo: Iwanami Shôten, c. 1932.

———. *Katsura Imperial Villa*. Tokyo: Mainichi Newspapers, 1953.

———. *Paintings and Studies by Kawanabe Kyôsai*. Tokyo: Maruzen, 1911.

Drexler, Arthur. *The Architecture of Japan*. New York: Museum of Modern Art, 1955.

Fischer, Felice, ed. *The Arts of Hon'ami Kôetsu: Japanese Renaissance Master*. Philadelphia: Philadelphia Museum of Art, 2000.

Fujioka, Hiroyasu, and Kentaro Mimura. "The Architectural View of the Architectural Critic Takao Itagaki." *UDC*, March 1972.

Harada, Jirô. *Japanese Gardens*. 1936. Reprint, London: The Studio, 1956.

Higuchi, Tadahiko. *The Visual and Spatial Structure of Landscapes*. Cambridge, MA: MIT Press, 1983.

Hitchcock, Henry-Russell, and Philip Johnson. *The International Style*. New York: W. W. Norton, 1932.

Itoh, Teiji. *The Japanese Garden: An Approach to Nature*. Translated by Donald Richie. New Haven, CT: Yale University Press, 1972.

———. *Kura: Design and Tradition of the Japanese Storehouse*. Tokyo: Kodansha International, 1973.

———. *Space and Illusion in the Japanese Garden*. Translated by Ralph Friedrich and Masajiro Shimamura. New York: Weatherhill / Tankosha, 1973.

Kawabata, Yasunari. *Thousand Cranes*. Translated by Edward G. Seidensticker. New York: Berkley, 1958.

Kawai, Kazuo. *Japan's American Interlude*. Chicago: University of Chicago Press, 1979.

Kinsaku Nakane: A Man and His Work. Niwa / The Garden 77, January 1991.

Kinsaku Nakane, Landscape Artist, Japanese Garden Exhibition. Yokohama: Yokohama City Art Museum, 1998.

"Kinsaku Nakane." Special Issue, *Tanko*, November 1994.

Kuck, Loraine E. *The World of the Japanese Garden: From Chinese Origins to Modern Landscape Art*. New York: Weatherhill, 1968.

Kuitert, Wybe. *Themes, Scenes, and Taste in the History of Japanese Garden Art*. Amsterdam: J. C. Gieben, 1988.

Kultermann, Udo, ed. *Kenzô Tange, 1946–1969: Architecture and Urban Design*. New York: Frederick A. Praeger, 1970.

Le Corbusier. *Towards a New Architecture*. 1923. Translated by Frederick Etchells, 1931. Reprint, New York: Dover, 1986.

Lippit, Yukio, and James T. Ulak. *Sôtatsu*. Washington, DC: Sackler Gallery, Smithsonian Institution, 2015.

Mares, Emmanuel, ed. *Shigemori Mirei, Creator of Spiritual Spaces*. Kyoto: Kyoto Tsushinsha Press, 2007.

McGrath, Raymond. *Twentieth-century Houses*. London: Faber & Faber, 1934.

McKelway, Matthew P. *Silver Wind: The Arts of Sakai Hôitsu (1761–1828)*". New York: Japan Society, 2012.

Mizuo, Hiroshi. *Edo Painting: Sôtatsu and Kôrin*. New York: Weatherhill; Tokyo: Heibonsha, 1972.

Morrison, Michael, and Lorna Price, eds. *Four Centuries of Fashion: Classical Kimono from the Kyoto National Museum*. San Francisco: Asian Art Museum, 1997.

Murase, Miyeko, and Takeshi Noguchi. *Irises and Eight Bridges: Masterpieces by Kôrin from the Nezu Museum and the Metropolitan Museum of Art*. Tokyo: Nezu Art Museum, 2012.

Ôhashi, Haruzô. *Japanese Gardens of the Modern Era*. Tokyo: Graphic-sha, 1987.

Oshima, Ken Tadashi. *International Architecture in Interwar Japan: Constructing Kokusai Kenchiku*. Seattle: University of Washington Press, 2010.

Reynolds, Jonathan M. *Allegories of Time and Space: Japanese Identity in Photography and Architecture*. Honolulu: University of Hawai'i Press, 2015.

———. *Maekawa Kunio and the Emergence of Modernist Japanese Architecture*. Berkeley: University of California Press, 2001.

Schaarschmidt-Richter, Irmtraud, and Osamu Mori. *Japanese Gardens*. Translated by Janet Seligman. New York: William Morrow, 1979.

Shigemori, Kanto. *Japanese Gardens: Islands of Serenity*. Tokyo: Japan Publications, 1971.

Shigemori, Mirei. *Gardens of Japan*. Kyoto: Nissha, 1949.

———. *Japanese Gardens Designed by Mirei Shigemori*. Tokyo: Heibonsha, 1964.

———. *Nihon Teien shi zukan* [An Illustrated History of the Japanese Garden]. 26 volumes. Tokyo: Yûkôsha, 1936–1939.

Shigemori, Mitsuaki. *Shigemori Mirei: The Artistic Universe of Stone Gardens, Part II*. Kyoto: Kyoto Tsushinsha Press, 2010.

Shirahata, Yôzaburô, ed. *Ueji, The Genius of Water and Stone*. Kyoto: Kyoto Tsushinsha Press, 2008.

Steele, Fletcher. "New Pioneering in Landscape Design." *Landscape Architecture*. October 1930. Reprinted in Treib, *Modern Landscape Architecture*.

Stewart, David B. *The Making of a Modern Japanese Architecture, 1868 to the Present*. Tokyo: Kodansha International, 1987.

Sutemi Horiguchi. Special Issue, *SD* [*Space Design*], 1996.

Suzuki, Hiroyuki. *The Life and Times of the Gardener Jihei Ogawa*. Tokyo: University of Tokyo Press, 2013.

Suzuki, Hiroyuki, Terunobu Fujimori, and Tokuzu Hara. *Josiah Conder: A Victorian Architect in Japan*. Tokyo: East Japan Railway Culture Foundation, 1997.

Tamura, Tsuyoshi. *Art of the Landscape Garden in Japan*. Tokyo: Kokusai Bunka Shinkokai, 1936.

Tange, Kenzô. *Katsura: Tradition and Creation in Japanese Architecture*. New Haven, CT: Yale University Press, 1960.

———. *Ise: Prototype of Japanese Architecture*. Cambridge, MA: MIT Press, 1965.

Tanizaki, Jun'ichirô. *Naomi*. 1924. Translated by Anthony Chambers. Rutland, VT: Tuttle, 1986.

Treib, Marc, ed. *The Architecture of Landscape, 1940–1960*. Philadelphia: University of Pennsylvania Press, 2002.

———. "Converging Arcs on a Sphere: Renewing Japanese Landscape Design." In Treib, *The Architecture of Landscape, 1940–1960*.

———. "The Japanese Storehouse." *Journal of the Society of Architectural Historians*, May 1976.

———. "Landscapes Transitional, Modern, Modernistic, Modernist." *Journal of Landscape Architecture*, Spring 2014.

———. *Modern Landscape Architecture: A Critical Review*. Cambridge, MA: MIT Press, 1993.

———. *Noguchi in Paris: Isamu Noguchi and the UNESCO Garden*. San Francisco: William Stout, 2003.

Tschumi, Christian. *Mirei Shigemori: Modernizing the Japanese Garden*. Basel: Birkhäuser, 2007.

Weisenfeld, Gennifer. *Imaging Disaster: Tokyo and the Visual Culture of Japan's Great Earthquake of 1923*. Berkeley: University of California Press, 2012.

Yoshida, Tetsurô. *The Gardens of Japan*. New York: Frederick A. Praeger, 1957.

———. *The Japanese House and Garden*. New York: Frederick A. Praeger, 1955.

Acknowledgments

The idea for this book began in 1989 with my rereading of Christopher Tunnard's *Gardens in the Modern Landscape* for an article I was writing on early modern landscape architecture. The illustrations of Sutemi Horiguchi's Kikkawa house caught my eye, in particular the incredibly subtle composition of its small interior court. While I had taught a survey course on Japanese architecture and gardens for several years, somehow I had never come across any mention of Horiguchi in the existing literature or from Japanese friends. David B. Stewart's definitive study, *The Making of a Modern Japanese Architecture, 1868 to the Present*, had not yet been published, but on a subsequent trip to Japan I asked David just who was this Horiguchi and what had he done. His reply provided my first knowledge of the architect and his work. Since then, both in his writings, and in person, I have benefited considerably from David's knowledge about Japan and its architecture, for which I am very grateful. In addition, I also wish to thank Makoto Suzuki, professor of landscape architecture at the Tokyo University of Agriculture, for his insights into Japanese garden art, for helping to gain access to several sites, and for aid with some translations. In the past few years, Giichi Kimura, now professor emeritus of architecture at Meiji University, has been a fruitful source of information and interpretation. As Horiguchi's last assistant at Meiji University, Professor Kimura has assembled and organized his professor's remaining documents and found a repository for them in the Meiji University library. I am most grateful for his assistance, conversations, clarifications, and for allowing the reproduction of materials from the archives.

For a book project such as this one, which has spanned so many years, numerous people have provided assistance without which it could never have been written. When work on this book began, Ken Tadashi Oshima (today professor of architectural history at the University of Washington) was my teaching and research assistant at the University of California, Berkeley. Over the years he has been instrumental in conducting research, introducing me to people, securing access to documents, and for reviewing a draft of the Horiguchi half of the book. His knowledge of the subject is evident in his own book, *International Architecture in Interwar Japan: Constructing Kokusai Kenchiku* (University of Washington Press, 2009) and his contribution has been significant. I am most thankful. Thanks also to Hugo Segawa, who facilitated my visit to the Japanese Pavilion in São Paulo.

      I can claim only a very rudimentary—more accurately, preschool—knowledge of the Japanese language, and through the years I have relied on a team of friends, colleagues, and students to aid me in my study. Ken Oshima, thanked above, was the first, followed thereafter by then-graduate students at the University of Tokyo, Kulapat Yantrasast (today a partner in wHY Architects, Los Angeles), and Jeeun Song (now Jeeun Song-Dusoir); Koichi Miura, then a graduate student at the University of California, Berkeley; and most recently, Melanie Hong, a doctoral candidate, also at Berkeley. I thank them warmly for their time and contributions. Interestingly, almost all of these assistants—all of whom were students at the time the project began—now have thriving careers as academics or design professionals.

      On the Christopher Tunnard side, I have had the most continued exchanges with, and hence the greatest education from, the British architectural historian Alan Powers and his encyclopedic knowledge of architectural modernism in Britain and Europe. He has kindly reviewed several of my earlier articles and books, and our exchanges over tea in London have always been lively and informative. Also in the UK are Jan Woudstra at the University of Sheffield, who with David Jacques, published a book on Tunnard, and who was helpful in pointing me to materials on the landscape architect in the archives. In the early phase of research, I benefited from rewarding conversations with Ian Kitson and Sheila Harvey (then at the Landscape Institute), who introduced me to information about Tunnard and sources of documents. Rusty Tunnard provided facts, some documents, and anecdotes about his father and family. I express my gratitude to all of those mentioned above, and ask forgiveness from those I have forgotten due to memories that have faded over this almost three decades.

      Let me also thank the staffs at the drawing collection at the Royal Institute of British Architects, the archives of the Landscape Institute (then in London, now housed at the Museum of English Rural Life at the University of Reading), the Yale University Library, Tate Britain, and the library of the Royal Horticultural Society in London.

      Research for this book was supported in part by the Graham Foundation for Advanced Studies in the Fine Arts; its production was supported by a generous grant from the Hubbard Educational Trust.

      Bonnie Lovell has gone beyond the call of duty in the copyediting phase of the process; her efforts to find just the right word and correct fact have added to the lucidity of the writing. And finally, at ORO Editions, I thank Jake Anderson for his expeditious management of the project.

Index